PUBLIC RECORD OFFICE HANDBOOKS

No. 13

The Records of the
FOREIGN OFFICE
1782-1939

LONDON

HER MAJESTY'S STATIONERY OFFICE

1969

SBN 11 440005 9

CONTENTS

III. Specimen Searches

IV. Annotated List of Record Classes

Appendices

INTRODUCTION

On 17 October 1968, while this handbook was in the press, the new Foreign and Commonwealth Office came into being and for the first time since the reign of Queen Elizabeth I one Secretary of State became responsible for the conduct of the whole of Britain's relations with countries overseas. The immediate ancestors of this new Office were the Foreign Office, formed, though not at first known by that name, in 1782, and the Commonwealth Office, formed as recently as 1966 by the merger of the Colonial Office and the Commonwealth Relations Office. The latter Office had itself been formed by the merger of the Dominions Office and the India Office in 1947. Also involved in the 1968 merger was the Diplomatic Service Administration Office, created on 1 January 1965 to administer the single Diplomatic Service which then replaced the separate overseas services of the Foreign Office and the Commonwealth Relations Office. This Diplomatic Service Administration Office had drawn its staff from the Diplomatic Service and had served the Foreign Office and the Commonwealth Office equally, while being part of neither.[1]

With the exception of the India Office (see p. 31, n. 4) the several ancestors of the Foreign and Commonwealth Office have transferred those of their records which have been selected for permanent preservation to the Public Record Office, where they are in general open to public inspection when thirty years old. The records of the Colonial and Dominions Offices to about 1929 have been the subject of a previous handbook in this series: R. B. Pugh, *The Records of the Colonial and Dominions Offices* (P.R.O. Handbook No. 3, 1964). This present handbook deals with the records of the Foreign Office from 1782 to the outbreak of war in 1939. It is intended to introduce the searcher to some nine hundred classes in the *Foreign Office* group and to related records in other groups in the Public Record Office. It is not a comprehensive guide to the sources for diplomatic history preserved in this country.

Part I is a brief history of the administrative machinery developed by the Foreign Office between 1782 and 1939 for the conduct of foreign affairs. Part II describes in some detail the records which were created in this process. Part III consists of four specimen searches chosen to illustrate the types of record and the means of reference produced by the registration and record-keeping systems employed before 1891, between 1891 and 1905, between 1906 and 1920, and after 1920 respectively. Part IV is an annotated list of all the classes which constitute the *Foreign Office* group, together with a few related classes from other groups; in the interests of comprehensiveness it includes classes created after 1939. Four Appendices deal with Foreign Office Clerks before 1852, with signs and codes used in Foreign Office registers and indexes, with private collections bearing on foreign affairs preserved in the Public Record Office, and with the location of private collections of papers of Secretaries of State for Foreign Affairs. The brief Index contains only such subjects as are not readily discoverable from the Table of Contents; no persons or places are included in it.

The whole of this handbook is the work of Mr. M. Roper, an Assistant Keeper of Public Records. He wishes to acknowledge his debt to his colleagues, whose

---

[1] For the background and structure of the Foreign and Commonwealth Office see *The Merger of the Foreign Office and the Commonwealth Office, 1968* (H.M.S.O., 1968).

enquiries stimulated much of his detailed research, to Mr. C. J. Child, the last Librarian of the separate Foreign Office, for his valuable comments on the draft of this handbook, to Mr. M. Moir of the India Office Records for guidance on relevant material among the holdings of that institution, and to Mr. H. M. G. Baillie of the Historical Manuscripts Commission, who provided the information upon which Appendix IV is based.

NOTES ON ILLUSTRATIONS

Front Cover: Circular of Charles James Fox, 29 March 1782 (F.O.211/1).

This constitutes the official notification to British diplomatic representatives abroad of the establishment of a separate Department for Foreign Affairs. Foreign ministers in London had been notified on 27 March, the date on which the offices of the Secretaries of State had been reorganised. This copy of the circular is from the archives of the British Legation at Copenhagen; there is another copy from the Berlin archives among the *Jackson Papers* (F.O.353/33) and the draft is in an entry book among the *State Papers Foreign* (S.P.110/83, p. 102). See p. 2.

Plate I: Lewis Hertslet, 1787–1870 (from a photograph in the Library of the Foreign and Commonwealth Office, by courtesy of the Secretary of State for Foreign and Commonwealth Affairs).

Lewis Hertslet was Sub-Librarian of the Foreign Office 1801–1810, Librarian and Keeper of the Papers 1810–1857 and Superintendent of the Queen's Messengers 1824–1854. He began the Library series of registers of correspondence (F.O.802) and extended the duties of the Librarian in many other ways. He inaugurated, as a semi-official venture, *Hertslet's Commercial Treaties* and *British and Foreign State Papers.* His family long maintained a connection with the Foreign Office. His father, Lewis Hertslet, was a Foreign Service Messenger 1797–1802 and his brother James was Sub-Librarian 1811–1855. His son, Sir Edward Hertslet, entered the Library in 1840, becoming Sub-Librarian in 1855 and succeeding his father as Librarian and Keeper of the Papers from 1857 to 1896. Edward also continued his father's publications and added to them the annual *Foreign Office List.* Three of his sons also served in the Foreign Office and in the Consular Service, Sir Cecil (1868–1919), Reginald (1870–1894) and Godfrey, who was a clerk in the Library 1890–1914, then served in the Consular Service until 1928 and continued as joint editor of the *Foreign Office List* until his death in December 1947. See pp. 20, 39–40, 90–91.

Plates II and III: A Docket Sheet, 1913 (F.O.371/1671, f.17).

This is a specimen of the docket sheets in use between 1906 and 1920. The year is printed in the top left corner and below this is written the country of origin and the date of the paper. In the top centre box is stamped the name of the country to which the paper relates and under which it is filed and below is written the paper's registry number. This registry number is also stamped in the top right corner, together with the date of registration; the same stamp is also put on the paper itself. On the next row is the name of the author of the paper and the number in his local correspondence series; as this particular paper is a telegram the word 'Telegram' is printed here and the whole docket sheet is printed in red instead of the normal black. Underneath is a box for the registry number of the last paper on the file for this particular subject. In the 'Subject' box appear the file title and a resumé of the paper's contents. In this particular example the file number is also stamped here, but it is more usual for it to be stamped or written below the registry number stamp in the top right corner. The minutes, which extend over the page, show the paper's progress from H. M. (later Sir Hughe) Knatchbull-Hugessen, a Junior Clerk in the American Department, to G. S. Spicer, the Senior Clerk in the Department, to Sir Lewis Mallet, the Assistant Under Secretary superintending the Department, to Sir Arthur Nicolson (later Lord Carnock), the Permanent Under Secretary, and finally to Sir Edward (later Earl) Grey, the Secretary of State, who writes in red ink. As this paper was not included in the Confidential Print there is no entry in the 'Print' box. The entries under 'How disposed of' show that the paper was repeated to the Ambassador in Washington and that arising from it a further telegram was sent to him and also a letter to the Admiralty. (Drafts ot these two papers are kept with the original telegram in this docket sheet.) Ticks indicate that the telegrams and draft have been entered in the General Register. The initials in the 'Action completed' box of O. Monk, the Sub-Registry Clerk responsible for the paper, indicate that he has checked that every direction given in the minutes has been carried out. In the 'Index' box is the index number of the division of the General Register in which the paper is entered (see Appendix 2(d)); the tick indicates that the papers in the docket sheet have been indexed. When the next paper on the file came in, its registry number was entered in the bottom left corner of this docket sheet. See pp. 61–65; this particular paper is mentioned on p. 104.

Plate IV: A Docket Sheet, 1931 (F.O.371/15150, f.73).

The form of docket sheet in use from 1920 differs from that in use between 1906 and 1920 chiefly in concentrating the information about the origin and contents of the paper on a typed docket slip, one copy of which is gummed to the docket sheet, others being used for the précis jacket and to make up the Day Book and the Chronological File. Other changes are the departmental designation in the top centre box, in this case that of the Central Department (see Appendix II(e)). A new 'References' box lists papers on the file, both forward and backward, which are particularly relevant to the paper in this docket sheet. The 'Index' box no longer contains the index number, as this is now included in the full registry number on the docket slip; the initials are those of the clerk in the Main Index Branch who indexed the contents of this docket sheet. See pp. 68–70; this particular paper is mentioned on p. 106.

I. The Foreign Office

Foreign Affairs before 1782[1]
Until 1782 there was no Foreign Office; indeed no single department of state was responsible for the conduct of British foreign affairs. The direction of foreign affairs had always been a matter for the royal prerogative and until the reign of Queen Anne it had been exercised to a very large extent by the Sovereign in person. Thereafter, although successive Sovereigns continued to take an interest in foreign affairs and at times even exerted considerable influence, direction increasingly passed, as in other fields of government, to ministers dependent upon a parliamentary majority.

In the execution of foreign affairs the main link between the Sovereign or ministry and British diplomatic representatives overseas was the Principal Secretary of State, although it was not unusual up to the end of the seventeenth century for the Sovereign to deal with diplomats either direct or through other intermediaries. Developing from the king's private secretary of the medieval period, the office of Principal Secretary of State had increased in importance and influence during the Tudor period and had since 1540 usually been shared by two persons. By the eighteenth century this dual secretariat had become so important that it was accepted as the sole means of communication between government and diplomat, while at the same time the Secretaries' influence in the direction of foreign policy had so grown that at times one or other of them might dominate the ministry of which he was a member.

The twin Secretaries were not concerned only with foreign affairs and the allocation of work between them varied from time to time. From 1640 there may be distinguished a rough geographical division of their work into what later became known as the Northern and Southern Departments or Provinces, a distinction which continued until 1782. Although the allocation of countries between the two Departments varied slightly from time to time to take account of particular circumstances, the general rule in the eighteenth century was that the Southern Department embraced France, Spain, Italy, Portugal, Switzerland, Turkey and the Barbary States, as well as Home and Irish affairs and (until 1768 when a third Secretary was added) the Colonies; the Northern Department was concerned with the remaining overseas countries with which diplomatic relations were maintained. In practice the distinction between the Departments was not a sharp one and since there was in theory only a single office, either Secretary could, if occasion arose, perform any of the functions of the other. It was not unusual, therefore, for one Secretary, particularly a dominant one such as the elder Pitt, to take an interest in the affairs of the other's Department.

Until 1698 the offices of the two Secretaries were housed in Whitehall, but the great fire there in that year necessitated their removal to the Cockpit.[2] There they remained, apart from brief intervals, until 1771, when both offices were firmly established in Cleveland Row, St. James's, after a decade of alternating between there and the Cockpit. The offices were associated with particular Secretaries and

---

[1] See F.M.G.Evans, *The Principal Secretary of State* (Manchester, 1923); M.A.Thomson, *The Secretaries of State 1681–1782* (Oxford, 1932); D.B.Horn, *The British Diplomatic Service 1689–1789* (Oxford, 1961), and 'The Machinery for the Conduct of British Foreign Policy in the Eighteenth Century' in *J. Soc. Archivists*, III (1967), pp.229–240.

[2] *Calendar of State Papers Domestic 1698*, pp.19, 20, 29; for the site of the Whitehall Cockpit see Sir E.Hertslet, *Recollections of the Old Foreign Office* (1901), pp.5–6 and plan facing p.4.

not with the Departments and when a Secretary was transferred from one Department to the other he did not necessarily remove from the office he already occupied but had the books and papers of his new Department brought to him there.[1]

Records relating to the conduct of foreign affairs from the reign of Henry VIII to 1781 are preserved in the Public Record Office among the records of the State Paper Office and are known from 1547 as *State Papers Foreign*.[2] A few records of an earlier date than 1782 will be found among the records of the *Foreign Office* group, particularly in the classes: *General Correspondence, Great Britain and General* (F.O.83); *King's Letter Books* (F.O.90); *Miscellanea, Series I* (F.O.95); and *Chief Clerk's Department, Archives* (F.O.366). Records of the conduct of foreign affairs will also be found in collections of privately preserved papers. Some of the more important of these collections have been calendared by the Historical Manuscripts Commission.[3]

The Foreign Office[4]

On 27 March 1782 Charles James Fox sent a circular to foreign diplomatic representatives in London beginning:

> Le Roi m'ayant fait l'Honneur de me nommer Son Secretaire d'Etat pour le Department des Affaires Etrangeres....[5]

Two days later he addressed a further circular to all British diplomatic representatives overseas:

> The King having, on the Resignation of Lord Viscount Stormont, been pleased to appoint Me to be One of His Majesty's Principal Secretaries of State and at the same Time to make a new Arrangement in the Departments by conferring that for Domestick Affairs and the Colonies on the Earl of Shelburne, and entrusting Me with the sole Direction of the Department for Foreign Affairs: I am to desire that You will, for the future, address Your Letters to me, which I shall not fail to lay regularly before the King, and to transmit to You such Orders and Instructions as His Majesty shall think proper to give for your Guidance and Direction.[6]

These circulars constitute the only record of the institution of the Office of Secretary of State for Foreign Affairs and of the founding of a separate Foreign Office. There is no reference to the new arrangement in the Privy Council Register, which records the taking of the oath of office by Fox as 'one of His Majesty's Principal Secretaries of State';[7] Fox's Patent of Appointment, dated 13 April 1782, refers to him in similar terms.[8] George III had proposed in 1772 that one of the Secretaries of State should 'transact the whole department of Foreign affairs', and had repeated the proposal at the end of 1781. He may, therefore, have played a significant role in the division of duties in 1782, although a draft in his hand of the new ministry of 27 March 1782 does not distinguish between the two Secretaries of State.[9]

The new department was referred to in more formal contexts as 'the Office of

---

[1] Hertslet, *Recollections*, pp.251–257.
[2] See *Guide to the Contents of the Public Record Office* (1963), II, pp.3–4, 11–13; *List of State Papers Foreign* (P.R.O. Lists and Indexes XIX, 1904); also p.33 below.
[3] See the Commission's *18th Report* (1917), App.II.
[4] See Hertslet, *Recollections; Cambridge Hist. of Brit. Foreign Policy*, III (Cambridge, 1923), pp.539–630; Sir J.Tilley and S.Gaselee, *The Foreign Office* (1933); F.Gosses, *The Management of British Foreign Policy before the First World War* (Leiden, 1948); Lord Strang, *The Foreign Office* (1955); D.G.Bishop *The Administration of British Foreign Relations* (Syracuse, U.S.A., 1961); D.Vital, *The Making of British Foreign Policy* (1968).
[5] F.O.95/433, p.2; S.P.104/262, p.203.
[6] S.P.110/83, p.102. This document has previously been cited only under an obsolete reference: '*S.P.Domestic, Entry Book* 416.' See also Front Cover and Notes on Illustrations.
[7] P.C.2/127, p.255.
[8] C.66/3793, no.7. So long as Secretaries of State were appointed by Letters Patent no distinction of office was made in the wording of their Patents.
[9] Sir J.Fortescue, *The Correspondence of King George the Third*, II (1927), no. 882; V (1928), nos. 3485, 3590; Horn, *Brit. Dipl. Service*, p.1.

His Majesty's Principal Secretary of State for Foreign Affairs', but for everyday use a number of shorter titles emerged. At first it was known as 'Mr. Fox's Office' and this linking of the department with the person of the Secretary of State continued until at least the Secretaryship of Castlereagh. Other titles such as 'Office of the Foreign Department', 'Foreign Department', 'Department for Foreign Affairs', and 'Office for Foreign Affairs' were in regular use by the beginning of the nineteenth century. 'Foreign Office' first occurs in 1807, when it became the standard address of the department,[1] but it did not supersede 'Foreign Department' and 'Department for Foreign Affairs' in general use until about 1810.[2]

The functions of the new department were described by Jeremy Sneyd, the Chief Clerk, for the Commission on Fees in 1785:

> The business of the Secretary of State's Office for the Foreign Department, consists in conducting the correspondence with all Foreign Courts, negotiating with the Ambassadors or Ministers of all the Foreign Courts in Europe, as well as of the United States of America, and receiving and making representations and applications to and from the same, and in corresponding with the other principal Departments of the State thereupon.[3]

This differs little in essence from a more recent definition of those functions:

> It is true to say, as a broad generalisation, that whereas the main function of the other British Departments of State is to carry out prescribed and fully realisable policies, that of the Foreign Office is to achieve as many of our national desiderata as can be made acceptable to other sovereign governments. This does not as a rule call for administrative science, but for diplomacy;...
>
> To some extent the Foreign Office may be regarded as the headquarters of British diplomatic activities and the establishments abroad as the front lines through which it operates.[4]

However, although the primary concern of the Foreign Office has always been the conduct of diplomatic relations with other sovereign states, it has at times also undertaken administrative responsibilities in overseas territories, although these might be thought to have been more properly the concern of the Colonial Office. These administrative responsibilities, mainly in Africa, came to an end only in 1955 when the Sudan became an independent state.[5]

The first Foreign Office was established by Fox in the office of the former Secretary of State for the Northern Department in Cleveland Row and there it remained until September 1786, when it was moved to the Cockpit in Whitehall. In December 1793 the Office moved to premises in Downing Street, where it was to remain for almost seventy years until the accommodation there became insufficient for the Office's expanding needs and it was decided to erect a new Foreign Office on the site as part of the general redevelopment of Whitehall. Accordingly on 27 August 1861 the Office took up temporary quarters at No.7 and No.8 Whitehall Gardens, where it remained until 1 July 1868 when the new Foreign Office building was opened.[6] This is the building which the Office has occupied ever since, although the vast increase in its work and staff since 1914 has made it impossible to accommodate the whole of the Office in the building and departments are now scattered among a number of other buildings in London.

[1] The earliest dating from the 'Foreign Office' appears to be 4 April 1807 (F.O.95/359, p.387) but examples of dating from 'Downing Street' continue until later in that year. The change in practice may be associated with the appointment of Canning as Secretary of State on 25 March 1807.
[2] The evolution of the department's title can be traced in F.O.366/669–672.
[3] *App. to 1st Rpt. of Commissioners on Fees, Gratuities, &c. of Public Offices*, H.C. 1806 (309) XI, p.27.
[4] Strang, *Foreign Office*, pp.10, 17.
[5] D.N.Chester and F.M.G.Willson, *The Organization of British Central Government 1914–1956* (1957), p.192.
[6] Hertslet, *Recollections*, pp.1–16.

Secretaries and Under Secretaries of State[1]

In 1786 the duty of the Secretary of State was said to be to lay the business of his Office before the King, to receive the King's commands thereupon and to give orders accordingly.[2] In reality this definition was already out of date. Although the Foreign Secretary was formally appointed (and still is) by the delivery of the three seals of office (greater and lesser signet, and cachet) by the Sovereign,[3] his selection was by the end of the eighteenth century a matter less for the Sovereign than for the Prime Minister, and the direction of foreign policy had also passed very largely from the Sovereign to a Cabinet within which the Foreign Secretary was a pre-eminent, often a dominant, member, able to pursue at times an almost independent foreign policy.[4]

Although the arrangement of 27 March 1782 had established separate Secretaries of State for Home and Foreign Affairs,[5] the theoretical unity of the Secretariat was maintained and any Secretary of State might act in the absence of another.[6] Thus while Castlereagh was attending the Continental Congresses after the Napoleonic Wars, Bathurst, the Secretary of State for War and the Colonies, signed most of the outgoing correspondence of the Foreign Office, although diplomatic representatives abroad were instructed to continue to address their despatches to the Foreign Office to Castlereagh.[7] However, a century later, when Balfour was at the Paris Peace Conference, his deputy at the Foreign Office was not one of the other Secretaries of State but Curzon, the Lord President of the Council. For shorter absences the greater ease of telegraphic communication and the increase in their own authority had meanwhile made the Under Secretaries the Foreign Secretary's usual deputies in all but the most formal matters.

At first and for some considerable time the Foreign Secretary required little more than clerical assistance in carrying out the functions of his office; he was able to deal personally with the diplomatic correspondence and to decide all matters except those of the merest routine. Even routine matters did not always escape his attention and Palmerston's frequent minutes on the handwriting and style of clerks and diplomats are famous.[8] However, as the business of the Foreign Office multiplied during the nineteenth century,[9] more and more of the work originally performed by the Secretary of State himself had to be delegated, at first to the Under Secretaries of State, but later to more junior officials.

The Under Secretaries of State were normally two in number[10] and they divided the work of the Office between them. Although at first both held office at the plea-

---

[1] For names of Secretaries of State for Foreign Affairs, 1782–1939, see Appendix IV; for Under Secretaries see Tilley and Gaselee, *Foreign Office*, pp.325–330, and *Foreign Office Lists*.
[2] *1st Rpt. of Commissioners on Fees*, p.4.
[3] *British Digest of International Law*, 7 (1965), p.160. The delivery of seals was followed, regularly until 1852 and intermittently thereafter until 1868, by the issue of Letters Patent of Appointment.
[4] Gosses, *Management of Brit. For. Policy*, pp.99–138.
[5] The office of Secretary of State for the Colonies was formally abolished by 'Burke's Act' (22 George III c.82) on 11 July 1782. The colonies remained the concern of the Home Secretary until 1801, when the Secretary of State for War (created in 1794) became Secretary of State for War and the Colonies. Later the number of Secretaries of State increased considerably. At present there are nine.
[6] 7 *B.D.I.L.*, p.158.
[7] F.O.83/1907: circular of 6 Aug. 1814.
[8] Hertslet, *Recollections*, pp.76–82; see also examples in F.O.96/17–23; F.O.800/382.
[9] The number of despatches, etc., received and sent increased from 12,402 in 1826 to 101,515 in 1900 (F.O.83/2194). The peak under the old registration system was 125,011 in 1904. The registration figures after 1906 are not strictly comparable as most outgoing correspondence was not registered separately; but see p.67, n.2.
[10] William Fraser was sole Under Secretary, 1783–1789; there was a third Under Secretary, 1824–1827.

sure of the Secretary of State,[1] the advantages of continuity were appreciated and one of the existing Under Secretaries was normally retained by a new Secretary of State; from this practice there developed the office of Permanent Under Secretary, who remained whatever the political complexion of the government in power for the time being. The other Under Secretary was identified more closely with the Secretary of State and was a political appointee. He was not at first necessarily a Member of Parliament or a Peer, indeed in the first half of the nineteenth century ten Government Under Secretaries held office without being members of either House. Only later in the century, when a succession of Foreign Secretaries in the House of Lords made it convenient to have an Under Secretary in the Commons, did the office become that of Parliamentary Under Secretary.[2]

The duties of the Under Secretaries were defined in 1828 as:

> to receive from the Secretary of State, and to carry into execution all Orders relating to the official business of the Department; in the absence, or under the direction of the Secretary of State, to receive and communicate with the Ministers and Consuls of Foreign Powers resident in this Country; to prepare Drafts of such special Letters and Instructions as occasion may require; to transact the details of whatever business is of the most confidential nature; to correspond with other Departments of the Government; and, generally, to be responsible to the Secretary of State for the due execution of the business of the Office in all its Branches.[3]

At first there was little distinction in importance or duties between the two Under Secretaries, and where one was more influential this was more often for personal reasons than because of the particular Under Secretaryship which he held, as in the case of Edward Cooke, a personal friend of Castlereagh, who was Government Under Secretary from 1812 to 1817. Only after the translation of his successor, Joseph Planta, to the Permanent Under Secretaryship in 1823 did the latter office commence to become the more important of the two, taking over in time more and more of the diplomatic business of the Office. Edmund Hammond's tenure of the office between 1854 and 1873, coinciding as it did with the increasing involvement of the other Under Secretary in parliamentary affairs, consolidated the influence of the Permanent Under Secretary and made him the acknowledged professional head of the Foreign Office. Before him only two Under Secretaries, George Aust (1790–1796) and Joseph Planta (1817–1827), had been appointed from the Clerks in the Foreign Office;[4] since his time every Permanent Under Secretary, with the special exception of Sir Julian Pauncefote (1882–1889), has previously served either as a Clerk in the Office or in the Diplomatic Service or both. As the importance of the Permanent Under Secretary grew, that of the Parliamentary Under Secretary declined until by 1876 his duties were confined to the parliamentary business of the Office,[5] although this was combined at times until the end of the century with superintendence of the Commercial Department.[6]

The need for a third Under Secretary had been apparent as early as 1824 and for two short periods between then and 1827 a second Government Under Secretary

[1] F.O.366/542, ff.2v–3.

[2] For the early history of the Under Secretaries see E. Jones-Parry, 'Under Secretaries of State for Foreign Affairs, 1782–1853' in E.H.R. XLIX (1934), pp.308–320.

[3] F.O.366/386: memorandum: Office of the Secretary of State for Foreign Affairs, June 1828.

[4] But William Fraser, the first permanent (if not Permanent) Under Secretary in the Foreign Office (1782–1789), and an Under Secretary of State since 1765, had begun his career as a Clerk in the Secretary of State's Office in 1753; W.R. Hamilton (Permanent Under Secretary, 1809–1822) had previously been Private Secretary and Précis Writer to the Secretary of State; and H.U. Addington (Permanent Under Secretary, 1842–1854) had served in the Diplomatic Service. In addition some Government Under Secretaries had previously served in the Diplomatic Service, and one (Charles Arbuthnot, 1803–1804) had been Précis Writer.

[5] F.O.366/386: minute by Tenterden, 17 July 1876.

[6] F.O. Lists; Gosses, Management of Brit. For. Policy, pp.161–163.

was appointed. Nothing permanent was done, however, until 1858 when the pressure of parliamentary business on the Parliamentary Under Secretary and the absence of Hammond through illness had made the need an urgent one. Accordingly, James Murray, a Foreign Office Clerk, was appointed as Assistant Under Secretary. He was, however, given little scope for initiative at first, all his activities being carefully supervised by one or other of the Under Secretaries. His duties were:

> to assist the Parliamentary Under Secretary whenever he is in attendance, but at such times he is to sign nothing. When the Permanent Under Secretary is absent then, in as much as at no time should both Under Secretaries of State be on leave, the Parliamentary Under Secretary will sign for him and vice versa, but if from any casualty both Under Secretaries of State should be away the Assistant Under Secretary will sign. When the Parliamentary Under Secretary is absent the Assistant Under Secretary will manage his division, and when the Permanent Under Secretary is absent he will do the same for him.[1]

In 1860 the Assistant Under Secretary was assigned the Consular Department as his special responsibility and permitted to dispose of the formal and routine business of that Department without reference to the Under Secretaries, but apart from such business he was still closely superintended by them.[2]

In 1876 a second Assistant Under Secretary, Sir Julian Pauncefote, a lawyer and former Legal Assistant Under Secretary at the Colonial Office, was appointed, primarily to conduct the legal business of the Office but with some diplomatic responsibilities.[3] On his promotion to Permanent Under Secretary in 1882 he retained his special responsibility for the conduct of legal business and his successor as Assistant Under Secretary, Philip Currie, was given a greater share of the diplomatic business[4]. The appointment of a Legal Assistant in 1886 (see p. 11) made it unnecessary thereafter for one of the Under Secretaries or Assistant Under Secretaries to be a lawyer.

A third Assistant Under Secretary was added in 1898[5] and the work of the Office was then divided as follows: the Permanent Under Secretary superintended the two main political departments, Western and Eastern (Europe), and also the Chief Clerk's, Treaty and Librarian's Departments; the Parliamentary Under Secretary conducted the parliamentary business and superintended the Commercial and Sanitary Department; and the three Assistant Under Secretaries superintended between them the American and Asiatic, the African and the Consular Departments and assisted the Permanent Under Secretary with some of the work of the Western and Treaty Departments.[6]

Apart from the short-lived posts of Superintendent of Protectorates, 1900–1905, and Controller of Commercial and Consular Affairs, 1912–1919 (see p. 17), which occupied an intermediate position between the Assistant Under Secretaries and the Senior Clerks, there were no further changes in the number of senior posts in the Office until February 1916. Then the Parliamentary Under Secretary, Lord Robert Cecil, was given the additional title of Minister of Blockade and an Under Secretary of State for Blockade was appointed to assist him. In the following year an Additional Parliamentary Under Secretary for Foreign Affairs was appointed. In July 1918 Cecil relinquished the Ministry of Blockade and became Assistant Secretary of

---

[1] F.O.366/675, pp.17–18, 36–39, 45–46.
[2] F.O.366/386: minute by Russell, 24 Dec. 1859.
[3] F.O.366/677, pp.427–429, 507–511; F.O.881/5941*, p.14; R.B.Mowat, *Life of Lord Pauncefote* (1929), pp.29–32, 37–39.
[4] F.O.366/678, pp.378–380; F.O.881/5941*, p.20.
[5] F.O.366/760, pp.257–258.
[6] *F.O. List 1899*, p.7.

State, but this title did not pass into permanent use. After the War the Additional Parliamentary Secretary remained, but the Minister and Under Secretary of Blockade disappeared when the Ministry was disbanded in 1919.

In 1919 the permanent senior establishment of the Office was one Permanent Under Secretary and one Assistant Under Secretary, with eight Assistant Secretaries (subsequently re-named Counsellors) corresponding to the former Senior Clerks but with rank equivalent to the pre-war Assistant Under Secretaries.[1] By 1922 the number of Assistant Under Secretaries had been increased to three, and in 1925 the senior Assistant Under Secretary was given the title of Deputy Under Secretary. Thereafter, apart from some variations in numbers the only innovations in the senior establishment before 1939 were the appointment of a second Parliamentary Under Secretary in 1935 and the creation of the post of Chief Diplomatic Adviser in 1938.[2] The need on occasion for a member of the Government above the rank of Parliamentary Under Secretary to assist the Secretary of State with specific subjects, such as League of Nations affairs, was met between the wars by assigning responsibility to a non-departmental Minister, such as the Chancellor of the Duchy of Lancaster.

Foreign Office Clerks, etc.[3]

In 1782 there were in the Office of the Secretary of State for Foreign Affairs one First or Chief Clerk, two Senior Clerks and five Clerks.[4] When the establishment of the Office was regulated by Order in Council in 1795, there were twelve Clerks, together with a Private Secretary and a Précis Writer to the Secretary of State, two Office Keepers and a Housekeeper.[5] In 1799 the twelve Clerks were graded as a Chief Clerk, two Senior Clerks, four Decypherers and five Junior Clerks.[6] By 1822 the establishment had been increased to one Chief Clerk, four First Class or Senior Clerks, six Second Class Clerks, six Third Class or Junior Clerks, three Assistant Junior Clerks, a Supplementary Clerk in the Chief Clerk's Department, a Private Secretary and a Précis Writer, a Librarian and Sub-Librarian, a Translator, two Office Keepers, a Door Porter and a Printer.[7]

In 1854 the establishment was a Chief Clerk, seven Senior Clerks, fourteen Second Class Clerks, ten Junior Clerks, six Assistant Junior Clerks, a Librarian, Sub-Librarian and five Supplementary Clerks in the Library, a Superintendent and Assistant in the Treaty Department, three Supplementary Clerks in the Chief Clerk's Department, a Translator, a Private Secretary, a Précis Writer, a Printer and ten Office Keepers, etc.[8]

In 1910 there were nine Senior Clerks, nine Assistant Clerks, twenty-eight Junior Clerks, two Legal Advisers, a Deputy Marshal of Ceremonies, an Oriental Translator, an Assistant and a First Class Clerk in the Financial Department, a Librarian and Assistant Librarian, a Superintendent and Assistant in the Treaty Department, a Registrar, eleven Staff Officers, thirty-seven Second Division Clerks, nine Typists, a Printer and eighteen Office Keepers, etc.[9]

---

[1] F.O.366/780–781.
[2] For details see the annual F.O. Lists.
[3] For the Foreign Office Establishment and details of the careers of the Clerks see the annual F.O. Lists from 1852 onwards; for Clerks serving before 1852 see Appendix I.
[4] F.O.366/669, pt.1, p.65.
[5] F.O.366/542, f.12.
[6] F.O.366/671, pp.118–123.
[7] F.O.366/542, f.41.
[8] Ibid., f.92.
[9] F.O. List 1910, pp.1–4.

By 1939 the establishment had increased almost fivefold. Then there were thirteen Counsellors, twenty First Secretaries, nineteen Second Secretaries, twenty-two Third Secretaries, three Legal Advisers, a Claims Adviser, a Librarian and Keeper of the Papers, a Vice-Marshal of the Diplomatic Corps, a Deputy Establishment Officer, a Deputy Finance Officer, twenty-one Establishment and Accounts Officers, a Superintendent of Printing, Stationery and Stores, a Chief Passport Officer, an Assistant Passport Officer and an Establishment Officer in the Passport Office, a Head of Department and an Assistant Head of Department in the Communications Department, seven Assistants, thirty-eight Staff Officers, three Assistant Press Officers, a Minor Staff Officer, a Second Division Clerk, 272 Clerical Officers, etc., 134 Typists, etc., nine Clerical Assistants, twenty-one Office Keepers, etc., and six Presskeepers.[1]

By the second quarter of the nineteenth century the Chief Clerk and the Senior Clerks had virtually ceased to have any direct dealings with the political (i.e. diplomatic) work of the Office, their duties being confined to the non-political departments.[2] The political departments were headed by Second Class Clerks who received special allowances as Clerks Assistant to the Under Secretaries. They had been known until 1831 as Private Secretaries to the Under Secretaries[3] and had originally been of less importance. In 1841 the Clerks Assistant were re-graded as Senior Clerks.[4] In 1857 a new class of Assistant Clerks was created from the senior Second Class Clerks to act as deputies to the Senior Clerks in the political departments; at the same time the remaining Clerks on the establishment were reorganized into three classes of Junior Clerks.[5] These Junior Clerks staffed the political departments, where much of their work was of a very routine clerical nature.[6]

In the non-political departments such work had been done since the early years of the nineteenth century by Supplementary Clerks, sometimes known as Supplemental, Extra, Temporary or Supernumerary Clerks. Originally these Supplementary Clerks were not on the establishment and were paid by special arrangement from the Contingencies Account; in some cases they worked for several years without pay before such arrangements were made. Before examinations were introduced, vacancies on the establishment were often filled from Supernumerary Clerks on probation.

In 1881 the classes of Junior Clerks were reduced from three to two and Lower Division Clerks (known as Second Division Clerks after 1890[7]) were introduced. The latter were not, however, permitted to work in the political departments, the first four being assigned to the Commerical and Consular Departments.[8] In 1896 the Supplementary Clerks in all the non-political departments were assimilated to the Second Division, certain of the senior ones being appointed Staff Officers.[9] Between 1906 and 1914 a few Boy Clerks were employed in the Registry.[10]

---

[1] *F.O. List 1939*, pp.1–12.
[2] F.O.366/386: memorandum of June 1828. Earlier Stephen Rolleston, as First Senior and later Chief Clerk, had acted as Assistant to the Under Secretaries (see pp. 17–18 below).
[3] F.O.366/673, p.162. For their duties see F.O.366/386: memorandum of June 1828.
[4] F.O.366/542, ff.75–80.
[5] F.O.366/386: draft, Clarendon to Treasury, 13 Jan. 1857; Treasury to F.O., 16 March 1857. The proposal had first been made in 1854, but had been rejected by the Treasury (F.O.366/449, pp.204–209, 251–258, 271–276).
[6] F.O.881/779, pp.2–3.
[7] F.O.366/724, p.403A.
[8] F.O.366/678, pp.159–160.
[9] F.O.366/760, p.99A.
[10] *App. to 5th Rpt. of R. Comm. on Civil Service*, H.C. 1914–16 [Cd.7749] XI, qq.36916–36921.

The two classes of Junior Clerks were amalgamated in 1908,[1] by which date they had ceased to be glorified copying clerks and were taking more and more part in the direction of foreign policy. This had been a gradual process, and it is a matter of opinion how far the reform of the registration system in 1906 contributed to it (see p. 63).

After World War I the class of Junior Clerks was divided once more in order to assimilate it with the Second and Third Secretary grades in the Diplomatic Service, with which the Foreign Office was now amalgamated. Diplomatic ranks were now generally applied to Foreign Office Clerks: Assistant Clerks became First Secretaries; the Senior Clerks of the six political departments and of the Political Intelligence Department, together with the Chief Clerk, were re-named Assistant Secretaries (and subsequently Counsellors), equivalent in rank to the pre-war Assistan-Under Secretaries.[2]

The amalgamation with the Diplomatic Service, although it had been coming for some time (see p. 26) was a break with the past which altered the character of the Foreign Office. It ended the continuity which the Clerks in the political departments had, by spending most if not all of their careers in London, hitherto brought to the work of the Office. From now on continuity had to be provided by the Second Division Clerks and their successors, who were not liable for foreign service. This meant that the keeping of proper records became more important than ever and it was fortunate that the reforms of the registry system of 1920 (see pp. 67–71) made this possible.

After 1920 no further appointments of Second Division Clerks were made, although the last survivor of this class continued to serve until after 1939. Their place at the bottom of the Foreign Office hierarchy was taken by Clerical and Executive Officers, both male and female.[3]

Until 1856 appointments to all posts in the Foreign Office were made by the Secretary of State without examination, and those appointed were often only sixteen or seventeen or even younger; but in that year Lord Clarendon introduced an examination for both Junior and Supplementary Clerks,[4] and thereafter the age of newly appointed Clerks rose to the early twenties and a University career became a normal prelude. The Foreign Office examination was not the general Civil Service one but was specifically devised to meet the Office's needs, particularly with regard to ability in foreign languages. The original subjects were Handwriting, Dictation, Précis and French[5] and the standards were not high; later the standards were raised and other subjects, including German and a choice of optional subjects, were added. At first the examinations were not competitive, only one candidate being nominated on each vacancy. An element of competition was, however, introduced within a few years, although even then the competition was not open, as only persons nominated by the Secretary of State (which in practice often meant by his Private Secretary) could compete. In the earliest competitions the number of candidates was limited to three and it was customary for these to work unpaid in the Foreign Office as Expectant Candidates while awaiting a competition. Later the number of candidates was increased and in 1907 the power to nominate was placed in the hands of a Board of Selection and the competition became virtually an open

[1] F.O.366/761, p.189.
[2] F.O.366/780–781.
[3] *F.O. Lists 1919–1939;* F.O.366/782, ff.103–196; F.O.366/783.
[4] There was a separate examination for Passport Clerks: see F.O.366/545: memorandum by Lenox Conyngham, 24 Dec. 1859.
[5] F.O.366/449, pp.411–412.

B

one. Meanwhile, in 1905 the examination had been assimilated to that for the rest of the Civil Service, although emphasis was still placed upon languages. Lower Division Clerks and their successors were appointed on the results of the normal Civil Service examinations for their grades.[1]

Secretaries of State had their Private Secretaries long before 1782, but it was only by the Order in Council of 1795 that this post was placed on the establishment. At the same time the Précis Writer was placed on the establishment, although an earlier Précis Writer is recorded.[2] In 1828 the duties of the Private Secretary were:

> to take charge of the Private Correspondence of the Secretary of State, and to make Copies of all Letters which he writes on private and confidential subjects;

those of the Précis Writer were:

> to make an abstract of all the official Dispatches which are addressed to the Secretary of State, and to copy all the Dispatches which he addresses to His Majesty's Ministers abroad. This abstract, and these Copies, are for the private use of the Secretary of State; and they are taken away by him when he quits the Office.[3]

Until 1812 the Précis Writer appears to have been the senior of the two, but thereafter the Private Secretary increased in importance and influence and by the middle of the nineteenth century he was beginning to play a part in deciding promotions and appointments both within the Office and in the Diplomatic Service.[4] Meanwhile the Précis Writer became in fact, although not in title, an Assistant Private Secretary;[5] the title survived until 1915. The Private Secretary and Précis Writer were not at first necessarily appointed from the Clerks in the Office; indeed when Brook Taylor became Private Secretary in 1796 he vacated his clerkship (see p.154). From about the middle of the nineteenth century, however, it became customary for appointments to be made only from the Clerks. Also from about the same time it became the usual practice to appoint one or more Assistant Private Secretaries, a post which is found occasionally at an earlier date. From 1866 the Parliamentary Under Secretary had a Private Secretary;[6] from 1875 the Permanent Under Secretary also had one.[7] Between 1915 and 1921 a Diplomatic Secretary handled those parts of the Private Secretary's duties which related to the Diplomatic Service, the holder of this post being a senior diplomat. After 1921 transfers and appointments in the Diplomatic Service were placed in the hands of a committee and the post of Diplomatic Secretary was reduced to that of Assistant Private Secretary, its holder doing the remaining diplomatic work but as a junior and with less authority.[8]

Two, and after 1858 four, Foreign Office Clerks were resident in the Office. The duties of these Resident Clerks were:

1. To open and distribute to the Under Secretaries of State Despatches arriving out of Office hours:
2. To decypher telegrams arriving from abroad out of Office hours and to send the contents at once to the Secretary of State . . . :
3. To send Copies of all such telegrams to the two Under Secretaries of State, to the Queen and the Prime Minister:

---

[1] Tilley and Gaselee, *Foreign Office*, pp.72–89; *Camb. Hist. of Brit. For. Policy* III, pp.615–616.
[2] *F.O. List, August 1854*, p.8.
[3] F.O.366/386: memorandum of June 1828. For the Précis Writer see also *Rpt. of Sel. Ctee. on Official Salaries*, H.C. 1850 (611) XV, q.3072.
[4] S. T. Bindoff, 'The Unreformed Diplomatic Service, 1812–60' in *T.R. Hist. Soc.*, 4th Series XVIII (1935), p.153.
[5] F.O.366/449, pp.552–553; *Rpt. of Sel. Ctee. on Diplomatic Service*, H.C. 1861 (459) VI, q.1473.
[6] F.O.366/676, p.94.
[7] F.O.366/258: draft salary list for quarter ending 29 March 1875.
[8] Tilley and Gaselee, *Foreign Office*, pp.206–208.

4. To put into Cypher and despatch all telegrams which are required to be sent out of Office hours:

5. The resident Clerk on duty to be always within reach and available if wanted; and specifically to be on duty throughout the day on Sundays for the receipt and despatch of telegrams.[1]

Mention should be made here of the Foreign Office Agency System which operated from before 1782 until its abolition in 1870. The Agents were Foreign Office Clerks who undertook, in return for a commission, to attend to the affairs and interests of members of the Diplomatic and Consular Services during their absence abroad.[2]

The appointment of Sir Julian Pauncefote as Legal Assistant Under Secretary in 1876 has already been mentioned (see p.6). After his promotion to Permanent Under Secretary in 1882 he retained his special responsibility for legal matters until 1886, when a Legal Assistant was appointed.[3] The title was changed in 1892 to the present one of Legal Adviser.[4] An Assistant Legal Adviser was appointed in 1902; a second was added in 1914; and a third in 1925. In 1929 one of the Assistant Legal Advisers became Claims Adviser.[5]

During World War I the Foreign Office had its own Naval Adviser (Admiral Sir Dudley de Chair) and Adviser on Arabian and Palestine Affairs (Sir Mark Sykes) (see p.170).

The post of Translator of the German Language, a sinecure, was put on the establishment in 1797,[6] but was abolished in 1809, the emoluments having been shared since 1806 by three persons, two of them Clerks on the establishment.[7] At about the same time the new post of Translator of the Spanish, Portuguese, Italian and Danish Languages was created.[8] This post (its title was later abbreviated to Translator) continued until 1886, when it was abolished and the duties shared among three Junior Clerks, each of whom dealt with translations from German, translation from other languages being divided between them; for this they received an extra allowance.[9] After World War I these Translator posts were restricted to Second Division Clerks and other clerical staff.[10] There was an Assistant Translator between 1823 and 1831.[11] The post of Oriental Translator appeared for the first time in the *Foreign Office List* for 1859 and continued until 1917. Special allowances were made to Clerical Officers and Typists[12] who were proficient in French.

The first Typist entered the Foreign Office in 1889.[13] Some years earlier Sir James Fergusson, the Parliamentary Under Secretary, had suggested the employment of Shorthand Writers and Lord Rosebery encouraged the Clerks in the Office to learn shorthand, but it was not until 1898 that the first Shorthand Writer was appointed.[14]

---

[1] F.O.366/675, pp.21–22. For the duties of the Resident Clerks in 1934 see F.O.366/938, ff.333–343.

[2] For a fuller account of the Agency System see Tilley and Gaselee, *Foreign Office*, pp.209–215. For a case of misappropriation by Agents see F.O.366/449, pp.85–104.

[3] F.O.366/724, pp.198–203.

[4] *F.O. List 1893.*

[5] *F.O. Lists 1903, 1915, 1926, 1930.*

[6] F.O.366/671, pp.20, 25–26. He had been paid from Secret Service funds previously: see K.Ellis, *The Post Office in the Eighteenth Century* (1958), pp.130, 133–134.

[7] F.O.366/380; F.O.366/671, p.303; F.O.95/9/4, f.322.

[8] J.C.Huttner was first paid for the quarter commencing in Oct. 1808 (F.O.366/380); according to the *D.N.B.* he was appointed in 1807.

[9] F.O.366/724, p.236; Tilley and Gaselee, *Foreign Office*, p.146.

[10] F.O.366/800, ff.318–353.

[11] F.O.366/672, p.338; F.O.366/673, pp.38, 167.

[12] F.O.366/800, ff.144–154.

[13] F.O.366/724, pp.361–362.

[14] *Ibid.*, p.191; F.O.366/760, p.293; Tilley and Gaselee, *Foreign Office*, p.84.

The numbers of Typists grew steadily from their first introduction; Shorthand Typists were not used to any great extent until after 1914.

The Foreign Office operated a printing press on its own premises from about 1825. This was for many years in the hands of the Harrison family. James Harrison was first paid as Printer to the Foreign Office on 15 May 1800.[1]

Departments of the Foreign Office: Political Departments

The internal divisions of the Foreign Office are known as departments and in general these can be divided into two categories: political and non-political. The political departments are those in which the diplomatic business of the Office is transacted, each department conducting diplomatic relations with a certain number of countries, the division being on a roughly geographical basis.

At first there were two political departments, one for each Under Secretary, divided on much the same lines as foreign affairs had been divided between the twin Secretaries of State before 1782. Austria, France, Spain, Italy, Portugal, Switzerland, Turkey and the Barbary States were the concern of the *Southern Department*; the other countries of Europe, together with the United States of America, which had formerly been the concern of the Colonial Secretary, were the concern of the *Northern Department*.[2] In general the Government Under Secretary took the Northern Department and the other Under Secretary the Southern, but there appears to have been no hard and fast rule on this until the second decade of the nineteenth century.[3]

The division of countries between the two Departments continued virtually unchanged for over thirty years, although the course of the long wars with France during that period meant that at times there were no diplomatic relations with many countries[4] and that some temporary rearrangements had to be made, the most important being the transfer of the U.S.A. to the Southern Department for a time. When diplomatic relations returned to normal after 1815 there was a rearrangement of the countries, the Northern Department taking the U.S.A., Denmark, Holland, Persia, Prussia and the other North German States, Russia, Sweden, Turkey, the Ionian Islands and (from 1823) Greece, China and India, with the Barbary Powers added in some years.[5] The other countries were assigned to the Southern Department.

In January 1824 there was another rearrangement of the departments, the U.S.A. and Holland being exchanged for Austria and the Italian States.[6] This arrangement was short-lived, however, for in May of that same year, the appointment of a third Under Secretary necessitated a further reorganization, the new Under Secretary taking the Netherlands, Sweden, Denmark, the German States, Portugal and Brazil. During the vacancy of the third Under Secretaryship from March 1825 to January 1826, the countries of that department were superintended by the Permanent Under Secretary, and when Clanricarde became third Under Secretary in January 1826 he took Prussia, the German and Italian States and Switzerland for his department.[7]

---

[1] F.O.366/556: memorandum by G.Lenox Conyngham, 23 March 1847; C.R. and H.G.Harrison, *The House of Harrison* (1914), pp.18–22.
[2] F.O.95/635: loose paper: *Correspondence in the State Paper Office*, 22 Feb. 1797.
[3] C.K.Webster, *The Foreign Policy of Castlereagh, 1812–1815* (1931), p.45.
[4] *Camb. Hist. of Brit. For. Policy* III, pp.553–554.
[5] F.O.95/446, 447; F.O.566/1: index at beginning of 1819 Diary. For relations with Persia, China and the Barbary States see also pp.30–31 below.
[6] F.O.83/82: circular, 8 Dec. 1823.
[7] *Ibid.*: circulars of 28 and 31 May 1824, 7 March 1825, 1 Jan. 1826.

Following the abolition of the third Under Secretaryship in 1827, the departments were rearranged as follows:

(i) Austria, France, Portugal, Spain, Italy, Switzerland, Turkey, Egypt, Greece;

(ii) Russia, Prussia, Netherlands, Sweden, Denmark, German States, North and South America, Persia.

The first of these departments was superintended by the Government Under Secretary, the second by John Backhouse, the Permanent Under Secretary. At about this time the use of North and South to describe the two departments appears to have been discontinued.

In June 1828 the two departments were completely rearranged, Backhouse taking France, Russia, Prussia, Spain, Turkey, Egypt, Greece, Persia, North and Central America, the Government Under Secretary being left with Austria, Netherlands, Portugal, Sweden, Denmark, Italy, German States, Switzerland and South America.

In 1831 each department was split into two divisions.[1] The arrangement of these was:

(i) France, Spain, North and Central America, Miscellaneous;

(ii) Russia, Prussia, Turkey, Greece, Persia;

(iii) Austria, Portugal, South America;

(iv) Holland, Belgium, Sweden, Denmark, Switzerland, Italy, German States.

The first two divisions were superintended by Backhouse, the other two by the Government Under Secretary. When responsibility for the Barbary States was transferred from the Colonial Office in 1836, it was assigned to the second of these divisions. In the previous year a separate *China Department* had been created on the ending of the East India Company's monopoly and this was placed under the superintendence of G.Lenox Conyngham, a Senior Clerk, who retained the superintendence until he became Chief Clerk in 1841, when it also passed to the second division.[2] In 1840 a minor rearrangement of the above divisions transferred Greece from the second to the first and Spain from the first to the third; Austria appears to have been transferred to the fourth division at about the same time and Prussia also joined this division in 1841.[3] By 1849 the Italian States had been transferred from the fourth to the second division.[4]

From 1852 the annual *Foreign Office Lists* give particulars of the composition of the several departments in the Office. In that year there were still four political departments, their arrangement being that of 1840 as subsequently amended. They were:

(i) France, Greece, North and Central America, Miscellaneous;

(ii) Austria, Prussia, German States, Belgium, Sweden, Switzerland, Netherlands, Lombardy, Denmark and Borneo;

(iii) Russia, Turkey, the rest of Italy, North Africa and the Middle East, China, Siam;

(iv) Spain, Portugal, South America.[5]

---

[1] Later the use of these terms was reversed, each Under Secretary taking a division of the Office, each division consisting of a number of departments.

[2] F.O.366/673, pp.261–263; V.Cromwell, 'An incident in the development of the Permanent Under Secretaryship at the Foreign Office' in *B.I.H.R.* XXXIII (1960), p.102.

[3] F.O.83/124 includes printed lists of the distribution of business in the F.O. for 1827, 1828, 1830, 1834, 1836(?), and 1840. F.O.366/386: memorandum by J.Backhouse, June 1838, has details of the 1831 arrangement and proposals for a rearrangement which appear to have been abortive.

[4] F.O.83/126: list of May 1849.

[5] *F.O. Lists 1852* and *1853*.

Thereafter the first major reorganization was in July 1854, when a fifth political department was added, the departments now being:

(i)   France, Greece, Switzerland, Miscellaneous;
(ii) Austria, Prussia, German States, Denmark;
(iii) Russia, Turkey, North Africa and the Middle East;
(iv) Spain, Portugal, Netherlands, Belgium, South America;
(v)   North and Central America, Sweden, Italy, China.[1]

In 1857 the number of departments was further increased to six with the new department taking Russia, Greece, Sweden and Italy.[2]

With a few minor alterations this arrangement lasted until January 1865, when the political departments were reduced to five:

(i)   the *French Department*: France, Switzerland, Italy, Madagascar and Miscellaneous;
(ii) the *German Department*: Austria, Prussia, German States, Belgium, Denmark, Netherlands, Sweden;
(iii) the *Turkish Department*: Russia, Greece, Turkey, North Africa and the Middle East;
(iv) the *Spanish Department*: Spain, Portugal, Mexico, South and Central America;
(v)   the *American Department*: China, Japan, Siam, U.S.A., Mosquito.[3]

This arrangement remained virtually unchanged until April 1881, when the political departments were further reduced to four with the abolition of the Spanish Department. South and Central America were transferred to the American Department and Spain and Portugal to the French Department.[4]

A little over a year later, in a general reorganization of the Foreign Office at the end of 1882, the political departments were reduced to three:

(i)   the *Western (Europe) Department*: Austria, Germany, Portugal, Spain, France, Italy, Madagascar, North Africa, Belgium, Denmark, Netherlands, Sweden and Norway, Switzerland, Miscellaneous;
(ii) the *American and Asiatic Department*: North, South and Central America, China, Japan, Siam;
(iii) the *Eastern (Europe) Department*: Greece, Montenegro, Roumania, Servia, Russia, Turkey, Egypt, Persia, Central Asia.[5]

The next major change was in 1899, when the American and Asiatic Department was divided into a *Far Eastern* (or *China*) *Department* and an *American Department*.[6] Thereafter there were no major changes until August 1914, when the Eastern and Western Departments were amalgamated in one *War Department* to deal with the general political, naval and military questions connected with the War, including censorship, in addition to the usual work concerning Eastern and Western Europe.[7] This arrangement continued throughout the War.[8]

During 1920 separate *Eastern, Central, Western* and *Northern Departments* emerged from the War Department, which was finally dissolved on 7 October 1920. The *American* (for a short while known as the *American and African*) and the *Far Eastern*

---

[1] T.1/5876A/14333/5512/54; *F.O. List, August 1854.*
[2] F.O.366/386: draft, Clarendon to Treasury, 13 Jan. 1857; Treasury to F.O., 16 March 1857; *F.O. List 1858.*
[3] F.O.366/386: minute by Russell, 29 Oct. 1864; *F.O. List 1865.*
[4] F.O.366/678, p.209; *F.O. List 1882.*
[5] F.O.366/386: minutes of Nov. and Dec. 1882; *F.O. List 1883.*
[6] F.O.366/386: minute by Sanderson, 9 Feb. 1899; *F.O. List 1900.*
[7] F.O.366/786, ff.144–146.
[8] For other departments created during the war see pp.23–24 below.

Departments continued. Later additional political departments were created. The resulting arrangement of departments between 1920 and 1939 was as follows:

(i)   *American and African* (from 1930 *American*): North, Central and South America; Abyssinia (to 1924); Liberia and Africa (to 1930);

(ii) *Far Eastern:* China, Japan, Siam;

(iii) *Eastern:* Turkey, Persia, the Middle East; Egypt (to 1924);

(iv) *Central:* Germany; Austria, Hungary, Italy and Albania, Czechoslovakia, Yugoslavia, Roumania, Bulgaria, Greece (to 1933); Belgium and Luxembourg, Danzig, France, Poland, Europe General, Peace Treaties, War Debts (from 1933); Holland (from 1937); Czechoslovakia (from April 1938);

(v)   *Western:* (from 1922 *League of Nations and Western*): Spain, Portugal; France, Belgium and Luxembourg (to 1933); Holland, Switzerland (to 1936); League of Nations (from 1922);

(vi) *Northern:* Russia (from 1918 to 1919 there had been a separate *Russian Department*), Finland, Sweden, Norway, Denmark, the Baltic States; Poland (to 1933); Afghanistan (from 1924);

(vii) *Egyptian* (formed in 1924): Egypt, the Sudan, Abyssinia (except for a short period in 1935–1936 when there was a separate *Abyssinian Department*), the Italian colonies in Africa; Africa General (from 1930);

(viii) *Southern* (formed in 1933): Austria, Hungary, Italy and Albania, Yugoslavia, Roumania, Bulgaria, Greece; Czechoslovakia (to March 1938); Switzerland from 1936).[1]

Departments of the Foreign Office: Consular, Commerical, Slave Trade and African Departments

Until 1825 no distinction was drawn so far as the organization of the Foreign Office was concerned between diplomatic (or political) and consular affairs. However, the reorganization of the consular system which followed from the Consular Advances Act of that year (6 Geo.IV c.87) involved the establishment of a separate *Consular Department* to deal with the consular correspondence of the Office under the superintendence of John Bidwell, the First Senior Clerk, who continued in this post until October 1851.[2] He exercised a considerable amount of initiative and was permitted to sign and receive despatches on behalf of the Secretary of State.[3] He was, however, nominally subject to the direction of the Under Secretaries[4] and under his successors the whole business of the Department, although still kept separate from the political business, passed more directly under the control of the Under Secretaries, each of whom was concerned with the consular affairs of the countries under his political superintendence. By 1854 the powers of the Superintendent of the Consular Department no longer differed from those of any other Senior Clerk.[5] In 1860 the Consular Department became the special concern of the Assistant Under Secretary, but the Under Secretaries still had an interest (see p.6).

Consuls did not necessarily deal exclusively with the Consular Department. Some consular posts, especially those in the Ottoman Empire, conducted both a political and a consular series of correspondence and dealt also, therefore, with the

[1] F.O.366/781; *F.O. Lists 1920–1939.*
[2] F.O.366/386: draft, Canning to Treasury, 25 Nov. 1825; F.O.366/674, pp.506–513. Bidwell had been dealing with the consular correspondence of North and South America since earlier in the year (F.O.83/82: circular, 17 March 1825).
[3] *Consular Instructions* (1833), para.IV, in *Rpt. from Sel. Ctee. on Consular Estabs.*, H.C. 1835 (499) VI, App. No. 1; F.O.83/86; circular of 15 May 1840.
[4] F.O.366/386: memorandum of June 1828.
[5] *Rpt. from Sel. Ctee. on Consular Service and Appointments*, H.C. 1857–58 (482) VIII, q.3.

appropriate political department.[1] Most posts corresponded to some extent with the other non-political departments. On the other hand in the case of the Far Eastern countries there was no distinction between political and consular correspondence until 1869 and even thereafter both were dealt with, in the first instance, by the appropriate political department until 1897 (see pp.44–45). Until 1836 correspondence with Consuls in the Barbary States was conducted not by the Consular Department of the Foreign Office but by the Colonial Office (see p.30).

The *Slave Trade Department* was responsible for executing the various treaties for the suppression of the Slave Trade which arose from the Congress of Vienna. The work was expected to be only temporary and the Department was not formally placed on the establishment of the Foreign Office until 1841.[2] However, as early as 1824 James Bandinel received a special annual allowance for superintending the Slave Trade business, together with a lump sum in recognition of his having conducted this business over the previous five years.[3] The Superintendent of the Slave Trade Department worked under the direction of one or other of the Under Secretaries. This Department gradually assumed in addition to its responsibilities under the Slave Trade Treaties, general direction of most other business relating to Africa.

A separate *Commercial Department* was established on 1 January 1865 to give effect to the recommendations of the Committee on Trade with Foreign Nations. It was given responsibility for correspondence on commercial matters with missions and consulates abroad, with representatives of foreign powers in England, with the Board of Trade and other government departments, and with Commercial Associations and private individuals.[4] Commercial matters relating to China, Japan and Siam were not included in this arrangement; these were dealt with in the appropriate political department until 1918.

This Commercial Department had a separate existence for less than two years. In October 1866 a combined *Consular and Commercial Department* was formed,[5] an arrangement which lasted until 1872, when a separate *Commercial Department* was again established. This revived Commercial Department was responsible for all matters connected with commercial treaties and tariffs, industrial questions, manufactures, railways and telegraphs, navigation questions, laws relating to commerce, shipping, trade marks, exhibitions and inventions.[6]

Also in 1872 a combined *Consular and Slave Trade Department* was created under a single Superintendent.[7] These two functions could not, however, be conveniently combined for long and in 1877 a *Consular Sub-Division* was created,[8] an arrangement which continued until 30 March 1880, when a separate *Consular Department* was re-established. At the same time sanitary affairs (cattle plague, quarantine and pilgrims), which had previously been dealt with by the Consular Sub-Division, remained with the Slave Trade Department, which was renamed the *Slave Trade and Sanitary Department*.[9]

[1] *2nd Rpt. from Sel. Ctee. on Diplomatic and Consular Services*, H.C.1871 (380) VII, qq.1651, 1653; *Rpt. from Sel. Ctee. on Diplomatic and Consular Services*, H.C. 1872 (314) VII, q.312.
[2] F.O.366/386: draft, Palmerston to Treasury, 9 Aug. 1841.
[3] F.O.83/40: draft, Planta to Bandinel, 4 Dec. 1824; Tilley and Gaselee, *Foreign Office*, p.217 (on p.47 the establishment of the Department is attributed to Canning 'about 1825').
[4] F.O.366/386: minute by Russell, 29 Oct. 1864; F.O.366/675, p.539a.
[5] F.O.366/676, pp.118–124.
[6] *Rpt. from Sel. Ctee. on Dipl. and Cons. Services* (1872), qq.2–5, 2199; F.O.366/677, pp.515–522.
[7] F.O.366/386: memorandum: *Proposed distribution of Clerks in attendance*, Feb. 1872; *F.O. List 1873*.
[8] F.O.366/386: minute by Derby, 15 Dec. 1876.
[9] *Ibid.*: minutes by Lister and Tenterden, Dec. 1879; F.O.366/678, pp.110–112.

In the general reorganization of Foreign Office departments at the end of 1882, consular, commercial, African (formerly Slave Trade) and sanitary affairs were reallocated between two departments, the *Consular and African (East and West) Department*, and the *Commercial and Sanitary Department*.[1] In 1893 separate *African (East and West)* and *Consular Departments* were established.[2] In 1894, 1898 and 1899 there were some minor rearrangements of functions between the three departments,[3] but there were no further major rearrangements until June 1900, when African affairs were divided between the *African Department*, responsible for South-East, West and South-West Africa, and the *African Protectorates Department*, under a Superintendent of Protectorates, responsible for the administration of East Africa, Uganda, British Central Africa and Somaliland.[4]

In April 1905 the post of Superintendent of Protectorates and the African Protectorates Department were abolished when the Colonial Office assumed responsibility for all the African Protectorates except Zanzibar, which remained with the Foreign Office until January 1914.[5] The African Department was abolished at the end of 1913,[6] its remaining functions being transferred to the *American* and later to the *Egyptian Departments* (see p.15).

In April 1912 the Commercial and Sanitary Department and the Consular Department, while remaining separate entities, were put under the superintendence of a Controller of Commercial and Consular Affairs.[7] From 1917 the new *Department of Overseas Trade* (see p.30) took over progressively more and more of the functions of the Commercial and Sanitary Department until in 1919 the post of Controller of Commercial and Consular Affairs was abolished and the Commercial Department itself was run down until it disappeared early in 1920, responsibility for sanitary or health matters passing to the Western Department (and subsequently in 1938 to the Library). At the same time the Consular Department passed partly under the direction of the Department of Overseas Trade.[8]

Departments of the Foreign Office: Chief Clerk's Department
In 1785 Jeremy Sneyd described his duties as Chief Clerk of the Foreign Office as being:

> to prepare all warrants which may arise in the Office for His Majesty's signature, and when signed, to see that they are correctly entered in the respective books; to take care that the public dispatches are punctually transmitted; to keep the accounts of the Office; to receive the Secretary of State's appointments, all the fees and gratuities, and to distribute them to whom they may belong; to pay all the Clerks salaries and contingencies of Office, and to prepare such bills for the Secretary of State's signing, of extraordinaries and extra-extraordinaries, as His Majesty may allow.[9]

Normally there was only one Chief Clerk, but in 1804 Stephen Rolleston was appointed Second Chief Clerk. The division of work at that period was that Thomas Bidwell, Senior, the First Chief Clerk, retained the establishment and financial business, while Rolleston acted as Assistant to the Under Secretaries in the political

[1] F.O.366/386: minutes of Nov. and Dec. 1882.
[2] *F.O. List 1894.*
[3] F.O.366/391: Sanderson to Rosebery, 22 Feb. 1894; F.O.366/386: minute by Sanderson, 8 Dec. 1897; various minutes, Feb. and March 1899.
[4] F.O.366/760, pp.340–358; *F.O. List 1901.*
[5] F.O.366/761, p.63a; Tilley and Gaselee, *Foreign Office*, pp.220–224.
[6] F.O.366/761, p.431a; *F.O. List 1914.*
[7] F.O.366/761, p.334; *5th Rpt. of R. Comm. on Civil Service* (1914–16), qq.37318, 37336–37339.
[8] F.O.366/781, f.339.
[9] *1st Rpt. of Commrs. on Fees*, p.28.

business of the Office, a responsibility which had already been his as First Senior Clerk, and which he continued to exercise, together with the establishment and financial business of the Office when he became sole Chief Clerk on Bidwell's death in 1817.[1] On his retirement in 1824 his successor's duties were confined to the establishment and financial business of the Office[2] and thereafter the Chief Clerk played virtually no part in the conduct of the political business. Also in 1824 the Chief Clerk ceased for a time to be responsible for the day-to-day work in connection with the accounts of diplomatic representatives abroad and of the King's Messengers, the first duty being assigned to the Third Senior Clerk and the second to the Librarian.[3]

In 1836 the Chief Clerk had custody of the three accounts of the Office: the Fee Fund, for the payment of all salaries and allowances to officers on the establishment; the Contingent Fund, for the payment of tradesmen's bills, rent, rates, taxes, wages and allowances; and the Messenger's Fund. He also recorded precedents of grants of money and appointments, prepared and sealed consular commissions and exequaturs, issued passports, dealt with the Treasury over the expenditure of the Diplomatic and Consular Services, dealt with correspondence respecting foreign orders and was responsible, under the direction of the Secretary and Under Secretaries of State, for the internal arrangements and discipline of the Office.[4]

In 1839 Palmerston considered abolishing the post of Chief Clerk, but its existence was defended by the Under Secretaries[5] and its duties were in fact increased. In that same year the day-to-day work in connection with the diplomatic accounts was restored;[6] two years later, on the appointment of Lenox Conyngham as Chief Clerk, the Treaty and Royal Letter business, which he had previously superintended as a Senior Clerk, was added, although he did relinquish the China Department.[7] In 1846 questions relating to foreign ministers' privileges (formerly the concern of the Librarian), to foreign orders and to births, marriages and deaths registered at British missions were also added.[8]

In 1854 the Treaty and Royal Letter business passed once more to a separate department; at the same time the Chief Clerk took over from the Librarian the superintendence of the Queen's Messengers.[9] Thereafter his duties remained virtually unchanged for the rest of the nineteenth century,[10] although free deliveries,[11] consular commissions and exequaturs and passport business were transferred to the Treaty Department in 1891[12] and certain routine functions were taken over from the African Department in 1899.[13]

In 1900 the title of the Department was changed to the *Financial Department*, and

[1] F.O.366/671, pp.119, 184, 292–293, 298; F.O.366/672, p.147.
[2] F.O.366/394: minute by Canning, 2 Feb. 1824; Canning to Treasury, 4 Feb. 1824.
[3] Cromwell, *B.I.H.R.* XXXIII, p.102.
[4] F.O.366/386: minute by Thomas Bidwell, Jr., 23 Aug. 1836. See also *Ibid.*: memorandum of June 1828; F.O.366/674, pp.71–76.
[5] F.O.366/674, pp.98–101.
[6] F.O.366/673, pp.376–377.
[7] F.O.366/386: draft, Palmerston to Treasury, 9 Aug. 1841; F.O.366/674, pp.50–70; Cromwell, *B.I.H.R.* XXXIII, p.102.
[8] Cromwell, *loc.cit.* Foreign ministers' privileges, or protections, concern the diplomatic immunity of the staffs of their missions in London. Registration of births, marriages and deaths by British Consuls was the responsibility of the Consular Department.
[9] T.1/5826A/14333/5512/54. The transfer to the Chief Clerk of the superintendence of the Messengers had been suggested (and rejected) as early as 1839 (F.O.366/674, pp.85–87).
[10] F.O.366/678, pp.316–339; *4th Rpt. of R. Comm. on Civil Estabs.*, H.C. 1890 [C.6172] XXVII, qq.26350–26355.
[11] That is correspondence relating to the custom free entry of the personal effects and baggage of diplomats.
[12] F.O.366/724, p.465.
[13] F.O.366/386: minutes of Feb.–Mar. 1899.

the Chief Clerk reduced to the rank of Senior Clerk and styled Chief Clerk of the Financial Department.[1] This arrangement continued until 1913, when the Department became known again as the *Chief Clerk's Department* under the Chief Clerk of the Foreign Office, who ranked immediately after the Controller of Commercial and Consular Affairs.[2]

Between the Wars there were a number of changes in the Department: a separate *King's Messengers and Communications Department* was established in 1921 (see p.23); a Finance Officer was appointed in 1922 to act as accounting officer for the Foreign Office;[3] the title of the Department was changed in 1933 to the *Establishment and Finance Department*, the Chief Clerk becoming the Principal Establishment Officer; and in 1938 the two posts of Principal Establishment Officer and Finance Officer were merged. At the beginning of the inter-War period the Chief Clerk ranked as an Assistant Secretary, but later the Chief Clerk or Principal Establishment Officer had the rank of Assistant (and even, in one case, Deputy) Under Secretary.[4]

Departments of the Foreign Office: Treaty and Royal Letter Department
Despite its title the Treaty and Royal Letter Department was not (and is not) concerned with the detailed negotiation of treaties with foreign powers. Its function was to prepare the formal documents required by those conducting negotiations, to deal with matters of protocol involved and to engross the resulting treaties. Detailed negotiations were conducted under the direction of the appropriate political department or, in the case of commercial treaties, of the Commercial Department.

The origins of a separate Treaty and Royal Letter Department are to be found in Castlereagh's direction in October 1813 that Henry Rolleston, a Foreign Office Clerk, should henceforth perform exclusively the duties of 'engrossing Treaties with Foreign Powers, Diplomatic Commissions and other Instruments for the signature of His Royal Highness the Prince Regent, and for passing His Majesty's Great Seal, [and] in copying and entering the same in the proper Books of the Office'.[5] At first Rolleston worked on his own, but from 1817 he had an assistant, J.B.Bergne, who was unpaid until 1824, when he was made a Supplementary Clerk paid from the Contingencies Fund; he was put on the establishment in 1841.[6]

Rolleston retained the superintendence of the Department when he became Fourth Senior Clerk in 1824 and the superintendence remained linked to that post when he was succeeded by Lenox Conyngham in 1834.[7] When Lenox Conyngham became Third Senior Clerk and subsequently, in 1841, Chief Clerk, he retained the superintendence of the Treaty and Royal Letter Department.[8] In 1854, however, a separate Treaty Department was re-established under the superintendence of Bergne.[9]

In 1874 the Department was responsible for treaties, ceremonial, full powers, commissions, credentials and sign manual instructions, royal letters, British and

---

[1] F.O.366/760, pp.340–358.
[2] F.O.366/761, p.433.
[3] F.O.366/789, ff.1–22; F.O.366/801, ff.17–37; F.O.366/805, f.321.
[4] F.O.366/781, ff.319, 343–344; F.O.366/918, ff.394–404; F.O.366/1031, file 653; *F.O. Lists 1922–1939.*
[5] F.O.366/672, pp.68–69.
[6] F.O.366/313: draft, Canning to Treasury, 10 Feb. 1824; F.O.366/542, ff.69–87; *F.O. List 1855,* p.31.
[7] For his duties in 1839 see F.O.366/674, pp.114–116.
[8] Cromwell, *B.I.H.R.* XXXIII, p.102; F.O.95/591/2, ff.206–209.
[9] T.1/5876A/14333/5512/54.

foreign orders, medals, shipwreck and honorary rewards, precedence, diplomatic privilege, presents, foreign titles of nobility and letters of introduction.[1] By 1882 extradition and naturalization, copyright and consular conventions had been added.[2] In 1891 free deliveries, consular commissions and exequaturs, and passports were taken over from the Chief Clerk's Department;[3] in 1894 Postal, Telegraph and Railway Unions and Conferences, and postal treaties and arrangements were taken over from the Commercial Department in exchange for trade marks, patents and copyright.[4]

At the beginning of World War I the Department was given special responsibility for Prize Court matters (a separate *Prize Court Department* was subsequently formed to deal with these), for questions arising in connection with the laws of neutrality, for the treatment of British armed merchant vessels and for the treatment of aliens in the United Kingdom, the Colonies and the Dominions (subsequently the concern of the *Prisoners of War and Aliens Department*).[5] During the War, the *Passport Office*, which had functioned under the direction of the Treaty Department since 1891, became virtually a separate department (see pp.22–23).

Departments of the Foreign Office: Library and Registry[6]

The first Librarian of the Foreign Office was Richard Ancell, appointed in 1801,[7] but it was under his two successors, Lewis Hertslet (1810–1857) (see Plate I) and his son, Edward (1857–1896), that the Library reached its eminence.

The Library had from the beginning concerned itself with the custody of and reference to both printed books[8] and the manuscript correspondence of the Office. Ancell had busied himself with 'arranging, methodizing and digesting the whole of the manuscript correspondences with the Foreign Department' and with discovering stray records.[9] To these duties Lewis Hertslet added: the making of a Register and Index (from 1810) (see pp.39–40); the preparation of memoranda, many of them of a kind which would later have been drawn up by the Legal Adviser (from 1816); the publication semi-officially of the series of *Hertslet's Commercial Treaties* (from 1820) and of *British and Foreign State Papers* (from 1824) (see pp.90–91); the cataloguing of the printed books (from 1848); and many other miscellaneous duties.[10] In addition he was Superintendent of King's (Queen's) Messengers from 1824 to 1854, having previously acted, like Ancell before him, as their Private Agent.[11]

By 1861 the Library was organized in four branches: the Manuscript Library and General Reference Room; the Printed Library; the preparation of memoranda; and the Registry.[12] By 1884 the Reference Room had become a separate branch and a

---

[1] F.O.881/2593, p.2.
[2] F.O.366/678, p.431.
[3] F.O.366/724, p.465.
[4] F.O.366/760, pp.9A–9B.
[5] F.O.366/786, ff.144–145.
[6] The records of the Library are not dealt with separately below. Before 1906 they will be found mainly in *General Correspondence, Great Britain and General* (F.O.83); after 1906 in *General Correspondence after 1906, Library* (F.O.370). See pp.56, 72 below.
[7] F.O.366/672, p.2.
[8] For the Printed Library and other non-record material see W.C.Dalgoutte and C.J.Child, 'The Foreign Office as a Source of Historical Information' in *Government Information and the Research Worker*, ed. R.Staveley and M.Piggott (2nd ed., 1965), pp.85–91.
[9] F.O.366/672, p.2; F.O.95/635; OBS 880.
[10] F.O.366/386: memorandum of June 1828; F.O.366/392: memorandum by Lenox Conyngham, 7 Feb. 1854; F.O.366/673, pp.470–471; F.O.83/181; F.O.83/636; Hertslet, *Recollections*, pp.144–145.
[11] T.1/5876A/14333/5512/54: memorandum by Hertslet, 5 Feb. 1854; F.O.366/471: Hertslet to Clarendon, 14 Oct. 1854. Hertslet's papers as Agent for the King's Messengers are in F.O.351 (see p.166 below).
[12] F.O.366/675, p.325.

General Duties branch had been added.[1] Strictly speaking the Library was required to produce memoranda only when papers over fifteen years old were involved, but in practice this limitation was not observed.[2] The Registry was something of a mis-nomer, since it did not register the incoming correspondence of the Office, as did the Colonial Office Registry of this period,[3] but dealt only with correspondence which had passed out of current use and had been arranged and bound. The regis-tration of incoming correspondence was carried out in the respective departments (see pp.34, 42). The General Duties involved a wide and varied range of subjects, including watching public sales to ensure that no diplomatic papers were sold or published without the sanction of the Government, questions relating to the inter-change of official documents with foreign governments,[4] and preparing tables showing the arrival and departure of Messengers and mails.[5]

Insufficiency of staff was the constant concern of the Librarian and the registra-tion work in particular was almost constantly in arrears, sometimes by a consider-able number of years.[6] In 1890 the Ridley Commission was critical of the existing registration system, which, even when kept as up to date as possible, involved a delay of possibly four years while papers were awaiting transfer to the Library (this took place when they were between one and two years old), arranging and binding.[7] As a result the making of registers and indexes in the Library was discontinued, after working off the existing arrears, and the work entrusted instead to the depart-ments. In practice the departments neglected their indexing work and from 1900 this was entrusted again to the Library (see p.45).

In 1906 the system of dealing with the correspondence of the Office was drasti-cally revised and for the first time a *Registry* was established which was responsible for the correspondence from the time of its receipt to the time of its transfer to the Public Record Office. This new Registry was a branch of the Library and the Registrar was subordinate to the Librarian. Within the Registry there were three Sub-Registries, one for each floor of the Office. In time this new system was found to involve too much duplication and to occasion too much delay in the circulation of papers. Consequently after World War I the Sub-Registries were abolished and the Registry was reorganized into four branches: Opening; Archives; Despatch; and Main Index. The Archives branch was in turn made up of divisions, each one corresponding to a department of the Office. This arrangement continued through-out the inter-war years (see p.67).

A *Historical Section* set up during World War I, and originally intended to be a temporary measure, was retained afterwards and made the responsibility of the Librarian.[8] Also after the War, the Library took over responsibility for Parliamen-tary Papers from the dissolved Parliamentary Department.[9]

---

[1] F.O.881/4905, p.1.
[2] *Ibid.*, pp.4–5.
[3] See R.B.Pugh, *The Records of the Colonial and Dominions Offices* (P.R.O. Handbook No. 3, 1964), p.22.
[4] For a period before 1894 this duty passed for a while to the Commercial Department: see F.O.366/391: minute, Sanderson to Rosebery, 22 Feb. 1894.
[5] See F.O.881/1869, pp.15–17, for the miscellaneous duties of the Library in 1871.
[6] F.O.366/392; F.O.366/673, pp.471–476; F.O.366/675, pp.327–329; F.O.881/5452.
[7] *4th Rpt. of R. Comm. on Civil Estabs.* (1890), p.6.
[8] F.O.366/762, pp.103–104.
[9] See pp.22, 90 below. The Librarian had had a certain amount of responsibility for the routine work of printing Parliamentary Papers from as early as 1853 (F.O.366/392; memorandum by Lenox Conyngham, 7 Feb. 1854).

Departments of the Foreign Office: Miscellaneous Departments

During the nineteenth century there was only one other department in the Foreign Office in addition to those mentioned above. This was the *Cyprus Department*, formed to administer that island when it was handed over to Britain by Turkey in 1878 and dissolved in 1880 when the administration was transferred to the Colonial Office.[1]

In the twentieth century, however, more new departments have come into existence, partly to deal with new functions but in some cases to deal with well established functions which have expanded to such an extent that they have outgrown their parent department.

A *Parliamentary* or '*Blue Book*' *Department* was established in 1903 to look after Confidential Print and the preparation of Parliamentary Papers,[2] the Assistant Clerks in the Department also acting for a time as secretaries of the Committee of Imperial Defence. In 1911 the Department was reorganized and its main occupation became that of ciphering and deciphering, the title being retained to some extent as camouflage. The Department was abolished at the end of World War I, the cipher work passing to the Communications Department and the 'Blue Book' work to the Library.[3]

The outbreak of War in 1914 led to an increase in the number of departments, most of which did not outlast it. These are dealt with separately below (see p.23). One which did survive was the *News Department*. This took over from the War Department responsibility for the collection of information from the foreign press, the supply of information to the press in London, including press censorship, and propaganda abroad. In 1917 it became a branch of the Department of Information so far as its propaganda work was concerned and with the establishment of the Ministry of Information in 1918 the Foreign Office ceased to have any formal connection with propaganda. After the War the need for propaganda was no longer felt to exist and the Ministry was wound up in November 1918. As censorship also had ended, the Foreign Office New Department's functions were thereafter confined to collecting information from and supplying it to the press.[4] Linked with News for a short time after 1918 was another war-time creation, the *Political Intelligence Department*, which had originally been the Intelligence Branch of the Department of Information. The function of this Department was to remedy from various sources the lack of information from countries in which diplomatic representation was no longer possible. With the return to normal relations after the War, this function was felt to be unnecessary and the Political Intelligence side of the News Department was wound up in 1920.[5]

The drastic restrictions imposed on the entry of foreigners by virtually all countries during the War and the continuation of these restrictions afterwards led to a tremendous increase in passport and visa business. The issue of passports was the responsibility of the Chief Clerk's Department until 1891, when it was transferred to the Treaty Department (see p.18). A separate *Passport Office* to deal with the routine business was opened in 1855;[6] a separate Passport Clerk had been pro-

[1] F.O.366/678, pp.30, 141–142. See p.96 below.
[2] F.O.366/386: minute by Sanderson, 19 Nov. 1903.
[3] Tilley and Gaselee, *Foreign Office*, pp.155–156, 297–298; F.O.366/789, ff.90–99.
[4] F.O.366/783, ff.331–372; F.O.366/787, ff.182–230B. See also the records of the Ministry of Information for this period (Inf.4).
[5] Tilley and Gaselee, *Foreign Office*, pp.190–191, 278–286; F.O.366/787, ff.12–59; F.O.366/790, ff.318–390.
[6] F.O.366/449, pp.395–396.

posed in 1853[1] and was in post by 1857.[2] In 1914 the staff of the Passport Office was one Second Division Clerk and a doorkeeper, but thereafter it increased considerably. After the War the Office became virtually independent, and a Branch Passport Office was opened in Liverpool.[3] A *Passport Control Department* was established to deal with visas.[4]

Another department with a long pre-history is the *Communications Department*, which became independent only after World War I, being known initially as the *King's Messengers and Communications Department*. This Department was made responsible for the ciphering and deciphering of telegrams (formerly undertaken in the Parliamentary Department) and for the transmission of despatches to and from diplomatic and consular posts abroad both by mail and by King's Messenger.[5] The Corps of King's (or Queen's) Messengers had its origins in the Messengers of the Great Chamber (controlled by the Lord Chamberlain), who were in existence long before 1782. For many years after that date the Foreign Office had no Messengers for its own exclusive use, but shared them with the Offices of the other Secretaries of State.[6] A major reorganization of the service took place in 1824, when it was divided into Home Service and Foreign Service Messengers,[7] eight of the former and all eighteen of the latter being placed under the immediate orders of the Foreign Office, with the Librarian of the Foreign Office as Superintendent of King's Messengers and Comptroller of their Accounts.[8] In 1854 the superintendence was transferred to the Chief Clerk (see p.18), under whose directions it remained until the separate Department was established.

Another post-War department was the *Dominions Information Department*, established in 1926 to supply information on foreign policy to the Dominions, to deal with Inter-Imperial relations, so far as they affected the Foreign Office, and to deal with matters of protocol affecting the foreign relations of the Dominions. After the passing of the Statute of Westminster in 1931, the changed status of the Dominions made the Department unnecessary and it was wound up in 1933,[9] its remaining functions being handled until 1939 by the Treaty Department.

Departments of the Foreign Office: Temporary War-time Departments 1914–1919[10]
During World War I a number of new Departments, mainly of a temporary nature, were set up to deal with certain special duties arising from the War. Of these the War Department, the Prize Court Department, the Prisoners of War and Aliens Department, the Historical Section and the News and Political Intelligence Departments have already been mentioned (see pp.14, 20–22) and the Department of Overseas Trade will be mentioned in another context (see p.30).

Of the remaining temporary departments the most important was the *Contraband Department* established early in the War to take over certain duties in connection with the blockade originally performed by the Commercial Department.[11] This

[1] F.O.366/545: memorandum by Hammond, 26 July 1853.
[2] F.O.366/449, pp.507–509.
[3] Tilley and Gaselee, *Foreign Office*, pp.192, 216, 293, 313–315; F.O.366/789, ff.141–272; F.O. 366/790, ff.273–288.
[4] Tilley and Gaselee, *Foreign Office*, p.315; F.O.366/791, ff.89–275.
[5] F.O.366/788, ff.1–292; *F.O. Lists 1922* and *1923*.
[6] Tilley and Gaselee, *Foreign Office*, pp.204, 297–298; V. Wheeler-Holohan, *The History of the King's Messengers* (1935).
[7] For Foreign Service Messengers' Regulations see F.O.881/7, 2036, 3074.
[8] F.O.366/672, pp.401–411.
[9] *F.O. Lists 1927–1933;* Tilley and Gaselee, *Foreign Office*, pp.264–265.
[10] See *F.O. Lists 1915–1919*; Tilley and Gaselee, *Foreign Office*, pp.172–200.
[11] F.O.366/786, f.145A.

developed in February 1916 into the *Ministry of Blockade*,[1] under a Minister of Blockade who was also a Parliamentary Under Secretary of State for Foreign Affairs. The Ministry was nominally under the control of the Foreign Office, but in practice it operated virtually independently. It provided a service of economic intelligence about enemy countries and enforced the policy of blockade. It was itself sub-divided into a number of departments: a *Finance Section*; the *Foreign Trade Department*[2] (which itself achieved a certain measure of independence); the *Restriction of Enemy Supplies Department*;[3] the *War Trade Intelligence Department* (originally the *Trade Clearing House*); and the *War Trade Statistical Department*.[4] Developing from the *Contraband Committee*, established at about the same time as the Contraband Department, several inter-departmental committees on which the Foreign Office was represented were also concerned with blockade matters. The Ministry was disbanded in May 1919, but a residual Contraband Department continued in the Foreign Office until November 1920.

A *Foreign Claims Office* to deal with claims by British subjects against enemy countries and by enemy subjects against the British Government was set up in 1915.[5] It worked with the Trading with the Enemy Department of the Public Trustee Office,[6] the Enemy Debts Committee and the Reparation Claims Department of the Board of Trade.[7] These claims were decided by *Mixed Arbitral Tribunals* established by the peace treaties after the War (see p.147). General questions relating to reparations were dealt with by an Inter-Allied *Reparations Commission* set up in 1919 (see p.147).

The Diplomatic and Consular Services[8]

The British *Diplomatic Service* has a long history, reaching back to the middle ages, but it was only during the eighteenth century that there was a marked development of professionalism, with a regular hierarchy of ranks.[9] The French wars between 1793 and 1815, with their consequent dislocation of diplomatic activity, interrupted this process, but from 1815 onwards the reconstituted Diplomatic Service expanded as Britain entered into diplomatic relations with more and more countries and the tempo and scope of those relations increased. In 1833 there were eighty-one paid members of the Diplomatic Service; within fifty years the numbers had doubled and by 1939 they had reached almost 400.[10]

Heads of diplomatic missions may have the title of *Ambassador* (at an Embassy),

---

[1] H.Hall, *British Archives and the Sources for the History of the World War* (1925), pp.69–72, 104–105 (some of his statements are at variance with the facts as ascertainable from other sources); A.C. Bell, *Blockade of the Central Empires, 1914–1918*, Official History of the War (1937); Chester and Willson, *Brit. Cent. Govt.*, pp.62, 386.
[2] For papers relating to the formation and organization of this Department see F.O.833/16–18.
[3] Formed in June 1916: F.O.382/1158, file 119660.
[4] The War Trade Intelligence and Statistical Departments were taken over from the War Trade Department in January 1917: F.O.382/1626, file 10654; Cab.15/6/24, pt.1, pp.23–31.
[5] F.O.366/761, p.517.
[6] Cab.15/6/6; Hall, *Brit. Archives*, p.87 and n.1.
[7] The records of the latter two are in B.T.8 and 102.
[8] Since 1852 the annual *Foreign Office Lists* have recorded the membership of the two Services. Before that date heads of mission (permanent and acting) are listed in *British Diplomatic Representatives, 1689–1789* and *1789–1852*, Camden 3rd Series, XLVI (1932) and L (1934). Other members of the Diplomatic Service may be identified in the *General Correspondence* of the Foreign Office and, especially, in the *Chief Clerk's Department Archives* (F.O.366). Consuls may be identified from the entry books of their commissions (F.O.83/1219, etc.) and from the *Chief Clerk's Department Archives*.
[9] Horn, *Brit. Dipl. Service*, pp.1, 13.
[10] *Diplomatic Service Return*, H.C. 1833 (267) XXIII, pp.367–375; *F.O. Lists*.

Envoy Extraordinary and Minister Plenipotentiary,[1] usually abbreviated to *Minister*, (at a Legation), or *Chargé d'Affaires*. The last title is generally used only for a temporary head of mission in the absence of the permanent head; it is also used occasionally on a more permanent basis where the head of a minor mission, exercising mainly consular functions, acts for a non-resident Minister or Ambassador accredited to a number of neighbouring countries.[2] In the nineteenth century heads of mission were more often Ministers than Ambassadors; indeed at one time there were only two ambassadorial missions, Paris and Constantinople.[3] More recently, however, Ambassadors have come to outnumber Ministers.

Heads of mission are appointed by royal commissions and are accredited to foreign governments by letters of credence ('credentials') signed by the Sovereign. Letters of recall notifying foreign governments of the termination of appointment of heads of mission are similarly signed by the Sovereign.[4] The role played by the Sovereign in the appointment of heads of mission has often been more than a formal one and at least as late as the reign of Edward VII could be decisive.[5]

The subordinate staff of missions were originally divided into two ranks: *Secretary* and *Attaché*. In time there developed from these a career structure which now consists of the following ranks: *Minister* (personal rank serving under an Ambassador); *Counsellor; First Secretary; Second Secretary; Third Secretary;* and *Junior Attaché*.[6]

The rank of Secretary is of considerable antiquity and was originally sub-divided into the ranks of *Secretary of Embassy* and *Secretary of Legation*, the former being the senior. Attachés, although not known by that name until about 1816, are found long before that date in the households of Ambassadors and Ministers, assisting with the secretarial work of the mission. Payment for some Attachés was introduced in 1823 and steps were taken at about the same time to secure more control by the Foreign Office over their appointment by requiring both *Paid* and *Unpaid Attachés* to obtain from the Foreign Secretary formal letters of appointment. As late as 1861, however, diplomats might still have in their households a number of unrecognized Attachés.[7] In 1862 the ranks of First, Second and Third Secretary were introduced and that of Paid Attaché abolished. Existing Paid Attachés became Second or Third Secretaries and thereafter Attachés were promoted to Third Secretaries on completion of probation. Attachés were not paid until after World War I.

Prospective Attachés often served a period of probation in the Foreign Office and from 1853 this was made compulsory. Three years later examinations were introduced for Unpaid Attachés and for promotion from Unpaid to Paid Attaché (after 1862 from Third to Second Secretary). The first examination tested handwriting, dictation (in English and French), languages (French and either German, Latin, Spanish or Italian), geography, précis and modern history; the second (abolished in 1872) tested ability to speak and write the languages of the countries in which the candidate had served, ability to draw up a report on the commercial and political relations of those countries, and knowledge of international law. The examinations were not competitive until 1883. In 1892 the examination for Attachés was assimilated to that for Foreign Office clerkships. There was a property

[1] In the nineteenth century it was possible to be a Minister Plenipotentiary without being also an Envoy Extraordinary and vice versa. There is also a lower rank of Minister Resident.
[2] Strang, *Foreign Office*, pp.55, 60; 7 *B.D.I.L.*, pp.656–657.
[3] *Rpt. of Sel. Ctee. on Official Salaries* (1850), q.354.
[4] 7 *B.D.I.L.*, pp.584–588. A reply to a letter of recall is known as a 'recredential'.
[5] See, for example, G.W.Monger, *The End of Isolation* (1963), pp.101–102.
[6] Strang, *Foreign Office*, p.55.
[7] Bindoff, *T.R.Hist.S.*, 4th Ser., XVIII, pp.144–148.

C

qualification of £400 a year for candidates for the Diplomatic Service until after World War I.[1]

Many of the Unpaid Attachés who served in the early part of the nineteenth century had no intention of making a career for themselves in the Diplomatic Service, but for those who had such an intention promotion was governed almost exclusively by favour and patronage. From 1853, however, seniority became the major factor in promotion to Secretary's rank, although patronage and influence continued for some time longer to play an important, though diminishing, part in promotion to the higher diplomatic ranks.[2]

In the nineteenth century the salaries attached to diplomatic posts tended to vary in accordance with the Secretary of State's ideas of their relative importance. Similarly the outfit allowance given to Ambassadors, Ministers and Secretaries on taking up appointments and the rent allowance for Ambassadors and Ministers varied considerably from post to post.[3] The latter was an important item, since heads of mission were expected to arrange and pay for their own official as well as private accommodation; it was not until after 1861 that the taking of a mission building on long lease became common, and even then it was a considerable time before it became the standard practice.[4] Standard scales of salaries and allowances for the Diplomatic Service were introduced only after World War I.[5] From 1871 special allowances were made for proficiency in difficult languages.[6]

Other reforms after World War I amalgamated the establishments of the Foreign Office and the Diplomatic Service (see p.9), although to some extent this was only making formal a process which had been developing naturally for some time. From an early date it had been common for exchanges, on a temporary or permanent basis, to take place between Foreign Office Clerks and members of the Diplomatic Service[7] and, particularly in the first half of the nineteenth century, for Private Secretaries and Précis Writers to find advancement in the Diplomatic Service; until 1834 it was also common for the Government Under Secretary to regard his post as a stepping stone to diplomatic preferment.[8] From the end of the nineteenth century it had also been common for Permanent Under Secretaries and Assistant Under Secretaries to be appointed to senior diplomatic posts and for appointments to the higher posts in the Foreign Office to be made from the Diplomatic Service.[9]

The negotiation of a treaty is often entrusted to the head of mission in the country concerned, a special full power being sent for the purpose. For major treaties, however, special *Plenipotentiaries* are appointed and in the case of important international congresses and conferences these include high-ranking diplomats, probably the Secretary of State himself and possibly even the Prime Minister.[10]

Diplomatic negotiations on matters of a technical or administrative nature may be conducted not through regular diplomatic representatives, but through *Commissioners*. These are specially appointed to deal with one particular subject or group of

[1] F.O.366/449, pp.405–409; *Rpt. from Sel. Ctee. on Dipl. Service* (1861), qq.955–956, App.2, nos. 23–24; F.O.881/693; Tilley and Gaselee, *Foreign Office*, pp.195, 257.

[2] Bindoff, *T.R.Hist.S.*, 4th Ser., XVIII, pp.160–167.

[3] Salaries and allowances of the Diplomatic Service, 1815–1850, are given in *Rpt. of Sel. Ctee. on Official Salaries* (1850), App.1. From 1861 they appear in the *F.O. Lists*. See also F.O.366/253–255, 283 for the period 1840–1876.

[4] *Rpt. of Sel. Ctee. on Dipl. and Consular Services*, H.C. 1870 (382) VII, q.53.

[5] Tilley and Gaselee, *Foreign Office*, pp.196–197, 255.

[6] F.O.366/795, ff.59–96; F.O.366/797, ff.375–379.

[7] See F.O.366/369; *Camb. Hist. of Brit. For. Policy* III, pp.593–594.

[8] Bindoff, *T.R.Hist.S.*, 4th Ser., XVIII, pp.152–157.

[9] Tilley and Gaselee, *Foreign Office*, pp. 198–199; *Camb. Hist. of Brit. For. Policy* III, pp.609–610.

[10] See, for example, *Brit. Dipl. Representatives, 1789–1852*, pp.2–4; F.O.83/2478: draft full powers for British Peace Conference Delegation, 1 Jan. 1919; also 7 *B.D.I.L.*, pp.588–593.

related subjects and are generally temporary. They have been used most frequently to deal with the settlement of claims between Britain and other countries, with the regulation of boundaries and, in the nineteenth century, with Slave Trade matters; they have also been used to conduct preliminary discussions leading to international agreements on technical subjects.[1] Commissioners are not necessarily appointed from members of the Diplomatic Service.

Specialists attached to missions, but not members of the Diplomatic Service are met with from the middle of the nineteenth century. *Military* and *Naval Attachés* first appear under those titles in 1857, although there had been a Military Commissioner at the Paris Embassy two years previously. These Attachés are serving Army and Naval Officers temporarily appointed to missions and returning to their normal careers after completing their period of service.[2] Later *Air Attachés* were also appointed. The more widespread appointment of specialist Attachés was a development of World War II, with the exception of the *Press Attachés* who appeared between the two Wars.[3] Though never a formally constituted branch of the Diplomatic Service, a *Chancery* or *Archivist Service*, composed of Second Division Clerks who could be prevailed upon to serve abroad, carried out registry and other similar functions in missions after World War I.[4]

A major feature of the 1920 reforms was the establishment of a *Commercial Diplomatic Service* under the direction of the Department of Overseas Trade. The origins of this Service are to be found in the *Commercial Attachés* (first appointed in 1880) and *Commercial Secretaries* (appointed after 1906) who had previously acted under the direction of the Commercial Department of the Foreign Office.[5] It was greatly influenced by the system established by the Germans before World War I for conducting their commercial diplomatic relations and by various war-time studies undertaken by Victor Wellesley as Controller of Commercial and Consular Affairs. The Commercial Diplomatic Service was amalgamated with the Foreign Office and Diplomatic Service into a single *Foreign Service* in 1943.[6]

Also involved in the 1943 amalgamation was the *Consular Service*, which, like the Diplomatic Service, had a long history before 1782.[7] The functions of these two Services are not dissimilar, differing mainly in scale. Thus:

> The head of a diplomatic mission represents his Sovereign . . . and his country in a foreign state; the head of a consular post is the agent for his country in one particular province or district or colony of that state, under the general direction and control of the head of the mission. The ambassador or minister plenipotentiary consorts and negotiates with the central authorities in the capital city; the consul consorts and negotiates with municipal and provincial officials. (. . . strictly speaking a diplomatic representative may negotiate with the Minister for Foreign Affairs and his staff only; whereas a consul is freer, and may deal with all those provincial authorities whose activities affect his official interests. . . .)[8]

The pre-1943 Consular Service was itself the product of an amalgamation in 1936

[1] 7 *B.D.I.L.*, pp.675–680.
[2] L.W.Hilbert, 'The Early Years of the Military Attaché Service in British Diplomacy' in *J. Soc. for Army Hist. Research*, XXXVII (1959), pp.164–171; A.Vagts, *The Military Attaché* (Princeton, 1967).
[3] Chester and Willson, *Brit. Cent. Govt.*, pp.195, 201–202; Strang, *Foreign Office*, pp.67, 107.
[4] Tilley and Gaselee, *Foreign Office*, pp.258–259; F.O.366/796, ff.1–88; F.O.366/804, ff.103–109.
[5] For their instructions see F.O.881/9421 and 8959* respectively.
[6] Tilley and Gaselee, *Foreign Office*, pp.242, 246–250; Strang, *Foreign Office*, pp.66, 68, 109–110; Sir H.Llewellyn Smith, *The Board of Trade* (1928), pp.79–80, 83–84.
[7] 8 *B.D.I.L.*, pp.3–7.
[8] Strang, *Foreign Office*, p.123. For detailed *Instructions to Consuls* see *Rpt. of Sel. Ctee. on Consular Estabs.* (1835), App.1; F.O.366/536 (c.1857); F.O.366/535 (c.1863); F.O.83/2498 (1907); F.O. 83/2499 (1916).

of three separate services: the *General Consular Service*, the *Levant Consular Service* and the *Far Eastern Consular Service*.[1] The General Consular Service, although the oldest of the three in origin, was the last to be fully organized as a career service. This occurred only in 1903 as the final stage in a cumulative process which had been going on since Canning's reforms of 1825.[2] The Levant Service had been taken over by the British Government in 1825 on the winding up of the Levant Company, but was not formally separated from the General Consular Service until 1877. The Far Eastern Service, which originally served China and later Japan and Siam, had been taken over in 1834 on the cessation of the East India Company's monopoly of trade with China and was put on a regular footing in 1854.[3]

The consular ranks are Consul-General; Consul; Vice-Consul; Consular Agent; and Pro-Consul. Consuls-General and Consuls were each further sub-divided into two grades by the 1903 reforms. *Consuls-General* are appointed where one consulate exercises some degree of supervisory control over other consulates in the area. Consular officers within a country are also subject to the control of the head of the diplomatic mission to that country.[4] A Consul-General may combine the headship of a minor diplomatic mission with his consular duties and be known as *Chargé d'Affaires and Consul-General*; similarly he may be *Agent and Consul-General*, a title now confined to areas such as the Persian Gulf, where the Consul-General, in addition to his consular duties, acts as Political Agent. *Vice-Consuls, Consular Agents* and *Pro-Consuls* are subordinate to *Consuls* and work under their instructions. Consuls and Consuls-General are appointed by royal commission and receive exequaturs from the Heads of State of the countries in which they reside; Vice-Consuls and Consular Agents are appointed by the Secretary of State on the recommendation of Consuls; Pro-Consuls are appointed by Consuls subject to the sanction of the Secretary of State. Pro-Consuls exercise only the notarial functions of a Consul. Consular Agents and Pro-Consuls are always unpaid; Vice-Consuls and, less frequently, Consuls, may also be unpaid and allowed to engage in trade. Various commissions and committees of enquiry during the nineteenth century looked upon the trading Consul with disfavour but could not secure his abolition. Consular officers, particularly in the three lowest grades, need not necessarily be British subjects.[5] In the Levant and Far Eastern Services there were additional ranks of *Interpreter* (also called *Dragoman* in the Levant Service), *Assistant* (divided into classes) and *Student Interpreter* (or *Student Dragoman*) below that of Vice-Consul. The *Superintendent of Trade* at Hong Kong was the equivalent of a Consul-General and at first Consuls in the Far East corresponded with the Foreign Office only through him.[6] Until 1883 this post was usually combined with that of Envoy Extraordinary and Minister Plenipotentiary to China.

Examinations for paid Consuls in the General Service were introduced in 1856, for the Far Eastern Service in 1859, and for the Levant Service in 1877. Newly appointed members of the General Service received virtually no training, but in the Far Eastern and Levant Services great emphasis was placed on learning languages (on the spot in the case of the former; usually at Cambridge in the case of the latter).[7]

[1] Strang, *Foreign Office*, p.67.
[2] Tilley and Gaselee, *Foreign Office*, p.246; 8 *B.D.I.L.*, pp.20–24.
[3] Tilley and Gaselee, *Foreign Office*, pp.236–237; D.C.M.Platt, 'The Role of the British Consular Service in Overseas Trade, 1825–1914' in *Economic Hist. Rev.*, 2nd Ser., XVI (1962–63), p.495.
[4] *2nd Rpt. of Sel. Ctee. on Dipl. and Consular Services* (1871), App.1, No.2.
[5] 8 *B.D.I.L.*, pp.24–56; Strang, *Foreign Office*, p.61.
[6] *Rpt. of Sel. Ctee. on Consular Service and Appointments (1857–58)*, qq.793, 5987.
[7] F.O.366/449, pp.409–411; 8 *B.D.I.L.*, pp.23–24; Tilley and Gaselee, *Foreign Office*, pp.236–237.

In general there was little movement between the Consular and Diplomatic Services before 1943, although members of the Levant and Far Eastern Services often obtained diplomatic appointments in their own specialized fields.[1] There was some movement from the Foreign Office (usually by Supplementary or Second Division Clerks) to the Consular Service.

One specialized function of Consuls in the Far Eastern and Levant Services merits special mention. This is the exercise of magisterial powers over their fellow countrymen by virtue of agreements known as capitulations. Above a network of local Consular Courts there were Supreme Courts covering a wider area with permanent *Judges* with legal qualifications.[2]

Other Departments of Government concerned with Foreign Affairs
The *Prime Minister* and the *Cabinet* and its many Committees were always concerned in the conduct of foreign affairs and saw all the important Foreign Office correspondence (see p.51). Salisbury and MacDonald combined the office of Prime Minister and Foreign Secretary, while other Prime Ministers, particularly Disraeli in the nineteenth century[3] and Lloyd George and Chamberlain in the twentieth, intervened in the conduct of foreign affairs to some extent independently of the Foreign Office. During the premiership of Lloyd George (1916–1922) the newly established *Cabinet Office* prepared summaries of events abroad for circulation to the Cabinet and to a wide range of Ministers and officials and provided the secretariat for the British Empire Delegation at the Peace Conference and at other international conferences. From November 1919 the Cabinet Office also handled relations with the League of Nations, the branch of the Office responsible for these being under an Assistant Secretary seconded from the Foreign Office. After 1922 work in connection with international conferences and with the League was handled by the Foreign Office.[4]

Although it is not a government department, mention should be made here of *Parliament*, which from time to time influenced foreign policy, or at least provided a forum in which policy could be outlined and discussed. Reports of its proceedings in *Hansard* and the 'Blue Books' published for its information are important source material for the diplomatic historian.[5]

The department with which the Foreign Office was most closely connected was the *Board of Trade*. In the field of commercial affairs the dividing line between the respective responsibilities of the Foreign Office and the Board was never easy to draw and a succession of committees and commissions of enquiry examined the problem in the nineteenth century, producing frequent reorganizations in both departments but failing to establish any lasting arrangements for dealing with commercial questions. The Commercial Department of the Board of Trade[6] was originally responsible for negotiating commercial treaties, but with the establish-

[1] *Camb. Hist. of Brit. For. Policy* III, p.621.
[2] Strang, *Foreign Office*, pp.131–133; 8 *B.D.I.L.*, pp.100–102; G.W.Keeton, *The Development of Extraterritoriality in China*, Vol. II (1928), pp.77–78.
[3] *Camb. Hist. of Brit. For. Policy* III, pp.601–602; Gosses, *Management of Brit. For. Policy*, pp.126–128.
[4] Chester and Willson, *Brit. Cent. Govt.*, pp.187, 289–291, 395; *Records of the Cabinet Office to 1922* (P.R.O. Handbook No. 11, 1966), pp.7–8, 20–23, 25, 27–28, 34–35. The relevant Cabinet Office records are in Cab.21, 23–25, 28–31. Records of the Prime Minister's Office are in Premier 1. For earlier Prime Ministers' papers in private collections see J.Brooke, *The Prime Ministers' Papers* 1801–1902, H.M.C. (1968).
[5] For the influence of Parliament on foreign policy see Gosses, *Management of Brit. For. Policy*, pp.81–98. For parliamentary questions see pp.52–53, 64, 70 below; for 'Blue Books' see pp.89–90.
[6] Records of this Department are in B.T.1, 3, 11, 12, 33, 35 and 36. See also B.T.2.

ment of the Commercial Department of the Foreign Office in 1865 (see p.16) the
Board's role became an advisory rather than an active one. Indeed the Board's Commercial Department was abolished, so far as overseas questions were concerned,
between 1872 and 1882. Even after the Department was revived in 1882 the Foreign
Office continued to conduct all negotiations, relying on the Board for advice and
information on commercial conditions and policy. Correspondence on commercial
matters with diplomatic and consular officials was conducted solely through the
Foreign Office.

In the last years of the nineteenth century the growing demand for commercial
intelligence led to the formation within the Board's Commercial Department of a
Commercial Intelligence Branch with a Commercial Intelligence Advisory Committee.[1] Information for this Branch was provided by the Commercial Attachés and
Secretaries, who continued, however, to correspond through the Foreign Office.
The Board did not undertake responsibility for the editing of their reports until
1907, although some had been published in the *Board of Trade Journal* since 1886
(see p.90).

In 1917 the *Department of Overseas Trade* was established under a Parliamentary
Secretary responsible jointly to the Foreign Secretary and the President of the
Board of Trade. This Department eventually took over the commercial work of the
Foreign Office and all the commercial work of the Board of Trade except commercial treaties and relations with foreign governments. These remaining functions of
the Board were dealt with by a Commercial Relations and Treaties Department.
Members of the newly created Commercial Diplomatic Service and Consuls, when
writing on commercial matters, corresponded direct with the Department of Overseas Trade, although their instructions were issued by the Department in the name
of the Secretary of State for Foreign Affairs.[2] The Department survived until 1946,
when its functions were handed over to the Board of Trade.[3]

The Foreign Office also dealt with the Board of Trade over several other
questions, particularly those relating to seamen and shipping, which were the
responsibility of the Board's Marine Department.[4] British Consuls might under the
Merchant Shipping Acts hold Naval Courts in which they exercised on behalf
of the Board semi-judicial powers over British ships and their crews; they corresponded direct with the Board on such matters.[5]

Another department with which there was an overlap of functions was the
Colonial Office, although here it was more a case of the Foreign Office undertaking
colonial administration (see p.3) than of the Colonial Office conducting foreign
affairs. The Colonial Office did, however, supervise the British Consuls in Morocco,
Algiers, Tunis and Tripoli between 1804 (before which date they had been supervised by the Home Office) and 1836 (after which supervision passed to the Foreign

[1] Llewellyn Smith, *Board of Trade*, pp.54–82; 7 *B.D.I.L.*, pp.225–228.
[2] F.O.366/787, f.80; Llewellyn Smith, *B. of Trade*, pp.82–88; Tilley and Gaselee, *Foreign Office*,
pp.248–249.
[3] Chester and Willson, *Brit. Cent. Govt.*, pp.109–110. The records of the Department of Overseas
Trade were taken over by the Board of Trade and will be found among the Board's records at the
Public Record Office (B.T.59–61, 90). See also the records of the Export Credit Guarantee Department.
[4] In 1939 this responsibility was relinquished and passed eventually to the Ministry of Transport,
where it remained until 1965, when it returned to the Board. The records are in B.T. 1, 2 and in
Ministry of Transport classes (M.T.4, 5, 9).
[5] For Board of Trade *Instructions to Consuls* see F.O.83/579, 2493, 2494, 2500; see also *Rpt. of Sel.
Ctee. on Trade with Foreign Nations*, H.C. 1864 (493) VII, q.1986; *5th Rpt. of R. Comm. on Civil
Service* (1914–16), q.37964; 7 *B.D.I.L.*, p.229; 8 *B.D.I.L.*, pp. 369–373, 378–384; Strang, *Foreign
Office*, pp.133–134.

Office).[1] The Colonial Office also for a time had an interest in the affairs of Persia and China.[2] After World War I the Colonial Office became mainly responsible for those areas in the Middle East which were under British mandate or within British spheres of interest, such as Arabia (to 1926), Iraq (to 1932), Palestine and Transjordan,[3] although the Foreign Office did continue to have some interest in them.

The *India Office* (and its predecessors the *East India Company* and the *Board of Control*) and the *Government of India* had Political and Secret Departments which, among other matters, dealt with relations with the countries of Asia, the Levant and the east coast of Africa.[4] They did this at times independently of the Foreign Office; at others they shared responsibility with the Foreign Office by interchanging copies of correspondence and by sharing the appointment of representatives in the countries concerned (occasionally, however, especially in the time of the East India Company, the Company might have a separate Agent in an area where the Foreign Office also had a Consul).

At the beginning of the nineteenth century the area with which the Company and the Board were concerned was an extensive one, but as the century progressed more and more of it became the responsibility of the Foreign Office, starting with China in 1834 (see p.13) and Persia in 1835.[5] By the end of the century the India Office was directly concerned only in Afghanistan, Nepal, the Persian Gulf and Turkish Arabia (Mesopotamia). The principal responsibility for the last of these passed to the Colonial Office in 1920 when, as Iraq, it was assigned to Britain under a mandate;[6] at the end of the mandate in 1932 responsibility passed to the Foreign Office. Responsibility for relations with Afghanistan passed to the Foreign Office in 1921,[7] and for those with Nepal in 1934,[8] although in both cases the India Office retained a significant interest. Relations with the Sheikhdoms of the Persian Gulf remained the responsibility of the India Office (except for a brief period from 1921 to 1926 when they were the concern of the Colonial Office[9]) until it was abolished in 1947,[10] when they passed to the Foreign Office. In January 1948 relations with Burma, which had chosen not to join the Commonwealth on becoming independent, passed to the Foreign Office from the Burma Office, which had itself taken them over from the India Office in 1937.[11]

Many other departments are concerned in some way or other in foreign affairs,

[1] M.I.Lee, 'The Supervision of the Barbary Consuls during the years 1756–1836' in *B.I.H.R.*, XXIII (1950), pp.191–199.

[2] The relevant records are in C.O.77; see Pugh, *Records of Col. and Dom. Offices*, p.76.

[3] *Ibid.*, pp.63, 84, 90, 99, 113–114.

[4] The records of the India Office and its predecessors are not in the Public Record Office but in the India Office Records at Orbit House, 197 Blackfriars Road, London, S.E.1. The Scheme of Classification of these records is given in S.C.Sutton, *A Guide to the India Office Library* (1967), pp.74–77; more detailed Guides are in preparation. The principal classes containing material dealing with external affairs are E/1 and L/P & S/3: Home correspondence, including that with the Foreign Office; E/4 and L/P & S/5–7: correspondence with India relating to areas outside India; G and L/P & S/9–12: correspondence with areas outside India (L/P & S/10–11 are general files dealing also with internal affairs); P: copies of correspondence of the Government of India, including that of its Political and Secret Department relating to external affairs; and R: collections received at a later date through official sources, including material akin to Foreign Office Embassy and Consular Archives.

[5] F.O.60/39: India Board to F.O., 22 Jan. 1835, and enclosures. Persia had previously been the concern of the Foreign Office until 1826 (F.O.60/27: Willock to Canning, No. 24, 17 Sept. 1826) and returned to the India Office again for a short period in 1858–1859.

[6] Pugh, *Records of Col. and Dom. Offices*, p.84.

[7] Chester and Willson, *Brit. Cent. Govt.*, p.188.

[8] F.O.371/18162–18164, file 1305.

[9] Pugh, *Records of Col. and Dom. Offices*, p.63.

[10] Chester and Willson, *Brit. Cent. Govt.*, p.191.

[11] *Ibid.*, pp.190–191.

either by advising or by acting through the Foreign Office in their own special fields; a few act independently.[1] Those departments which were most involved before 1939 were: the *Law Officers of the Crown* and the *Lord Chancellor*, who advised on international law and, before 1876, on often quite trivial matters of domestic law; the *Service Ministries*, which had their own Attachés at missions abroad (see p.27); the *Home Office*, which was involved in questions of extradition, aliens and foreign ministers' privileges, and also superintended the Barbary Consulates between 1782 and 1804 (see p.30); the *Treasury*, which was concerned with establishment and financial matters and, in the twentieth century, with international economic questions; the *Office of Works*, which was responsible for Foreign Office, embassy, legation and consular buildings and furniture;[2] the *Ministry of Agriculture and Fisheries*, which was interested in trade relations so far as they affected agriculture and fisheries;[3] the *Registrars General*, to whom returns of births, marriages and deaths of British subjects abroad were made; the *General Post Office* and the *Ministry of Labour*, which supplied the British representatives to the Universal Postal Union and the International Labour Organization respectively;[4] and the *British Council*, which was founded in the early nineteen thirties, with the co-operation of the Foreign Office, to conduct cultural propaganda overseas.[5]

[1] 7 *B.D.I.L.*, pp.219–281.
[2] See Works 10 and Works 40.
[3] See especially M.A.F.40.
[4] Chester and Willson, *Brit. Cent. Govt.*, p.185. For papers of the Ministry of Labour's Overseas Department see Lab.13.
[5] *Ibid.*, p.193.

II. The Records

The Foreign Office Group

The establishment of the Foreign Office in 1782 had no immediate effect upon the system of keeping records relating to foreign affairs. These extend in a virtually unbroken series back to the sixteenth century and it was general usage for over a century after 1782 to consider them collectively as Foreign Office records.[1] Not until 1909 was any formal distinction made between those created before and those created after 1782, the former being then classed as *State Papers Foreign*, and put into the *State Paper Office* group.[2] The remainder, together with subsequent accruals, constitute the *Foreign Office* group, and it is with these that this Handbook is primarily concerned.

General Correspondence before 1906: Registration 1782–1810

A series of registers of Foreign Office correspondence commencing on 1 January 1782 will be found in the class of *Miscellanea, Series I* (F.O.95/93–97). These have daily entries of despatches received and sent, those received being grouped by the mail (the Flanders, Dutch, French, Lisbon and New York mails are mentioned) or other means of conveyance. The information entered for each despatch is the name of its sender or addressee, the despatch number and, for incoming despatches, the date of despatch. From January 1787 the subject is also given, at first only briefly in one or two words, but later more fully; there are still periods, however, during which subject entries do not appear. These registers appear to have been overlooked in the past because they were listed among the entry books in their class as 'Flanders, etc., Letters Received'.

The registers end abruptly with the entries for 25 August 1789; as these occur in the middle of a volume we must presume that for some reason the keeping of the registers in this form was then discontinued.[3] However, in 1799 the duties of Stephen Rolleston, the First Senior Clerk, included responsibility 'for the Registry of the Mails upon their Arrival and Departure', a duty which he still performed as Second Chief Clerk in 1806.[4] Moreover, a register, presumably compiled in the course of this duty, survives from the Northern Department for 1798 (F.O.95/601).[5] It is not very informative, since it gives no details of the contents of despatches, although there are occasional notes of the contents of enclosures to outgoing despatches. Other information given for outgoing despatches is the name of the addressee, the despatch number, the date and, occasionally, the means of conveyance. For incoming despatches the name of the sender and the place from which he writes, the number and date of the despatch, the date of receipt and the means of conveyance (usually the American or Hamburg mails) are given.

A series of 'so-called' Registers of Correspondence for the period 1781–1796 compiled at a later date in the State Paper Office was destroyed under the schedule of 1910 (see p.94).

Another series of registers covers the period 1805–1810. It starts with a register

[1] For example, S.R.Scargill-Bird, *Guide to the Various Classes of Documents preserved in the Public Record Office* (3rd ed., 1908), p.369.
[2] *Guide to the Public Records: Part I, Introductory* (1949), pp.15–16.
[3] It may be linked with the appointment of J.B.Burges as Under Secretary on 22 Aug. 1789: see p.57 below.
[4] F.O.366/671, pp.119–120, 126–127, 293.
[5] The cover is incorrectly stamped '1796'.

of Northern Department despatches received January–September 1805 and sent January–October 1805 with separate sections for correspondence with representatives in Russia February 1805–January 1806 and in Prussia September–October 1805 (F.O.95/350). It is followed by another Northern Department register of despatches received February 1806 and sent January–September 1806 (F.O. 95/351). No Southern Department register for 1805 has survived, but there is one of despatches received January–May 1806 and sent January–March 1806 (F.O. 95/352). These departmental registers are continued, with some gaps and overlappings, in separate country registers,[1] extending in the main until the summer of 1807, although those for America (F.O.95/28), Austria (F.O.95/47), Italy (F.O. 95/162) and Portugal (F.O.95/183) continue into 1808 and the last has a few entries for September 1809. A register in the same style, in the volume intended but never used for France from 1806,[2] was used for all countries during the Secretaryship of Bathurst (October–December 1809) and continued under his successor, Wellesley, until March 1810 (F.O.95/102).

Entries in this series of registers are in roughly chronological order, the information given being for despatches received (left-hand page): from whom and means of conveyance, despatch number, date sent, number of enclosures, date received and subject; and for despatches sent (right-hand page): to whom, despatch number, date, number of enclosures and subject. The subject entries are usually very full. The registers were not kept up consistently and there are many gaps, not only between successive registers (which may be attributable simply to the accident of survival), but even within individual registers. The registers do not include domestic correspondence.

From these early essays in the registration of Foreign Office correspondence, incomplete and inconsistent though they were, there emerged at the end of the first decade of the nineteenth century the series of departmental diaries and Library registers. These were kept up in parallel until the end of 1890, after which the departmental diaries alone continued.

General Correspondence before 1906: Departmental Diaries 1809–1890
There was no central registry in the Foreign Office until 1906, but from 20 December 1809 each department kept a daily record of its correspondence, both foreign and domestic, in its own registers,[3] more often called 'diaries' to distinguish them from the registers compiled after the records had passed to the Library. Each department kept its diaries in its own particular fashion and throughout the period before 1891 there was never complete uniformity of practice, although towards the end the differences were only in the size of the pages and in the conventional signs used.

The Southern Department's diaries begin on 20 December 1809 and extend in their original form in an unbroken sequence to 31 December 1816 (F.O.95/383–386); the early diaries of the Northern Department are less complete, covering the periods 20 December 1809 to 7 February 1812, 11 January 1813 to 20 December 1814 and 1 January 1816 to 3 January 1818 (F.O.95/353–354, 381–382, 446–447).[4]

---

[1] F.O.95/28, 47, 84, 145, 162, 183, 205, 225, 249, 308, 332.
[2] The spine is stamped 'France 1806 to . . .' and the volume was formerly listed under this title and date.
[3] In 1828 the diaries were entered up by the 'Private Secretaries' to the Under Secretaries (F.O. 366/386: memorandum of June 1828).
[4] Attention was first drawn to these early diaries by C.S.B.Buckland, 'Some Early Foreign Office Registers at the Public Record Office' in *E.H.R.* XXXVII (1922), pp.567–568.

The first system of registration devised by the Southern Department involved the entry of each incoming despatch or letter in order of receipt and the assigning to it of a register number, which was docketed on the paper itself; outgoing correspondence was not given register numbers. The first series of numbers runs from the commencement of the diaries to the end of 1811, the second continues until March 1814 and the third until the end of 1814; thereafter there are separate annual series for 1815 and 1816. Until the middle of the third series gaps were left from time to time in the sequence of numbers, originally, one might assume, for the use of the Northern Department; at times, particularly during the latter part of 1813, many incoming papers were not assigned numbers. Occasionally from about June 1813 and regularly from September 1813 to the end of 1814 correspondence of the Northern Department was also entered in these Diaries.[1] During this period register numbers are also to be found on the dockets of Northern Department correspondence.

The Southern Department's diaries, although now bound up in four volumes, were originally in fifteen separate parts. The first of these parts, which extends to 17 May 1810, deals directly only with incoming correspondence. The information given in each entry is register number, name of sender and despatch number, date, country, subject and nature and date of action taken. With the second part the system is varied somewhat and this revised system remains virtually unchanged thereafter until the end of 1816. Incoming correspondence is entered on the left-hand page of an opening and outgoing correspondence on the right. The information given for incoming correspondence is register number, name of sender and despatch number, date and subject; for outgoing correspondence that given is addressee and subject. The date is given at the beginning of the entries for each day. Register numbers are used for cross-references to the incoming correspondence; until early in 1812 entries of outgoing papers are preceded by letters in alphabetical order intended for the same purpose.

There is also a separate diary of the Southern Department's outgoing correspondence for the period 28 June 1810 to 1 January 1811, with one entry of 17 September 1811 (F.O.95/380). The left-hand page of each opening relates to 'domestic' correspondence, that is correspondence with persons in this country, principally in other government departments, and the right-hand page to despatches to diplomatic representatives abroad. Most of the entries also appear in the contemporary register from the main series (F.O.95/383), but there are many out-letters in the latter, particularly domestic ones, which do not appear in F.O.95/380. Where entries are unique to F.O.95/380 no date of despatch is given; it seems possible, therefore, that these were never sent and that the purpose of this diary was to record business in hand in the Department rather than correspondence sent out.

The diaries of the Northern Department took longer to establish a settled form. The earliest (F.O.95/353) covers the period 20 December 1809 to 7 February 1812 and is in three sections. The first (pp.1–20) relates to despatches received to 17 September 1810, entries being by date of receipt and mail (Heligoland or Gothenburg). The information given is name of sender, despatch number, date, number of enclosures and subject. The second (pp.21–22) relates to despatches sent between 2 February 1810 and 4 October 1810 and is arranged chronologically. The information given is addressee, despatch number, date, number of enclosures and subject. The third section (from p.26) relates to despatches received between September 1810 and December 1811, with a few earlier and later entries. This has a separate

---

[1] F.O.95/384–385; both are labelled 'South'.

series of entries for each correspondent with an index to correspondents on the fly leaf; within each series the entries are chronological. The information given is date received, despatch number, date, number of enclosures and subject (this last is not always entered).

A second diary (F.O.95/354), relating to despatches sent in 1811 (with one entry of 12 January 1812), is arranged by correspondents like the third section of the first diary, with an index on the fly leaf; it gives the same information as in the second section of the first diary. A third diary from this same period (F.O.95/381) covers the period 20 February to 2 March 1811 and relates only to domestic correspondence. It covers both in- and out-letters, but the entries are few. It is the only Northern Department diary of this period to have register numbers; these are from gaps in the Southern Department series.

The next Northern Department diary (F.O.95/382) is for the years 1813[1] and 1814. The entries for individual correspondents are no longer in separate sections, but are continuous in a roughly chronological order with batches of correspondence with a single person grouped together. Despatches sent are entered on the left-hand page; despatches received on the right. There are indexes to correspondents at the end of the volume.

In January 1816 the Northern Department introduced a new system of keeping its diaries. Annual volumes are divided into country sections, distinguished by 'tags' or 'cuts', the entries within each being chronological and including both despatches and domestic correspondence. Incoming correspondence is entered on the left-hand page, the information given being name of sender, despatch number, dates sent and received and subject. On the right are entries of outgoing correspondence giving name of addressee, despatch number, date sent and subject. Entries are normally confined to a single line. In 1817 the same system was adopted by the Southern Department and thereafter the system continued virtually unchanged until the end of 1890, each political department keeping an annual register with a separate section for each country with which it dealt.[2] The system was also adopted, as we shall see, in several of the non-political departments.

One exception is a diary for the whole Office arranged by countries and covering the period September to November 1818 (F.O.95/448). The evenness of the ink and writing suggests that it was not entered daily but made up carefully at intervals. Its purpose is not clear.

The Northern Department diaries for 1816 and 1817 have survived in their original form (F.O.95/446–447) but all other diaries kept on this system in the political departments were subsequently transferred to the Library with the correspondence to which they related[3] and there separated and rebound in a country arrangement, with several years' diaries for each country (or occasionally, especially for South and Central America, groups of neighbouring countries) bound in a single volume. These rearranged diaries are now in the class of *Registers of General Correspondence* (F.O.566).

When it adopted the new system in 1817, the Southern Department continued to assign register numbers to incoming correspondence and to enter these on the dockets. However, now instead of a single numerical series for the whole Department there was a separate series for each country section. This system of register

---

[1] The date 1812 also appears on the spine and flyleaf and in the index; this refers to the date of despatch of some of the incoming correspondence, which was not received and registered, however, until 1813.
[2] *4th Rpt. of R. Comm. on Civil Estabs.* (1890), q.26058.
[3] *Ibid.*, q.26053.

numbers for incoming correspondence was adopted by the Northern Department in 1822.

The numbering of entries of outgoing correspondence was introduced later and at different times in the different divisions and departments. The division of the Government Under Secretary's department which dealt with Austria, Portugal and South America began this in 1834; its example was followed by the other division in that department (that dealing with the German[1] and Italian States, Denmark, Sweden, Belgium and the Netherlands) in 1839. Also in 1839 numbering of out-letters appears in the diaries for France and Spain, which formed part of one of the Permanent Under Secretary's divisions, and in the following year when Greece was transferred to this same division its diaries were brought into line; but the diaries for the other countries in the division, the U.S.A. and Mexico, did not follow suit until 1841. The fourth division did not start to number its out-letters until 1844, except for Prussia which had its out-letters numbered in 1839 and again from 1841. The China out-letters were numbered, as we shall see, before China was transferred to this division in 1841, but were not numbered in 1842 or 1843. From the beginning it was usual for the register numbers of out-letters to be entered in the diaries of the political departments in red ink.

The register numbers, although noted on the dockets, were used only for cross-referencing within the diaries; they were not used as references on any other occasion.

In some country sections of the diaries there are separate sub-divisions, marked by 'tags' or 'cuts', for embassy, consular (where consuls carried on a separate political correspondence) and domestic correspondence; separate sub-divisions might also be used for correspondence on special subjects (the correspondence itself is often to be found in separate 'case' volumes). The Eastern Department kept separate cuts for telegrams between 1881 and 1890 and most of these are now bound up in a single volume (F.O.566/487). Other departments used special signs in their diaries to distinguish between telegrams and despatches and for other similar purposes.[2]

From 1816 to 1823 such correspondence relating to China and India as the Foreign Office had was entered in the Northern Department diaries in the normal way and the sections from 1818 to 1823 were subsequently bound up together (F.O. 566/109). When the Foreign Office began to take an interest in China again in 1833 a separate diary section was again started and the sections for 1833 and 1834 were subsequently bound up with those for 1818–1823. In 1835 a separate China Department, with its own diary, was created.[3] The correspondence for 1833 and 1834, including some material omitted from the original diary sections, was reregistered, the incoming correspondence being renumbered in a single series covering both years. The numbers on the dockets of the original correspondence were amended accordingly. Outgoing correspondence was also numbered serially. At the beginning of 1835 new series of numbers were started for both incoming and outgoing correspondence and these continued until 1841, when China ceased to be dealt with by a separate department and became the concern of one of the Permanent Under Secretary's divisions. The revised diary for 1833 and 1834, the diary from 1835 to 1841 and the diary sections from 1842 to 1848 are now bound in a single volume (F.O.566/110).

The method of registration developed in the political departments was adopted

---

[1] The outgoing correspondence relating to Saxony, however, was not numbered until 1840.
[2] For signs in use in departments in 1890 see Appendix II(a).
[3] F.O.366/673, p.263.

subsequently by the Consular, Commercial and Treaty Departments, each of which kept an annual diary, or diaries, divided into country sections. Separate diaries of consular correspondence for the U.S.A. and other American countries start in 1825, when John Bidwell became responsible for this correspondence.[1] For most other countries they commence in 1826, exceptions being Belgium (1832), Persia (1833), Greece (1834), the Barbary States (1836) (see p.16) and the Far Eastern countries (1869).[2] There are separate diaries of commercial correspondence for most countries[3] between 1865 and 1868 and again from 1872. Between 1869 and 1871, when there was a combined Consular and Commercial Department,[4] consular and commercial correspondence is entered in the same diaries. A separate series of Treaty Department diaries has survived from 1867, although they appear to have been kept in the Department from an earlier date. Before 1882 these diaries, each of which covers several years, include some correspondence which had already been registered in other departments of the office before being passed to the Treaty Department. From 1882 the Department's diaries are annual ones, and deal only with correspondence coming into the Department in the first place.[5]

Out-letters of the Consular Department are numbered serially in the diaries from 1841 and those of the Commercial and Treaty Departments from the introduction of their separate diaries. In the consular diaries to 1878 and the commercial diaries to 1884 the register numbers of out-letters are in red ink, as in the political diaries, but thereafter they are in black ink and the numbers appear with a line above when used in cross-references. This method of cross-referencing was also adopted by the Treaty Department in 1882. From 1873 consular diaries are divided into separate sub-sections for each consulate, together with one for domestic correspondence; a similar sub-division into embassy, consular and domestic appears in the commercial diaries from 1881.

Like the political departments' diaries, those of the Consular, Commercial and Treaty Departments have been separated and re-bound in a country arrangement and will be found in the class of *Registers of General Correspondence* (F.O.566).

The Slave Trade correspondence had been entered with the Barbary Powers in one or other of the departmental diaries until 1823; in 1824 entries appear to have been made in both. These sections were subsequently made up into one volume together with the Barbary Powers sections for 1825 and an incomplete Slave Trade section for 1826 (F.O.566/509).

The main series of separate Slave Trade diaries starts in 1824. At first two, three or even four years' correspondence is entered in a single volume, but in 1845 annual volumes begin. Until 1846 the first part of each volume is a subject index and the second a chronological diary, with incoming correspondence on the left and outgoing on the right. There are register numbers for both in- and out-letters, with each series continuing uninterrupted throughout a volume, even when it covers more than one year. The diary section has cross-references to the subject index. From 1845 entries in the subject index become infrequent[6] and in 1847 the arrangement of the volumes changes, the diary being divided into country sections, with a

---

[1] See p.15 n.2 above. Some of the earliest entries in these diary sections give the appearance of having been made retrospectively.
[2] The consular sections of the diaries for the Far Eastern countries were kept in the political department and bound with the political sections from 1869 to 1896.
[3] There were no separate commercial diaries or registers for the Far Eastern countries until 1918.
[4] The Departments merged in Oct. 1866 (see p.16) but separate commercial and consular diaries were kept up to the end of 1868.
[5] F.O.366/678, p.429.
[6] See F.O.881/5452, p. 1.

separate section for domestic correspondence, and being placed before the subject index, which is now always blank and is omitted from 1851. From 1847 each country has its own separate annual series of register numbers for both incoming and outgoing correspondence. This system continues in use until 1872, when the Slave Trade and Consular Departments were united.

Entries of Slave Trade correspondence from 1873 to 1876 appear in the consular diaries, sometimes in separate 'cuts', but with the sub-division of the Consular and Slave Trade Department in 1877 the Slave Trade diaries resume on the old system, with added sections for East and West Coasts of Africa. Previous consular correspondence concerning these had been entered in sections of the Consular Department diaries: West Coast of Africa correspondence in the Miscellaneous sections from 1848 to 1857 (now bound up in F.O.566/276) and in separate sections from 1858 to 1877 (F.O.566/1628–1630);[1] and East Coast of Africa correspondence in separate sections from 1872 to 1877 (F.O.566/1630). In 1884 the diaries change their title from 'Slave Trade' to 'Africa' as a consequence of the change of departmental title at the end of 1882.

Other Slave Trade Department diaries which have survived are for January 1852 (F.O.96/151) and January 1877 (F.O.566/546), each of which was subsequently re-entered in the appropriate annual volume. The former is particularly valuable since it supplies some deficiencies in the 1852 diary (F.O.566/525), which is damaged. A précis book of Slave Trade correspondence for 1823 (F.O.95/474) has also survived; this appears to have been compiled for the use of Canning as Secretary of State.

Certain matters relating to Africa were dealt with in other departments and correspondence will be found entered in diaries other than the 'Slave Trade' or 'Africa' ones. For example, there are separate political diary sections for Madagascar, 1863–1883 (F.O.566/260–261); consular correspondence relating to Madagascar is entered in consular diary sections which also cover the Pacific Islands and Borneo, 1858–1884 (F.O.566/310–312). Some West Coast of Africa entries appear between 1881 and 1883 in diary sections of the French Department; these also deal with Newfoundland and Raiatea (F.O.566/1632) and concern Anglo-French differences in those places.

During the period 1880–1882 there was a separate 'sanitary' series of correspondence, which was dealt with in the Slave Trade Department (see pp.16, 44). It was not, however, entered in the Slave Trade diaries and the separate diaries which presumably existed at the time have not survived. Before 1880 correspondence on sanitary matters is in the consular series of correspondence and is entered in the consular diaries; after 1882 it is similarly entered in the commercial diaries.

General Correspondence before 1906: Library Registers before 1891

On 18 July 1810 Lewis Hertslet, then newly appointed as Librarian of the Foreign Office, set down a scheme for a register and index of the entire correspondence of the Office. This was as follows:

    1. The Series of Papers belonging to the different countries to be arranged in conformity with the list subjoined, assigning to each country two or more specified letters, for the purpose of distinguishing them in the Index.

    2. The Number, Date, Name of Person, and Description of each Dispatch, Letter, etc., to be regularly entered, monthly, in to the Book appropriated for the Register according to the said Order of Arrangement.

---

[1] These appear to relate to correspondence which is in *General Correspondence before 1906, Africa* (F.O.2); see p.55 below.

3. The Dispatches from the British Ministers, Consuls, and Agents at Foreign Courts, and the Colonies dependent thereon, with the drafts of their Instructions, and all Letters and Communications from the different parts of the said Countries, and the Answers thereto, to constitute the Foreign part of the Register, and to be entered separately in the Order above mentioned.

4. The Notes, etc., of the Ministers, Consuls, and Agents from Foreign Courts resident in England, together with the Communications from the different Departments of State, and all other Letters or Papers relating to each particular country forwarded from any part of Great Britain, when arranged in order of date and divided according to the List above mentioned, to be considered as forming the Domestic part of the Register.

5. The Foreign and Domestic parts of the Digest to be bound together, comprising a year's correspondence.

6. The Indexes, entered in a separate volume, to include the names of the Persons, Places, Ships, and Subjects adverted to, and principally concerned in the Register – referring to the year (by the insertion of the terminating Figures), the abridged name of the Country, and the Pages of the Register wherein the Papers or Subject required is contained – to be arranged in alphabetical order, and, for the greater facility of access to the reference, the left-hand side of the Book to contain the Names of Persons, Places, and Ships, and the opposite Pages to be appropriated solely for the insertion of the Matter or Subject.[1]

This scheme was accepted and became the basis of registration in the Foreign Office Library for the next eighty years, although the details, particularly of indexing, were amended somewhat in practice and the final form of registers and indexes emerged only gradually in the course of Lewis Hertslet's Librarianship.[2] The registers and indexes compiled in the Library now constitute the class of *Registers (Library Series) and Indexes of General Correspondence* (F.O.802).[3]

Registration on a monthly basis, as Hertslet had envisaged, was not attempted; it did not take place until the records had passed out of current use and been transferred to the Library (normally when they were between one and two years old) and had been arranged and bound.[4] The registers were kept by countries and each was arranged as proposed by Hertslet: that is under the headings Foreign (or Embassy or Diplomatic or Political), Consuls, Consular Domestic, Domestic (i.e. Foreign Ministers in London) and Domestic Various. This followed the order in which the general correspondence itself was arranged and bound (see pp. 53–54). Later the commercial and treaty correspondence concerning each country was similarly registered in the order in which it was bound among the general correspondence. The registers were, however, bound not annually as Hertslet had intended but so as to make convenient sized volumes. The volumes in each country series were numbered for purposes of reference.

The Slave Trade and Africa correspondence was not registered in the Library until 1876.[5] Registration was then taken back only to 1845, to which date the departmental diaries were indexed, and was done in a separate series within the class (F.O.802/503–533). The Library's own correspondence and any correspondence of the other departments which did not fall conveniently under any country was registered under 'Great Britain' (F.O.802/259–263) or 'General' (F.O.802/228–241). The Chief Clerk's correspondence did not pass to the Library during the period in which the Library registers were being compiled and, therefore, escaped registration there (see p.74).

[1] Hertslet, *Recollections*, pp.29–30.
[2] F.O.366/392: L.Hertslet to Clarendon, 31 Dec. 1853.
[3] Microfilm copies are also preserved (F.O.605).
[4] *Rpt. of Sel. Ctee. on Official Salaries* (1850), q.3072; *Rpt. of Sel. Ctee. on Dipl. Service* (1861), p.75; *4th Rpt. of R. Comm. on Civil Estabs.* (1890), q.26441.
[5] F.O.881/5452; F.O.366/392: minute by E.Hertslet, 1 Aug. 1876.

Each register entry gives the despatch number, date and place and sender or addressee; it also includes a full description of the subject of the paper, including the names of any persons mentioned in it. Where the subject entry is very brief and is followed by the note 'Diary', this indicates that the paper is not in its expected place in the bound correspondence and that the particulars of the registry entry have been taken from the departmental diary. Such papers may be in the correspondence for some other country to which they are relevant or in 'case' volumes (see p.54). Cases relating to a single country are registered separately at the end of that country's series of registers; those relating to general subjects (such as replies to circulars) will be found entered in the Great Britain or General registers. Occasionally papers which appear in the registers will not be found in their proper place in the correspondence. This would occur if a case volume was made up retrospectively after registration (e.g. the removal of Law Officers' Reports in 1909) (see p.56).

The main country series of registers start in 1810, but they are preceded by a register entitled 'North and South', compiled at an early date,[1] and relating to the 1808 correspondence for Portugal and the Brazils and Spain and the 1809 correspondence for these same countries and also for America, Austria, Sardinia, Seven Islands, Sicily, Sweden and Turkey (F.O.802/380). Later, in about 1867,[2] the America register was carried back to 1793 (F.O.802/4) and a register of what are now *State Papers Foreign, France* (S.P.78) was compiled for the period 1761 to 1768 (F.O.802/223).

Hertslet's scheme for a comprehensive index to the whole series of registers was not put into operation although it bears a close resemblance to that projected again in 1891 (see p.43). In practice the compilation of the indexes lagged considerably behind that of the registers. Indexing was in progress by 1844,[3] but at the beginning of 1850 only 1,677 volumes of correspondence had been indexed, 1,081 during the previous year, and 5,698 remained unindexed.[4]

The system of indexing eventually put into operation involved separate country indexes, references being by volume and page to the corresponding registers. The earliest indexes (e.g. F.O.802/220)[5] have alternate pages for 'Correspondents' and 'Subjects' (the latter including persons mentioned in the correspondence), but the form generally adopted later was to divide the index by 'Persons' and 'Subjects' (the latter including places and ships) with one column for the former and two for the latter on each page. The arrangement of entries was alphabetical by the first two letters of the name or subject, with no attempt thereafter at a lexicographical arrangement. Registers of cases and the two registers of early correspondence relating to America and France were indexed separately. The subject indexes vary in quality and should be used with caution.

In general the Library registers now provide a better means of reference to the records than the departmental diaries, because they are indexed, give fuller details of subjects and are arranged in the same order as the correspondence. In 1870 Edmund Hammond thought the system 'perfect'.[6] It had, however, one weakness, which detracted seriously from the registers' value so far as the current work of the Office was concerned – it required a considerable amount of time and effort, and

---

[1] The watermarks are 1811 and 1812.
[2] F.O.366/676, p.223.
[3] F.O.83/241: memorandum by L.Hertslet, 2 July 1844.
[4] F.O.366/392: memorandum, *State of Register of Correspondence and Index to Register*, 30 Jan. 1850.
[5] Compiled after 1827, the date of the watermark.
[6] *Rpt. of Sel. Ctee. on Dipl. and Consular Services* (1870), q.61.

D

registration and, even more, indexing were perpetually in arrears, often by a considerable number of years.[1] Even if sufficient staff could have been provided to keep
registration and indexing up to date, account had still to be taken of the delay
before papers passed to the Library and could be arranged and bound; this delay
might be as much as four years.[2] For this reason, therefore, the Library registers
and indexes were condemned in 1890 by the Ridley Commission[3] and were brought
to an end when the arrears up to that year had been made good.

General Correspondence before 1906: Registers and Indexes 1891–1905

In 1890 the Ridley Commission recommended that:

> a regular register of all papers should be kept in each department, that it should be duly entered
> up and indexed every day, and that at the expiration of two years, the papers with the registers
> and indices complete, should be handed over to the librarian for custody, and eventual binding.[4]

This was accepted by the Foreign Office, standard signs and abbreviations for
use in the registers were drawn up to replace the individual systems previously
employed in the several departments, and printed instructions were issued to index-
makers. The new arrangements had what was considered to be a satisfactory trial in
November 1890 and came into effect on 1 January 1891.[5]

The new registers kept in the departments did not differ appreciably from the old
diaries, although at first an attempt was made to enter the subject of each paper in
more detail. Like the earlier diaries the new registers, with a few exceptions, do not
now retain their original annual departmental arrangement, but have been separated
and re-bound in a country arrangement with several years' register sections to a
volume. They are in the class of Registers of General Correspondence (F.O. 566).

Until 1896 the diplomatic and consular correspondence for China, Japan and
Siam were both dealt with in the political department, being registered in separate
sections of one register, the consular correspondence being in separate 'cuts'. These
registers have now been separated by countries, but the diplomatic and consular
sections for each country remain together. From 1897 consular correspondence was
dealt with in the Consular Department and that Department's register sections for
these countries have been made up into separate country volumes. The sections of
the Treaty Department registers relating to these three countries have not been
sub-divided and are bound up together in two volumes (F.O. 566/653, 580).

Separate sections were not assigned in the registers to all the individual countries
of South and Central America. The nature and extent of the groupings varied from
department to department.[6] In order to locate a particular register for any of these
countries it may be necessary to look in the class list under various headings.

The Commercial Department registers between 1899 and 1905 and the African
Department registers alone retain their annual departmental form.[7] There are three
volumes to each commercial register: volume one includes France, Belgium,
Netherlands, Austria, Germany, Switzerland, Sweden, Denmark and Norway;
volume two Russia, Italy, Spain, Portugal, Turkey, the Balkan States, Persia and

---

[1] F.O.366/392; F.O.881/5452; F.O.83/241; 4th Rpt. of R. Comm. on Civil Estabs. (1890), qq.
27538–27539.
[2] 4th Rpt. of R. Comm. on Civil Estabs. (1890), q.26441.
[3] Ibid., paras.7–11.
[4] Ibid., para.10.
[5] F.O.97/565; F.O.366/724, pp.474–476; F.O.881/6017. For the new standard signs see Appendix
II(b).
[6] They can be deduced from the list of country codes: Appendix II(c).
[7] The original form of the Consular Department's registers may be deduced from the arrangement of the country code lists at the beginning of F.O.804/51.

Greece; and volume three Egypt, Morocco, U.S.A., Central America, South America and Miscellaneous. A few of these registers appear in the main body of the class list under Egypt (F.O.566/712, 715), France (F.O.566/736, 740) and Russia (F.O.566/929, 932); the rest appear in a special Commercial sub-division towards the end of the list (F.O.566/1663–1677). Except for 1899, when each country section has its pages numbered separately, the pages are numbered consecutively from the beginning of volume one to the end of volume three; the page numbers included in each volume have been entered in the search room copy of the class list.

The annual Africa registers (F.O.566/1640–1662) continue unchanged the Africa diaries before 1891. From 1898 the register is divided into two: 'Africa' and 'African Protectorates'. Except for 1905, when the order is reversed, the page numbers of the Protectorates register follow on from those of the Africa register;[1] the page numbers included in each volume have been entered in the search room copy of the class list.

It was originally intended that the indexes should be compiled daily in the departments, but work soon fell into arrears and there were also complaints from the Librarian of the inadequacy of both indexes and registers. Accordingly in 1900 the task of working off arrears and continuing the indexes was entrusted to the Library, the keeping of the registers remaining the responsibility of the departments.[2]

The indexes for the period 1891–1905 now form the class of *Indexes to General Correspondence* (F.O.804).[3] They relate not to the original correspondence but to the departmental registers and, apart from those for the political departments, they were kept on a departmental basis even after they had been taken over by the Library. A system of country code letters was devised for use in the index references; as these were assigned in the individual departments, they vary from department to department.[4]

There are separate country indexes (sometimes with more than one volume to a country) to the political departments' registers (F.O.804/4–50). Where the registers relate to a group of countries (e.g. Central America), this grouping is maintained in the index. Because of this country arrangement the country code letters are not used in these indexes. On each page of the index there are three columns, one for persons and the other two for subjects; entries are alphabetical by the first two letters of the name or subject; reference is by the year and the page of the register section.

The Consular Department index is in four volumes (each covering the whole period) arranged alphabetically: A–C, D–K, L–R and S–Z (F.O.804/51–54). There are alternate pages for persons and subjects; references are by the year, the country code letter and the page of the register section.

The first part of the Commercial Department index is in two alphabetically arranged volumes (A–J and K–Z) covering the period 1891–1899 (F.O.804/57–58).[5] The arrangement and references are the same as those in the Consular Department index. The index for the period 1900–1905 (F.O.804/59)[6] has the same three column arrangement (one for persons; two for subjects) as the political indexes. References are by the year and the page of the register; the search room class list must be

---

[1] In 1902 (F.O.566/1651, 1659) there is an overlap, pp.317–320 appearing in both registers.
[2] F.O.366/760, pp.240–242, 256; F.O.366/787, f.170 (p.2); Z.Steiner, 'The Last Years of the Old Foreign Office, 1898–1905', in *Historical Journal*, VI (1963), p.86.
[3] Photocopies are also preserved (F.O.738).
[4] For these country codes see Appendix II(c).
[5] Formerly F.O.833/1–2. See p.126 below.
[6] Formerly F.O.833/3.

consulted to see in which of the three register volumes for a year a particular page comes.

The Treaty Department index for 1891–1899 is wanting. That for 1900–1905 (F.O.804/56) has the three column arrangement of persons and subjects; reference is by the year, the country code letter and the page of the register section.

The African Department index is in three volumes covering the years 1891–1896, 1897–1902 and 1903–1905 respectively (F.O.804/1–3). From 1898 it relates to both the Africa and the Protectorates registers. It has the three column arrangement of persons and subjects. Reference is by the year and the page of the register; whether the latter is in the Africa or Protectorates register can be determined by reference to the search room class list.

General Correspondence before 1906: Original Correspondence

The original correspondence received at the Foreign Office was classified in this period first by the country to which it related and then under two main heads: 'foreign' and 'domestic'. The foreign correspondence consisted of despatches from British diplomatic and consular representatives abroad, together with 'foreign various' (letters from individuals writing from the country concerned); the domestic correspondence consisted of notes from foreign diplomatic representatives in London and 'domestic various' (letters from other government departments and from individuals and institutions in this country). The basic distinction between foreign and domestic correspondence was retained throughout the period, although as the former grew in size and was further sub-divided and referred to by departmental series (e.g. 'consular', 'commercial'), the term 'foreign' rather passed out of use.

British diplomatic and consular representatives were expected to write frequently to the Foreign Office[1] and to acknowledge all despatches received from the Office. Each diplomatic and consular post had its own annual series of 'local' or 'despatch numbers';[2] the enclosures in each despatch were numbered and noted in the margin of the despatch. At the end of each year a return was made of the number of despatches sent. This numbering of despatches had been ordered for diplomats by the two Secretaries of State in 1766;[3] there appears to have been no general order for numbering consular despatches until 1824,[4] although individual consuls had numbered their despatches from a much earlier date. Those consular officials in the Ottoman Empire who had diplomatic as well as consular functions started separate series of diplomatic (or political) and consular despatches in the 1830s.[5] A separate series of Slave Trade despatches was ordered in 1823;[6] this became the Africa series in 1883.[7] Separate series of commercial, sanitary and treaty despatches started in 1865, 1880 and 1883 respectively.[8] Correspondence from representatives in the Far Eastern countries was not divided into political and consular until 1869, and even thereafter the consular series continued to be dealt with in the first instance in the

---

[1] '. . . at least once by every post' (F.O.95/377, p.74); '. . . at least once every week' (F.O.83/81: circular of 1 Jan. 1816).
[2] A new series of despatch numbers was sometimes started during a year on a change of head of mission or consul or of Secretary of State.
[3] S.P.78/271, ff. 17–18; S.P.90/85, f. 160.
[4] F.O.83/82: circular, 1 Jan. 1824.
[5] The first to do so was the Consul General at Alexandria in 1833 (F.O.78/227–228, 231).
[6] F.O.84/24: draft circular, Slave Trade No.1, July 1823.
[7] F.O.83/775: circular, 23 Feb. 1883.
[8] F.O.366/675, p.539a; F.O.83/589: circular, 22 Dec. 1879; F.O.83/738: circular, 23 Dec. 1882. The sanitary series merged in the commercial in 1883 when responsibility for such matters passed from the Slave Trade to the Commercial Department.

political department until 1897; there was no separate commercial series until 1918. Where despatches were not immediately related to any of the normal series they were left unnumbered and marked 'Separate' or 'Private'.

The forms to be observed in official despatches were laid down from time to time in considerable detail. Despatches and enclosures were to be written in a large round and distinct hand on folio paper with a margin of one-quarter of the page on the inner side; each despatch was to be confined to a single subject; enclosures in foreign languages other than French were to be accompanied by translations and where printed papers were enclosed two copies were to be sent if possible; newspaper cuttings, etc., sent as enclosures were to be pasted on despatch paper.[1]

Despatches were normally addressed to the Secretary of State, although it was not unusual, particularly towards the end of the period, for them to be addressed to the Under Secretaries or even, in special circumstances, to others, as when the consular correspondence was addressed to the Superintendent of the Consular Department during the superintendence of John Bidwell (see p.15). A separate correspondence was also carried on with the Chief Clerk (see pp.49, 76).

Despatches might arrive at the Foreign Office by the ordinary mails, by Foreign Service Messenger or by the hand of a trustworthy traveller. The mails had been used for carrying despatches since the late seventeenth century[2] and were by the nineteenth century the normal means of transmission. Despatches might be entrusted to travellers only if it involved the Office in no expense; the employment of special couriers was permitted only under extraordinary circumstances.[3] Where there was a risk of loss or delay *en route* despatches might be sent in duplicate by different means of conveyance.[4]

Confidential despatches were normally sent where possible in the diplomatic bag entrusted to a Foreign Service Messenger. Bags containing such confidential material, known as 'crossed bags', were carried in special valises and were kept in the constant custody of the Messenger. Opportunity might also be taken to send by Messenger non-confidential material, particularly that of a bulky nature, in 'un-crossed bags'. For the major diplomatic posts, Paris, Berlin, Vienna, St. Petersburg and Constantinople, there was a frequent and regular Messenger service; Madrid and Italy had a regular but less frequent service. Messengers' routes varied with circumstances, but in the latter part of the nineteenth century there were seven regular journeys: to Paris; to Berlin; to St. Petersburg via Berlin; to Vienna via Berlin; to Constantinople via Paris, Vienna and the Balkans; to Madrid via Paris; and to Italy via Paris.[5] By the beginning of the twentieth century regular journeys had been reduced to three: to Paris and, on alternate weeks, to Constantinople via Berlin and Vienna and to St. Petersburg via Berlin.[6] Bags from and for posts off the main route were picked up and handed over at various intermediate stations. Special arrangements were made to take account of special circumstances, such as the absence of Queen Victoria abroad.[7]

Diplomatic and consular representatives often sent their despatches to the Foreign Office, particularly when using the Messenger Service, under 'flying seal',

---

[1] For example, F.O.83/82: circular to Consuls, 1 Jan. 1824; F.O.83/85: circular, 1 March 1836; F.O.96/27: Hammond to Alston, 9 Feb. 1862. See also H.Temperley, *The Foreign Policy of Canning, 1822–1827* (1925), p.264.

[2] Horn, *Brit. Dipl. Service*, pp.217–218.

[3] F.O.83/81: circular, 1 Jan. 1816; F.O.83/82: circular, 19 Dec. 1823.

[4] See, for example, F.O.95/11–17.

[5] F.O.366/263–274 give details of individual journeys.

[6] F.O.366/761, p.48; Tilley and Gaselee, *Foreign Office*, p.205.

[7] For example, F.O.96/27: memorandum by Hammond, 1 Sept. 1862.

that is with a seal attached but not closed, to some intermediate post. In the case of a consul this would be to the Consul-General or the head of mission to whom he was subordinated; in the case of a diplomat, to a colleague at another post. For example, in the middle of the nineteenth century despatches from Bavaria and Württemberg went under flying seal to Frankfort and then in the same state to Paris; despatches from Persia passed under flying seal through Constantinople.[1]

Despatches of a secret or confidential nature which were sent by the ordinary mail were put into cipher. The ciphers, of which a number were current at any one time, were usually numerical and there were complicated rules for their employment. In the early years of the Foreign Office these ciphers were devised, as they had been throughout the eighteenth century, by members of the Willes family in the Secret Department of the Secretaries of State.[2] But with the abolition of that Department in 1844 fresh arrangements had to be made and at some date before 1874 cipher making was entrusted to certain Foreign Office Clerks.[3] In order to make it more difficult for a foreign power to break a cipher, diplomats were forbidden to put into cipher any document received from or known to a foreign court. Similarly they were forbidden to give or even read to a foreign court copies or translations of any document or part of a document received in cipher from the Foreign Office without careful paraphrasing.[4] Invisible ink was not used in despatches to the Foreign Office, although its use in correspondence between diplomats is known.[5]

The introduction of the electric telegraph in the middle of the nineteenth century gave diplomats and consuls another means of communicating with the Foreign Office. The first use of this appears to have been by the Paris Embassy in December 1852[6] and by the middle of the following year Florence, Berlin and Vienna were also in telegraphic communication with the Office.[7] Thereafter, as the telegraph lines were extended more and more posts were able to avail themselves of this means of communication and this they did with increasing frequency. By 1878 telegraphic communication was so extensive that telegrams were numbered like despatches and from some missions might run to several hundred a year.[8] In 1884 the telegraphic addresses 'Prodrome' and 'Breastrail' were registered. 'Prodrome London' was used for diplomatic telegrams to the Foreign Office and 'Prodrome' followed by the name of the mission for telegrams from the Office; 'Breastrail' was used in the same way for consular telegrams.[9]

Telegrams were normally sent in cipher. At first they were followed by 'recorders', duplicates sent through the normal channels of correspondence as a check on decipherment, or by 'extenders', longer despatches giving in more detail the reasons for instructions given by telegram. In 1890 the former were replaced by 'paraphrases',[10] sent through the normal channels, conveying the substance of

[1] F.O.96/24: Malet to Clarendon, 1 July 1854; minute by Clarendon, 4 July 1854; minute by Hammond, 4 May [? 1855].
[2] Tilley and Gaselee, Foreign Office, p.147. See also p.47 below. For eighteenth-century ciphers see S.P.106.
[3] F.O.366/677, pp.357–359. Ciphers of 1820 and 1830 were still in use in 1861: Tilley and Gaselee, Foreign Office, p.148.
[4] F.O.83/81: circular, 1 Jan. 1816; F.O.96/25: lithographed circular, Information for the employment of Cyphers, undated but paper watermarked 1828.
[5] P.R.O.30/29/12, no.4/20, ff.107–108.
[6] F.O.27/940: Cowley to F.O., 10 Dec. 1852.
[7] F.O.79/165: chargé d'affaires, Florence, to F.O., 18 March 1853; F.O.65/427: Bloomfield to F.O., 5 June 1853; F.O.7/420: Westmorland to F.O., 26 June 1853.
[8] In 1897 the Constantinople Embassy sent 702 diplomatic telegrams (F.O.78/4813–4814).
[9] F.O.83/1275.
[10] F.O.366/1136: minute, Currie to Salisbury, 21 Feb. 1890.

telegrams without repeating the wording and thus not compromising the cipher if they were intercepted. Whenever a telegram had to be repeated for any reason, the second version was known as a 'repeater'.

Domestic correspondence was of too miscellaneous a nature for any general comments to be made about it. A word should, however, be said about the language employed by foreign ministers in London in their notes to the Secretary of State. Until the latter part of the eighteenth century this was invariably French, but the ministers of the United States of America used English from the beginning of their representation and during the nineteenth century more and more foreign ministers came to use their own language or, in some cases, English.[1] One exception was the Russian Embassy which continued to use French until 1917.

Throughout the eighteenth and early nineteenth centuries foreign mails passing through the Post Office, including despatches to and from foreign ministers in London, were regularly opened and copied in the Secret Office maintained there by the Secretaries of State. Any necessary deciphering was done in the Secret Department or Deciphering Branch, staffed largely by the descendants of Edward Willes, Bishop of Bath and Wells, Decipherer of Letters from 1716 to 1773. This title was abolished in 1812, but the interception of foreign mails continued until criticism in press and Parliament led to the abolition of the Secret Office in February 1844 and of the Deciphering Branch in October of the same year.[2] After 1766 intercepted despatches and correspondence came to be regarded as private papers and were not normally kept among the official records.[3] However, covering letters from the Secret Office, 1781–1806, will be found in the *General Correspondence, Great Britain and General* (F.O.83/5)[4] and some intercepted despatches are among the supplementary correspondence in *Miscellanea, Series I* (F.O.95/1–10). There are intercepted despatches for the period 1824–1828 in the *Howard de Walden Papers* (F.O.360/3–5).

General Correspondence before 1906: Minutes, Drafts, Circulation
The way in which the business of the Foreign Office was conducted in the middle of this period was described in detail in a draft report of the abortive committee of enquiry into the state of the Office of 1850.[5]

The letters and despatches which arrive before 12 o'clock, are dealt with as follows:
1st. They are opened by one or other of two clerks, called Resident Clerks, who occupy apartments in the Foreign Office.

2ndly. They are immediately forwarded to the Under-Secretary to whose division of labour they belong.

3rdly. They are forwarded by the Under-Secretary, with or without observation, as the case may require, to the Secretary of State.

4thly. They are returned to the respective Under-Secretary by the Secretary of State, accompanied by such directions for their further treatment as the Secretary of State may think fit to give.

---

[1] 7 *B.D.I.L.*, pp.961–967.

[2] Ellis, *Post Office*, pp.60–77, 127–131, 138–142; *Rpt. from Lords' Sel. Ctee. on Post Office*, H.C. 1844 (601) XIV, p.503.

[3] Before 1766 they are in *State Papers Foreign, Confidential* (S.P.107).

[4] This volume also includes a warrant for intercepting mail issued by the Duke of Grafton on 5 Aug. 1765. *Home Office Entry Books, Private and Secret* for the period 1806–1855 (H.O.79/1–5) contain similar warrants.

[5] There is an undated printed copy of this draft in the Foreign Office Library, *General No. 4.* There appears to be no copy in either Foreign Office or Treasury records in the Public Record Office. On the committee of enquiry see F.O.366/386: copy, Addington to Malmesbury, 17 July 1852, and copy memorandum by Sir Charles Trevelyan, 30 July 1852; also Tilley and Gaselee, *Foreign Office*, pp.62–69.

5thly. They are then sent by the Under-Secretary to the department to which they respectively belong, where they are entered in a register which is kept of the papers which pass daily through each department.

6thly. The drafts of answers, or the memoranda containing information called for by the Secretary of State, having been prepared by each head of department, and delivered to the respective Under-Secretary, are by him sent to the Secretary of State; who, after giving the drafts his final sanction, returns them to the Under-Secretary for completion in their several departments.

Such letters and despatches as arrive after 12 o'clock are similarly dealt with, except that, as the clerks are then assembled, they are opened in the department to which they belong, and are registered *before* they are sent to the Under-Secretary.

The foreign correspondence of the office is extensively circulated for the information of the Diplomatic Officers serving abroad; and it is the duty of each senior clerk to call the attention of his fellow senior clerks to such correspondence as ought to be so circulated, in order that it may be copied in its proper department, and sent to the officers serving abroad, who are to be made acquainted with its contents.

The outstanding feature of this system is the concentration of initiative in the hands of the Secretary of State and, to a lesser extent, of the Under Secretaries. In this it contrasts with the Colonial Office system in which the Senior Clerk of a department took the initiative, and papers moved up the chain of command.[1]

That the system described in 1850 had long been in existence is clear from the duties assigned to the Foreign Office clerks in a memorandum by Lord Grenville of 1799.[2] Indeed it seems probable that the system had changed little since 1782.

In one respect there had been a change since 1799. Then the Under Secretaries had been responsible for docketing incoming despatches,[3] but in December 1805 heads of mission were instructed to docket their own despatches, giving the place and date, their name, the number of enclosures and the means of conveyance; a year later they were further instructed to include in the docket the 'Heads or Précis of Principal Facts'.[4] All that needed to be added to the docket in the Foreign Office was the date of receipt. Similar instructions were given to consuls in 1824.[5] Thereafter, only the domestic correspondence and, from 1882, telegrams[6] were docketed in the Office. From 1887 to 1889 special docket sheets, with a space for minutes, were used in the Commercial Department for domestic and other correspondence not docketed at source.

The Under Secretaries were permitted to make observations on the despatches which passed through their hands, but the surviving minutes from the various Foreign Secretaryships of Lord Palmerston (F.O.96/17–23) do not suggest that in his time they took much advantage of this opportunity to express their opinions, at least not in writing. Where there are minutes by the Under Secretaries, they are mostly replies to specific enquiries from Palmerston. Minutes by Foreign Office clerks are extremely rare for this period; they appear to be always replies to specific enquiries and, except for those by the Chief Clerk, they are not generally initialed by their authors but simply subscribed 'F.O.' with the date. However, under Palmerston's successors minutes by the Under Secretaries, particularly by Edmund Hammond, increase in number and importance; minutes also appear more frequently from Foreign Office clerks, who gradually begin to initial their contri-

[1] Pugh, *Records of Colonial and Dominions Offices*, pp.36–37.
[2] F.O.366/671, pp.119–123.
[3] *Ibid.*, p.126.
[4] F.O.95/377, pp.106, 154.
[5] F.O.83/82: circular to consuls, 1 Jan. 1824.
[6] F.O.366/391: minute by Tenterden, 13 Feb. 1882.

butions.[1] When memoranda requiring recourse to correspondence in the Library were called for, the Librarian was responsible for their production (the rule that he was to do so only when the correspondent was over fifteen years old was ignored).[2] Many of these memoranda were printed in the series of Confidential Print.

The clerks were further involved by a change in practice at some date between 1869 and 1886 by which despatches arriving out of office hours went first from the Resident Clerks to the Senior Clerks of the responsible departments, who, before passing them on to the Under Secretaries, noted on them 'such explanations as seem necessary', although it remained, except in special cases, 'not the practice to draw up Memoranda or detailed observations on the despatches which come in, such a practice tending to occasion delay'.[3] On the other hand the opening of letters and despatches arriving during office hours in the appropriate department did not continue for very long after 1850, at least so far as the political correspondence was concerned. From 1855 this was usually opened by the Under Secretaries or by their Private Secretaries, sent to the departments for entry in the departmental diaries and then returned to the Under Secretaries for transmission to the Secretary of State.[4] Correspondence addressed to the Chief Clerk, however, was sent direct to his department,[5] while before 1883 and again from 1886 consular correspondence arriving out of office hours was sent unopened by the Resident Clerks direct to the Consular Department.[6]

At first minuting was mostly on separate octavo sheets of paper, brief minutes and circulation lists only being endorsed on despatches. As time went on, however, endorsement of minutes became more common until in 1887 instructions had to be given that special octavo minute sheets should be used for minutes which, owing to the limited space below the docket, would extend to a second page.[7] Three years later, however, there were renewed complaints that 'serious inconvenience and confusion are caused by Despatches being covered with a variety of Minutes and Initials' and orders were given that 'Minutes should be as clear as possible and should leave room for the Initial of the Secretary of State and for any observations he may wish to add'.[8] Minutes were supposed to be dated by their writers, although neglect of this resulted in the issue in 1879 of a reminder that the writers of minutes and those through whom papers passed should date them.[9] Printed circulation slips for papers passing within the Office had been used since at least 1848.[10]

Lord Salisbury made use of a stamped monogram 'S', said to have been applied on occasions by his Private Secretary, to indicate that he had seen and approved papers submitted to him.[11] Papers passing through the Chief Clerk's hands were from about 1872 stamped 'Seen by the Chief Clerk', a date stamp being subsequently incorporated. Attempts to introduce stamped signatures for the Under Secretaries and Assistant Secretaries in 1881 were unsuccessful,[12] but in 1895 a

---

[1] Minutes for the period 1854–1867 are in F.O.96/24–27.
[2] See p.21 above. For a list of Library memoranda see F.O.881/8159. Material collected for the production of memoranda is in F.O.95/783–800.
[3] Confidential Print No.5228, pp.2, 4. There is a copy of the 1886 version in F.O.366/724, pp.168–173; F.O.881/5228 is the 1890 version. Compare F.O.881/1726, a version of 1869.
[4] F.O.881/5941*, p.9 (No.16); Rpt. of Sel. Ctee. on Dipl. Service (1861), q.679 (p.74); F.O.881/1726, p.3; F.O.881/5228, p.3; 4th Rpt. of R. Comm. on Civil Estabs. (1890), qq.26075, 26383.
[5] 4th Rpt. of R. Comm. on Civil Estabs. (1890), q.26383.
[6] F.O.366/386: various minutes of July–Aug. 1886.
[7] F.O.366/391: minute by E.Barrington, 3 Feb. 1887.
[8] Ibid.: copy minute by P.Currie, 5 March 1890; F.O.881/7034*, p.13.
[9] F.O.366/678, p.66.
[10] Papers of this date with circulation slips still attached will be found in F.O.366/280.
[11] F.O.366/391: minute by T.V.Lister, 7 April 1881; Camb. Hist. of Brit. For. Policy III, p.606.
[12] F.O.366/391: various minutes, March–April 1881.

stamp with the Chief Clerk's name on it was introduced for use by his clerks to sign certain papers.[1]

Many of Palmerston's minutes were instructions for replying to despatches and the resulting drafts often incorporate these instructions verbatim. However, even Palmerston, for all his concern with the *minutiae* of his Office had occasionally to leave matters to the discretion of his Under Secretaries.[2] The preparation of drafts, with the exception of circulars, was confined at first to the Secretary of State and the Under Secretaries.[3] By 1828 the Superintendents of the Consular and Slave Trade Departments also prepared drafts, but in the political departments they were still prepared by the Under Secretaries.[4] By 1850 their preparation had devolved upon the Senior Clerks in the departments, although they might have to work within strict limits set by the full instructions which came down from the Secretary of State or the Under Secretaries. However, within a decade Senior Clerks (especially the Senior Clerk in the Consular Department) were distributing the work of drafting despatches as they saw fit among the Junior Clerks, while in matters of routine despatches might be prepared for signature without a draft being first submitted.[5] In 1889 instructions were given that drafts should bear the names of those who prepared them,[6] and it is clear from an examination of subsequent drafts that their preparation was by that date largely carried out by the Junior Clerks. Between 1887 and 1889 special printed sheets for drafts were used in the Commercial Department.

Fair copying and ciphering of despatches approved in draft by the Secretary of State or the Under Secretaries was in 1799 and 1806 the responsibility of the four 'Decypherers',[7] and more particularly of the two senior ones; fair copying might also be required of the other clerks.[8] In 1828 ciphering was 'confided to those Clerks who are habitually employed in the confidential business of the Office' and the making of fair copies of despatches was the duty of the Junior Clerks.[9] Throughout this period the ciphering of despatches and telegrams in the political departments continued to be done by the Junior Clerks. Printed and lithographed circular letters are known from as early as 1814 and 1820 respectively;[10] later printed letters were used for transmitting papers to other departments and for certain types of routine correspondence with diplomatic and consular representatives. But with these exceptions the making of fair copies of despatches remained the duty of the Junior Clerks until the advent of the typewriter at the end of the nineteenth century. A typist was first employed in the Office in 1889 (see p.11), and was used at first mainly for copying. Not until 1896 were the political departments allowed to send papers for typing and then only non-confidential ones[11] but by 1900 many drafts were being typewritten and by 1905 so were most outgoing despatches.

The signing of despatches was for many years reserved for the Secretary of State and the Under Secretaries, although John Bidwell had been permitted to sign

[1] F.O.366/760, pp.86–87.
[2] F.O.96/20: minute by Palmerston, 17 Jan. 1841.
[3] *1st Rpt. of Commrs. on Fees* (1806), p.4; F.O.366/671, pp.118, 293.
[4] F.O.366/386: memorandum of June 1828.
[5] *Rpt. of Sel. Ctee. on Consular Service and Appointments* (1857–58), q.2; *Rpt. of Sel. Ctee. on Dipl. Service* (1861), q.679 (p.74).
[6] F.O.366/724, p.374; F.O.881/7034*, p.13.
[7] Not to be confused with the Decipherers of Letters in the Secret Department of the Secretaries of State (see p.46 above).
[8] F.O.366/671, pp.120–122, 294–295.
[9] F.O.366/386: memorandum of June 1828.
[10] F.O.83/81: circular of 26 Sept. 1814; circular of Nov. 1820.
[11] F.O.366/760, pp.109–111.

despatches as Superintendent of the Consular Department (see p.15). At first the Under Secretaries had signed only in the absence of the Secretary of State or on his specific instructions; they signed domestic correspondence more frequently than despatches, although Palmerston permitted them to sign circulars[1] and in 1860 they were permitted to sign 'merely transmitting despatches'.[2] However, as the nineteenth century advanced more and more despatches were signed by them as a matter of course. When the first Assistant Under Secretary was appointed in 1858 he was permitted to sign only in the absence of both the Under Secretaries; not until 1860 was he permitted to sign consular despatches of the kind which they had previously signed (see p.6). Subsequently, however, the Assistant Under Secretaries were permitted, as a matter of course, to sign the more routine correspondence, even of the political departments. Where the Under Secretaries or Assistant Under Secretaries signed as a matter of course they did so 'for' the Secretary of State; otherwise they signed 'in the absence of' the Secretary of State.[3]

Despatches from the Foreign Office were dated from 'St. James's' until 1786, then from 'Whitehall' until 1793 and thereafter until 1807 from 'Downing Street'; since 1807 it has been customary to date from the 'Foreign Office'.[4] The date was added after signature and was normally that on which the despatch was sent off,[5] but on occasions despatches might be ante-dated.[6]

Despatches and drafts on matters of any importance were circulated to the Prime Minister and the Sovereign, normally in that order, although it was at times reversed and at other times originals would go to the Sovereign and copies to the Prime Minister simultaneously.[7] Replies to despatches might be sent off before the drafts had returned from the Sovereign,[8] although this was not supposed to happen with the more important drafts.[9] The sending of despatches before the Queen had returned the drafts led to a famous conflict between Palmerston and Queen Victoria. For a while the Queen reaffirmed her right to have all drafts for her approval sent in sufficient time to make herself acquainted with their contents before they had to be sent off, but by the end of her reign it had again become a common practice for despatches to be sent off before she had seen the drafts. In such cases it was accepted that despatches should be subsequently confirmed or cancelled by telegram. Drafts and copies sent to Queen Victoria continued to be handwritten even after the introduction of typewriters to the Office.[10]

Despatches and drafts, or more frequently copies of them, were also seen by the Cabinet. The practice in the early nineteenth century was for an abstract to be circulated to ministers[11] and then for despatches and drafts returned by the Sovereign and Prime Minister to be left in boxes in the Cabinet Room at the old Foreign

[1] F.O.96/19: minute by W.Fox Strangways, 13 June 1837.
[2] F.O.366/675, p.209.
[3] F.O.366/724, pp.121–122; F.O.881/7034*, p.12.
[4] F.O.366/669–671; Hertslet, *Recollections*, pp.58–59. See also p.3 n.1.
[5] F.O.366/671, pp.119, 293.
[6] F.O.96/19: minutes by J.Backhouse and Palmerston, 27–28 Oct. 1837.
[7] F.O.96/18: minutes by Palmerston, 11–12 Oct. 1835; F.O.96/22: minute by Palmerston, 24 June 1849. Minutes by the Private Secretaries to the Sovereign and by Prime Ministers will be found in F.O.96/17–27 and scattered through the *General Correspondence* classes. Correspondence with Sir H.F.Ponsonby, Private Secretary to Queen Victoria, 1870–1895, is in F.O.800/3 (see p.169 below).
[8] F.O.96/17: minute by Palmerston, 1 Sept. 1832.
[9] F.O.96/21: minute by Palmerston, 19 Nov. 1847. See also F.O.366/280, pp.37–52.
[10] *Camb, Hist. of Brit. For. Policy* III, pp.571–577; Tilley and Gaselee, *Foreign Office*, p.136; F.O.881/7034*, pp.5–6. For the confirmation of despatches by telegram see F.O.96/27: minute by J.Murray, 18 April 1865.
[11] For a specimen abstract of 1833 see F.O.366/280, pp.93–96.

Office,[1] where any minister who wished might read them. Palmerston, however, preferred that copies of the more important papers should be circulated to ministers and this was generally done throughout the rest of the nineteenth century.[2] Printed circulation slips were used for this.[3] It is possible that despatches were still being formally read at Cabinet meetings in 1856.[4]

The widespread circulation of copies of all important despatches and drafts to British diplomatic representatives was freely practised, although not originated, by Palmerston.[5] Even after the series of Confidential Print was commenced in 1829,[6] most copies for immediate circulation were made by hand until the introduction of the telegraph brought about a change in practice. Copies of telegrams both received and sent were duplicated by the manifold process for urgent distribution within the Office and to the Queen, while printed sheets of the day's more important telegrams and despatches, known as daily print sections,[7] were subsequently circulated to the Prince of Wales,[8] to members of the Cabinet and occasionally to missions abroad. Telegrams in cipher were printed in paraphrase.[9] The regular Confidential Print series was widely circulated to missions abroad as well as within the Foreign Office and to other government departments. From time to time special arrangements were made for their distribution.[10]

Copies of individual despatches and drafts might also be sent to other interested government departments. In some cases enclosures to despatches which were of particular interest to other departments were forwarded in original without any copy being made in the Foreign Office.[11] This happened most frequently with Commercial Reports, which went to the Board of Trade,[12] and the reports of Military and Naval Attachés, which were forwarded to the War Office and Admiralty respectively. Originals transmitted in this way were supposed to be returned when the other department had finished with them,[13] but this does not always appear to have happened. When such papers are not to be found in the Foreign Office General Correspondence, search should be made in the records of the department to which they were sent; if they do not appear there, it is often worth looking in the appropriate class of Embassy and Consular Archives for the draft.

Special arrangement were made in the Foreign Office for dealing with parliamentary questions and references to the Law Officers of the Crown. The identification of parliamentary questions relating to the Foreign Office was the responsibility of the Librarian, who circulated copies of questions to the Secretary of State, Under Secretaries and heads of departments, who between them decided what

---

[1] The Cabinet met there until 1861: see Hertslet, Recollections, p.22.
[2] F.O.96/17: minute by J.Backhouse, 28 March 1833; F.O.96/18: minutes by Palmerston and others, 2 Oct. 1835; F.O.96/21: various minutes, 19 May 1847; F.O.366/391: minutes of Jan.–Feb. 1853; F.O.881/7034*, p.4.
[3] For specimens, 1841–1854, see F.O.366/280, pp.313–333.
[4] F.O.96/25: minute by Palmerston, 7 Dec. 1856.
[5] Sir C.Webster, The Foreign Policy of Palmerston, 1830–1842, Vol. I (1951), p.71.
[6] 7 B.D.I.L., p.ix; see also pp.88–89 below.
[7] Many daily print sections will be found bound up with the originals in the General Correspondence. Bound chronological sets for certain periods may also be found in Private Collections (e.g. P.R.O.30/29/371–381) and in the Miscellanea classes of Embassy and Consular Archives (e.g. F.O. 287/2–14; F.O.300/3–9, 12–16, 18).
[8] Officially from 1886; informally for some years previously. See Gosses, Management of Brit. For. Policy, pp.105–106.
[9] Tilley and Gaselee, Foreign Office, pp.135–137; F.O.881/7034*, pp.1–3.
[10] See F.O.83/909, 1460, 2034.
[11] F.O.881/3264.
[12] They were usually printed; see p.90 below.
[13] The return of such material is recorded in the departmental diaries and registers by underlining the words 'in original' in the entry of the letter transmitting the papers to the other department.

answers were to be given.[1] Detailed rules were drawn up for the submission of papers to the Law Officers and for printing the resulting reports.[2]

General Correspondence before 1906: Make up
Arrangements for keeping the official correspondence of the Foreign Office were laid down by Lord Grenville in a memorandum of 7 April 1799.[3]

> The Dispatches [*sic*] received and Drafts transmitted, shall be collected at the end of every Month, and shall, after they have been checked by the Under Secretaries of State and the Clerk whose duty it is to register the Mails, with the Entries in the proper Book, be deposited in the Presses appointed for that purpose, in the Rooms of the Under Secretaries of State. . . .
>
> At the Expiration of every three Months, the Correspondence of the Year up to that Period, is to be again looked over, and the proper Steps taken for restoring to their Places all Dispatches that may have been previously removed therefrom.
>
> In the Month of February the whole of the Correspondence of the preceding Year is to be opened out into the Official Port Folios; and in the Month of June, to be permanently bound up. . . .

In 1801 arranging the correspondence became the responsibility of the Librarian,[4] who took charge of it when it had passed out of current use in the departments. In the second half of the nineteenth century this was one year from the end of the calendar year in which it was created.[5] Prior to their transfer to the Library papers were kept folded in presses in the departments, their arrangement being by countries with drafts kept apart from despatches; this basic arrangement was retained in the bound volumes subsequently made up in the Library[6] and now constituting the several country classes of *General Correspondence before 1906* in the Public Record Office.[7]

Within each country class the primary division of each year's[8] correspondence is into foreign and domestic. The foreign correspondence consists mostly of despatches and drafts of despatches, arranged in separate series for each diplomatic and consular post[9] within the country and its dependencies. Where Secretaries of Missions or Vice-Consuls conducted an independent correspondence with the Foreign Office, this is kept as a separate series, but where Chargés d'Affaires or Vice-Consuls carried on the normal numbered series of correspondence in the absence of their superiors, this is normally to be found in its proper place in the correspondence of the post. Consular, commercial and treaty series of correspondence are included in the general country classes (as is the separate sanitary series, 1880–1882) but are kept distinct from the diplomatic or political correspondence. Drafts remain separate from despatches, which they precede in the general arrangement. Telegrams and paraphrases are generally kept in separate series once they reach significant proportions. The several series which result from this arrangement are bound up in order of despatch numbers, with unnumbered 'Separate' and

---

[1] F.O.881/1869, p.16.

[2] F.O.881/7034*, pp.7–10; F.O.881/7727.

[3] F.O.366/671, pp.124–127.

[4] F.O.366/672, p.2.

[5] F.O.881/2470, p.3; *4th Rpt. R. Comm. on Civil Estabs.* (1890), q.27535.

[6] F.O.95/794: memorandum of 22 Aug. 1848; *Rpt. of Sel. Ctee. on Dipl. Service* (1861), q.679 (p.75); F.O.881/1726, p.4; F.O.881/5228, p.4.

[7] For a list of these country classes see pp.109–124 below. For many classes the numeration of the volumes is that given in the Foreign Office Library before transfer.

[8] Before 1906 the date of the document, not the date of its receipt, decided the year under which it was arranged.

[9] Until 1843 (later in the case of some countries) the *List of Foreign Office Records to 1878* gives only the names of consular officers, not their posts.

'Private' despatches placed by their dates, and their division into volumes varies in accordance with their bulk. Thus for some countries the political despatches may occupy several volumes, while the various series of both drafts and despatches for several consulates may be in a single one.

Until 1806 the domestic correspondence was not included in the country classes of *General Correspondence*. Correspondence with certain government departments before this date is in the *Great Britain and General* class (F.O.83/1–7); the rest is in the *Supplement to General Correspondence* (e.g. F.O.97/58–60). After 1806 the domestic correspondence for each country is in two main series: that with foreign diplomatic representatives in London; and domestic various. From the latter a separate series of 'consular domestic' is generally distinguished from the late 1820s and separate commercial and treaty series from 1866 and 1883 respectively. The correspondence with foreign diplomatic representatives is arranged in separate chronological series of drafts and notes received; the several series of domestic various are arranged in date order, no distinction being made between drafts and letters received. The domestic correspondence for a year follows immediately after that year's foreign correspondence. Its division into volumes depends upon its bulk. Sometimes the consular, commercial and treaty series of domestic various are bound up with, although kept distinct from, the corresponding foreign series.

Thus if we take as an example the correspondence relating to Sweden for 1891 (F.O.73/542–551) we shall find that it consists of one volume of diplomatic drafts to the Minister and Chargé d'Affaires; one volume of diplomatic despatches; one volume containing both consular and treaty drafts and despatches; one volume of commercial drafts; one volume of commercial despatches; one volume of correspondence with the Consuls-General at Christiania containing diplomatic, consular, commercial and treaty drafts and despatches; a similar volume of consular, commercial and treaty correspondence with other consuls; a volume of correspondence with the Swedish Minister in London containing diplomatic, consular, commercial and treaty drafts and notes; one volume of domestic various, sub-divided into diplomatic, consular and treaty; and one volume of domestic various, commercial.

Correspondence on a question of continuing active interest after two years might be retained in departments and not transferred to the Library until that question was settled. Then it was not normally integrated into the annual volumes of correspondence but bound up in separate 'case' volumes.[1] On occasions correspondence on a particular subject might be removed from the bound volumes in the Library and made up into cases retrospectively.[2] Cases relating to a single event are normally placed in the appropriate country class in accordance with the date when they were closed. Thus, among the many cases following the 1871 correspondence relating to the U.S.A. are sixty volumes of Claims arising from the Civil War and containing papers of the period 1861–1871 (F.O.5/1236–1295). On the other hand cases relating to perennial questions are normally made up in annual volumes, which take their place at the end of the correspondence for the year to which they relate. For example, case volumes relating to Newfoundland Fisheries occur annually in the correspondence relating to France from 1877 (e.g. F.O.27/2276–2277).[3]

Some cases were held back in departments longer than others. The reason for this was often one of confidentiality, but this does not always appear to have been

---

[1] F.O.881/2470, p.3; *4th Rpt. of R. Comm. on Civil Estabs.* (1890), qq.27562–27568.
[2] F.O.366/675, p.341.
[3] Earlier case volumes on this subject are arranged in blocks covering several years (F.O.27/553, 1226–1232, 2195–2213).

so. When ultimately transferred to the Library, they were put in their proper places in the country series, where, since there were no vacant numbers for them, they were given the number of the preceding piece followed by * or **. They retained these 'starred' numbers for a time after transfer to the Public Record Office, but were subsequently taken from their country classes to form the class of *Supplement to General Correspondence* (F.O.97). The arrangement within this class is by countries.

A copy of a register and index of cases to 1905 made in the Foreign Office Library is kept in the search rooms of the Public Record Office. It is arranged by countries with a subject index; it is keyed up with current Public Record Office references.

The Slave Trade correspondence was originally retained in the Department, no transfers being made to the Library until 1861.[1] When transfers did commence in the normal way, this correspondence was not integrated into the various country classes[2] but kept separately in a class now known as *General Correspondence before 1906, Slave Trade* (F.O.84), a title which continued in use until 1892, despite the change of departmental title to Consular and African and the change in name of the 'Slave Trade' series of correspondence to the 'Africa' series as a consequence the merger with the Consular Department of 1882 (see p.17). The only effect of the 1882 reorganization on the arrangement of the records was the separation of the Muscat consular correspondence into the class of *General Correspondence before 1906, Muscat* (F.O.54), where correspondence before 1867 is also to be found.[3]

The arrangement of each year's Slave Trade correspondence is as follows: correspondence with Slave Trade Commissioners (this becomes less important as the century continues and from 1871 the residual correspondence is included in the next group); Slave Trade correspondence with British diplomatic and consular representatives and with foreign diplomatic representatives in London, arranged by countries; correspondence with officials in the African protectorates (after 1882); of the remaining domestic correspondence that with government departments is arranged separately from that with other individuals and institutions (domestic various). Drafts and despatches are kept apart as are drafts and letters to government departments, each series being arranged in order of date or despatch number; the domestic various is arranged by date with no separation of drafts and letters received. There are also some case volumes.

With the formation of the separate African (East and West) Department in 1893 (see p.17) the arrangement of the correspondence changes. That relating to the West Coast, Uganda and Central Africa is in the class of *General Correspondence before 1906, Africa* (F.O.2),[4] where it follows earlier material relating to Africa from departments other than the Slave Trade Department, including Consular Department correspondence with consuls on the West Coast, 1850–1866 and 1872,[5] domestic various and consular domestic correspondence, 1825–1866, and records relating to various African expeditions. The East Coast correspondence is in the new class of *General Correspondence before 1906, Zanzibar* (F.O.107) and the Liberia

[1] F.O.366/675, p.336.
[2] Except for the sanitary correspondence, which was the concern of the Slave Trade Department from 1880 to 1882.
[3] The correspondence before 1867 relates mainly to Zanzibar, which had been part of the Imamate until 1856 (see p.119). Muscat Slave Trade and Africa correspondence continues in F.O.84 until 1892.
[4] Some records relating to British Central Africa, 1892–1895, are in *Miscellanea, Series II* (F.O. 96/191–193).
[5] Consular correspondence for 1849, the year in which consuls were first appointed for the West Coast of Africa, is mixed with Slave Trade correspondence in F.O.84/775.

correspondence returns to the class of *General Correspondence before 1906, Liberia* (F.O.47), in which it had been placed before 1860. From 1899 the Africa series of correspondence with representatives on the East Coast transfers to the *Africa* (F.O.2) class, the *Zanzibar* (F.O.107) class continuing only for the consular, commercial and treaty series and certain case volumes. From 1893 to 1900 the Africa series of correspondence with diplomatic and consular representatives in or of other countries are in the appropriate country classes of *General Correspondence before 1906* arranged in separate sections corresponding to those for consular, commercial and treaty correspondence; from 1901 to 1905 they are in *General Correspondence before 1906, Africa* (F.O.2). The Africa domestic various correspondence, 1893–1898, is in the *Great Britain and General* class (F.O.83); from 1899 to 1905 it is in the *Africa* (F.O.2) class.

A considerable amount of correspondence which could not be put in any of the country classes of *General Correspondence before 1906* because it was of a miscellaneous, general or domestic nature was made into an artificial class of *General Correspondence, Great Britain and General* (F.O.83). This includes early correspondence with other government departments, some going back to 1745; miscellaneous domestic correspondence; copies and drafts of circulars; cases of a general nature, including replies to circulars; Library correspondence and papers; parliamentary questions (from 1890); and some case volumes and formal records of the Treaty Department (see pp.78–80). The class continues after 1905 for certain formal records of the Treaty Department and a few volumes of printed *Instructions to Consuls*.[1]

Also in the *Great Britain and General* class are 202 volumes of Law Officers' Reports arranged by countries and covering the period 1764–1876 (F.O.83/2203–2404). These had originally been bound in their appropriate places in the country classes of *General Correspondence*, but were removed, returned to the Foreign Office and put into their present arrangement in 1909 so that none should become open to public inspection when the general open date for Foreign Office records was extended to 1837.[2] They were returned to the Public Record Office and opened to public inspection after the extension of the open period to 1878 in 1925.[3] From 1877 original Law Officers' Reports and the related correspondence will be found in the appropriate country classes of *General Correspondence* among the domestic various correspondence, usually, after 1883, in the treaty series. From 1861 Law Officers' Reports have been printed in annual volumes in the series of Confidential Print (see p.88).

Some supplementary general correspondence for the period 1767–1847 is to be found in the class of *Miscellanea, Series I* (F.O.95/1–10). Also in this class is a series of volumes of material collected for the production of Library memoranda (F.O. 95/783–800).

Until the latter part of the nineteenth century it was the regular, although not invariable, practice for incidental papers to be separated from the drafts and despatches to which they related before binding. Some such loose papers survive in the class of *Miscellanea, Series II*. They include rough drafts, deciphers, duplicates and copies for the period 1820–1884 and minutes and memoranda for the period 1830–1867 (F.O.96/2–27). They also include some private correspondence as well

---

[1] The numerical lists of this class in the *Lists of Foreign Office Records* (P.R.O. Lists and Indexes No. LII and Supplementary Lists and Indexes No. XIII, Vol. 5) have been supplemented in the search rooms of the Public Record Office by a typescript list arranged on a departmental/subject basis.

[2] F.O.370/23, file 7526.

[3] F.O.370/203, file 1399.

as minutes by Prime Ministers and the Sovereign's Private Secretaries. There are also Slave Trade drafts and minutes for the period 1833–1872 (F.O.96/28–33). The arrangement of these loose papers is roughly chronological.

General Correspondence before 1906: Entry Books

Entry books have never been an important element in the Foreign Office system of official record keeping. A few such books do, however, survive and are now mainly preserved in the class of *Miscellanea, Series I* (F.O.95). They relate principally to the domestic correspondence, their main date range being from 1794 to 1839, although some go back earlier and continue from series of entry books in the *State Paper Office* group. Certain specialized entry books were kept in the Chief Clerk's and Treaty Departments and some of these continue to a later date (see pp.75–80). More numerous are the private entry books of official correspondence kept for the use of the Secretaries of State which survive in the same class of *Miscellanea*.

When James Bland Burges became Under Secretary of State in 1789, he wrote:

> The immense number of despatches which come from agents to Foreign Courts are filed up in large presses, but no note of them is taken, nor is there even an index to them; so that, if anything is wanted, the whole year's accumulation must be rummaged over before it can be found, and frequently material concerns must be forgotten for want of a Memorandum to preserve their sense. As to the past, it would be a Herculean task to attempt to put things right; but it is my intention to take better care in future, and to enter the purport of every despatch in a volume properly prepared for that purpose. By this means the Duke [of Leeds, the Secretary of State] will be enabled at a glance to recollect everything that has passed, and public affairs will be reduced to a regularity they have never yet attained.[1]

Burges was mistaken in stating that up to then no note of despatches had been made, for, as we have seen (p.33), a series of registers, inadequate though they may have been as finding aids, had been kept up from 1782 until 25 August 1789, three days after his own appointment. Certainly he appears to have been thinking of something much fuller than these registers and it is undoubtedly to his initiative that we owe the surviving examples of précis books by countries which start in January 1790 and in which the entries are largely in Burges' own hand. They relate to Austria (F.O.95/40), Flanders (F.O.95/98), Italy (F.O.95/158), Poland (F.O.95/176), Spain (F.O.95/270) and Sweden (F.O.95/301). Except for the Austria volume they include despatches of 1789 received after 1 January 1790. They were intended to relate to both despatches and drafts, but the latter are entered only in the Austria and Flanders volumes. They were not kept up for long; that for Austria continues to August 1790, the others cover an even shorter period.

The series of entry books was, however, revived in the following year for Lord Grenville, with separate volumes for précis of despatches received and copies of despatches sent; again entries are to be found in Burges' own hand. This time the series was kept up rather longer. The entry books for Spain (F.O.95/271–278) commence at the end of March 1791 and continue to the beginning of November 1796, when entries cease part way through both volumes, suggesting that the series was then discontinued. A précis book of despatches received, 1791–1792, and an entry book of despatches sent, 1791–1793, have also survived for France (F.O. 95/99–100); there is a blank volume labelled '1794' (F.O.95/101); a précis book of despatches received, 1791–1792, relating to Prussia is now among the *Chatham Papers* (P.R.O.30/8/338, pt.3). That these entry books were regarded as the private records of the Secretary of State is clear from their labelling: 'Lord Grenville Private'.

---

[1] Quoted in Tilley and Gaselee, *Foreign Office*, pp.34–35.

E

In 1795, the first Précis Writer on the establishment was appointed and the keeping of private entry books of official despatches was thereafter his responsibility. These were normally taken away by a Secretary of State on leaving office, but some remained in the Foreign Office and are now in the Public Record Office; they are arranged by countries, normally with separate volumes for précis of despatches and copies of drafts. They include fairly complete series from the Secretaryships of Hawkesbury (1801–1804)[1] and Mulgrave (1805–1806)[2] and a series started for Fox (1806) and continued for Howick (1806–1807).[3] In addition there are two volumes from the Secretaryship of Harrowby (1804–1805) (F.O.95/281, 329), six volumes relating to Sicily from Canning's first Secretaryship (1807–1809) (F.O. 95/253–258), two general volumes from the brief Secretaryship of Bathurst in 1809 (F.O.95/470–471), two blank volumes from the Secretaryship of Wellesley (1809–1812) (F.O.95/185, 240), and, from Canning's second Secretaryship, a Slave Trade précis book for 1823 (F.O.95/474). These entry books often have stamped on their covers the name of the Secretary of State for whom they were kept, but unused volumes of one Secretary of State might be used for his successors.[4]

The most complete set of entry books comes from the Secretaryship of Castlereagh (1812–1822); their survival among the Foreign Office records is probably to be attributed to his having died in office. They are in three distinct but overlapping series. One series is arranged by countries with separate volumes for despatches received and sent, the entries in each volume being chronological.[5] This series is labelled 'Viscount Castlereagh' and was undoubtedly compiled by the Précis Writer for Castlereagh's private use. Linked with it are thirteen volumes known as 'Précis Appendix Volumes'. Twelve of these consist of duplicate despatches arranged by countries in date order (F.O.95/11–18, 20–23). Précis of these despatches are often omitted from the main series[6] and the binding of duplicates when these were available appears to have been employed to save the Précis Writer the task of abstracting them. The remaining volume (F.O.95/415) is an entry book of some of the more important drafts of 1816; these relate to several countries.

The status of the two other series is less certain. One is arranged by countries with separate domestic volumes (F.O.95/455–469). It covers the period 1812–1816 and appears to relate to the Southern Department only; entries consist of précis of despatches received arranged under various subject headings. The other series consists of chronological entries of foreign and domestic drafts arranged by departments. The Southern Department volumes (F.O.95/416–432) start in January 1812 and include, therefore, some drafts by Wellesley as Secretary of State, but entries cease with the notification of Castlereagh's death; the Northern Department volumes (F.O.95/407–414) start in January 1815 and end a few days before Castlereagh's death. Despite this coincidence of date, the apparent restriction of the former series to one department and the departmental arrangement of the latter suggest a connection with the Under Secretaries rather than with the Secretary of State and it may be that both should be regarded as official. Neither is labelled

---

[1] F.O.95/24–25, 41–43, 79–80, 125–129, 147–148, 159, 168–169, 177–179, 197–200, 217–220, 279–280, 302–303, 326–328.

[2] F.O.95/26, 44, 81, 130, 134, 160, 180, 201–202, 221, 304.

[3] F.O.95/27, 29–30, 45–46, 48, 82–83, 85, 131–133, 141–144, 161, 163, 181–182, 184, 203–204, 206, 222–224, 226–227, 252, 305–307, 309, 330–331, 333.

[4] For example, F.O.95/26 is stamped 'Lord Hawkesbury', but was used for correspondence of 1805–1806 when the Secretary of State was Lord Mulgrave.

[5] F.O.95/31–39, 49–78, 86–92, 103–124, 135–140, 149–157, 170–175, 186–196, 207–216, 228–239, 241–248, 250–251, 259–269, 282–300, 310–325, 334–349.

[6] See F.O.95/34, p.2.

'Viscount Castlereagh' as is the main Précis Writer's series. Neither appears from the handwriting to have been kept up by the Précis Writer. The Northern and Southern volumes of the latter series were entered by different copyists.

With these possible exceptions, official entry books relating to the foreign correspondence of the Office are very few. They include an entry book of drafts labelled 'Foreign Miscellaneous, 1782–8' and relating mainly to Prussia and France (F.O. 95/405); and two entry books of confidential despatches and drafts, 1810–1812 (F.O.95/378–379). There is also an entry book of circulars to diplomatic and consular representatives abroad and to foreign ministers in London, 1800–1822[1] (F.O. 95/377); this continues an entry book of circulars, 1799–1800, now in the class of *State Papers Foreign, Supplementary* (S.P.110/84). An earlier volume in this class (S.P. 110/83) ends with Fox's notification to British diplomatic representatives of his appointment as Secretary of State for Foreign Affairs in March 1782 (see p.2). The Foreign Office class of *Miscellanea, Series I* also contains an entry book of despatches to and from the Hague in 1771 (F.O.95/146), which belongs more properly to *State Papers Foreign*.

Entry books of domestic out-letters until 1822 are arranged in five series, each divided from 1794 into separate volumes for the Northern and Southern Departments. These five series are: Admiralty, Law Officers, Domestic General, Foreign Ministers[2] and Treasury. They are now for the most part in *Miscellanea, Series I* (F.O.95).

The earliest volume in the Admiralty series (F.O.95/355) dates back to 1761. This and part of the second volume (F.O.95/356, pp.1–211) are entry books of the Secretary of State for the Northern Department before 1782, continuing a series in *State Papers Domestic, Entry Books* (S.P.44). From 1782 to 1793 there is a single series of Admiralty entry books (F.O.95/356, from p.212, and F.O.95/362, pp.1–109), which continues from 1794 for the Southern Department (F.O.95/362, from p.110, to F.O. 95/369); a separate series starts in 1794 for the Northern Department (F.O.95/357–361).

The Law Officers entry books also continue in an unbroken series from before 1782. A volume started for the Secretary of State for the Northern Department in 1764 continued in use in the Foreign Office until 1793.[3] It is now in the class of *Home Office, Law Officers, Letter Books* (H.O.49/2). From 1794 to 1822 there are separate Northern and Southern series of Law Officers entry books (F.O.95/370–376).

The first Foreign Ministers entry book (F.O.95/433) overlaps and partly duplicates one in the class of *State Papers Foreign, Entry Books* (S.P.104/262). The former, which consists mainly of circulars, was kept up regularly only until 1783 and thereafter intermittently until 1789.[4] Not until 1794 do the Foreign Ministers entry books resume with a series for the Northern Department, which thereafter is continuous until 1819 (F.O.95/434–438); the Southern Department series does not commence until 1796 and also continues until 1819 (F.O.95/439–443).

The Domestic General and Treasury series of entry books do not appear before 1794. From that date there is a Northern series of Domestic General entry books to 1822 (F O.95/388–393) and a Southern series from 1799 to 1822 (F.O.95/387, 394–404). There are Treasury entry books for the Northern Department from 1794

[1] With one entry of 1833.
[2] For the separate series of entry books of foreign ministers' protections see p.78 below.
[3] With one entry of 1796.
[4] A loose draft of 1791 follows the last entry.

to 1821 (F.O.95/476–480) and for the Southern Department from 1799 to 1822 (F.O. 95/481–490).[1]

After 1822 out-letters to government departments are entered in a single series of entry books now forming the class of *Letter Books, Public Offices* (F.O.91).[2] Until 1824 there are separate volumes for the Northern and Southern Departments, but thereafter this distinction lapses. The series ends in 1839.

It is convenient to mention here a series of entry books which did not originate in the Foreign Office but have subsequently come to be among its records. These are the entry books for the period 1801–1836 of outgoing correspondence relating to the Barbary States of Algiers, Morocco, Tripoli and Tunis. They were compiled in the Home Office (to 1804) and subsequently in the Colonial Office and were transferred to the Foreign Office when it took over responsibility for the Barbary consuls in 1836 (see p.30). The series has been distributed on no systematic basis between several classes of Foreign Office records.

These entry books consist of separate volumes of 'Instructions to Consuls', that is outgoing despatches, and, from 1816, domestic out-letters. Until the beginning of 1825 the volumes cover all four countries, the entry books of Instructions being divided into country sections until 1816 and thereafter being entered chronologically and indexed by countries; the domestic entry books are chronological with indexes of departments and correspondents. From 1825 to 1836 entries are in separate volumes for each country.

The entry books to 1825 are now in the class of *General Correspondence, Barbary States* (F.O.8/5–8, 11–12) and the Algiers entry books from 1825 are in the same class (F.O.8/9–10, 13). The post-1825 entry books for the other three countries have been placed in other classes: those for Morocco in *Miscellanea, Series I* (F.O. 95/164–167); those for Tripoli in *General Correspondence, Tripoli, Series I* (F.O.76/40–43); and those for Tunis in *General Correspondence, Tunis, Series I* (F.O.77/27–28). Entry books of treaties relating to the Barbary States, which originally belonged to the same series, are in *Miscellanea, Series I* (F.O.95/510, 518–521; cf. F.O.96/136).

General Correspondence since 1906: Registration, Action, Indexing 1906–1920

The registration and indexing system introduced in the Foreign Office in 1891 never worked satisfactorily, even after indexing was resumed by the Library in 1900. Recognition of this resulted in the appointment of a departmental committee 'to examine whether any improvements can be made in our existing arrangements for registering and keeping the correspondence'. This committee's report, presented on 18 May 1904, recommended that the registration, keeping and indexing of papers be divorced from the departments and entrusted to a separate Registry.[3] Further study of the problems involved followed; and an experiment in keeping papers unfolded in printed docket sheets was held in the Commercial Department.[4] Eventually, after a delay of six months occasioned by the Treasury,[5] a system based upon the recommendations of the committee and devised by E.A. (later Sir Eyre)

---

[1] There is also a Chief Clerk's series of Treasury letter books, 1761–1881: see p.76 below.
[2] F.O.91/5 was returned to the Foreign Office and thought to have been lost there; it was recently discovered to have been retransferred as F.O.95/472. F.O.91/11 is an entry book of foreign ministers' protections (see p.78 below).
[3] F.O.881/8616*.
[4] F.O.366/761, pp.26–27. The docket sheets used in this Department in 1905 were similar to those used there previously, 1887–1889 (see p.48), and to those generally adopted in 1906.
[5] F.O.366/1136: draft, Sanderson to Sir G.Murray, 5 Jan. 1906.

Crowe, then an Assistant Clerk in the Office, was put into operation under his supervision on 1 January 1906.[1]

A Registry was established under the direction of a Registrar, who was subordinate to the Librarian. It consisted of a Central Registry and three Sub-Registries, one for each floor of the Office. At first Sub-Registry I served the Eastern and Western Departments, Sub-Registry II the China, Commercial and Treaty Department, and Sub-Registry III the American, African and Consular Departments. The correspondence of the Chief Clerk's Department and the Library passed through the Central Registry but not through the Sub-Registries. An attempt in 1913 by the Consular Department to secure a separate Sub-Registry was unsuccessful.[2]

Official correspondence was opened in the Central Registry and placed inside docket sheets[3] (despatches from abroad arrived already enclosed in these). Each docket sheet was stamped with the name of the country and the series (if not political), with the date of receipt and with a registry number, of which there was a single annual series for the whole Office.[4] Each paper was then entered in the Central Register in the order of its registry number. Ephemeral papers might be excluded from registration, but if it was subsequently decided to register them, they were not given 'back dates' or 'back numbers' but stamped with the date of actual registration and given the next registry number. Similar treatment was given to other papers which escaped registration on first coming into the Office and were registered later. Conversely gaps were not left in the series of registry numbers for missing numbered despatches.

The Central Registers from 1 January 1906 to 20 November 1920 are now in the Public Record Office, where they form the class of *Numerical (Central) Registers of General Correspondence* (F.O.662). Each page is divided into columns for (i) registry number; (ii) mission; (iii) consuls; (iv) date or despatch number; (v) office; (vi) name; (vii) country; (viii) subject; and (ix) a series of columns for each department of the Office, distribution being indicated by a mark in the appropriate one. The origin of a paper is indicated by an entry under either (ii), (iii), (v) or (vi); in (ii) and (iii) the name of the place not the name of the person is entered; in (v) the government department of origin is indicated by its initials; Foreign Office memoranda and drafts not linked to registered papers are indicated by the initials 'F.O.' in this column; (vi) is used for domestic correspondence other than that with government departments. Where there is no entry in columns (ii), (iii), (v) or (vi), the correspondent is the same as in the preceding entry. The country named in column (vii) is that to which the paper relates and under which it has been kept, and not necessarily that from which it originated; where the country of origin and the country to which a paper relates are the same, this column may be left blank. An entry is not always made in column (viii); where it is, it is only a brief note. The date of registration is stamped at the top of each page.

Telegrams were placed in distinctive docket sheets marked 'Telegram' and printed in red, and were treated in a similar manner to letters and despatches, except that those arriving out of office hours were acted upon by the Resident Clerks and then sent to the Central Registry next morning and that those arriving in the

---

[1] F.O.366/761, p.133; Tilley and Gaselee, *Foreign Office*, p.156; Steiner, *Hist. J.* VI, pp.86–87. The system is described in F.O.881/8550 and 8552; *5th Rpt. of R. Comm. on Civil Service* (1914–16), qq.36915–36938, 37837–38008.

[2] F.O.366/761, p.452.

[3] See Plates II and III.

[4] Each new annual series started with papers received on 1 Jan., even though they were dated the previous year, except in 1920 when the 1919 series was continued for correspondence of those departments which did not change at once to the new system of registration (see p.68).

General Registry in cipher were sent for deciphering to the appropriate department,[1] passed to the proper Sub-Registry for manifolding and then returned to the Central Registry, while those in code were sent for decoding in the Sub-Registry concerned and then returned to the Central Registry. All telegrams were manifolded or printed on white paper and one copy was treated as the registered paper. Another copy was sent direct to the Permanent Secretary and copies of the more important to the Parliamentary Under Secretary and, if received too late for inclusion in the day's telegram sections, to the Assistant Under Secretaries. The printed telegram sections (on distinctive blue-green paper) went to the Secretary and all the Under Secretaries of State. Telegrams in cipher were paraphrased in the departments and it was the paraphrases not the originals which were printed in the telegram sections. Telegrams are indicated in the earliest Central Registers by a T in the left-hand margin or in the registry number column; from 1910, however, they are distinguished by being entered in red ink.

Secret papers were placed in distinctive docket sheets (with a band of green stripes across the top of page one)[2] in the Central Registry and sent from there direct to departments, where they were entered in a Secret Register and where they remained after action had been taken on them. Only a dummy docket sheet was sent in such an instance to the Sub-Registry and this gave only sufficient indication of the paper's contents for identification purposes.

From the Central Registry all other papers passed to the appropriate Sub-Registry, where the dockets of despatches were checked and amended if necessary, and other papers were docketed, after which they were entered in the General Register. This was divided into annual volumes with a separate series for each department and a separate volume or division of a volume for each country. Cuts were used to separate correspondence of a particular sort, such as the political correspondence with consuls in the political series of registers. The General Registers of the political, Commercial Consular, Treaty and (to 1913) African Departments are now in the Public Record Office in the class *Registers of General Correspondence* (F.O.566). As with previous registers in this class, the original annual arrangement of each departmental series has been disturbed and the registers within each series are now bound up in a country arrangement. The General Registers of the Library and Chief Clerk's Department have not been preserved.[3]

As in the departmental diaries and registers before 1906, incoming correspondence is entered on the left-hand page of the General Register; however, more detail is given than previously. The page is ruled into columns for (i) date registered; (ii) registry number; (iii) whether printed (indicated by inserting the letter 'P'); (iv) name; (v) despatch number; (vi) office; (vii) date of paper; (viii) last paper; (ix) subject; (x) contents; (xi) kept with; and (xii) forward reference. Origin is indicated by the entry under (iv) or (vi); (iv) is used both for despatches and for domestic correspondence other than that with government departments; when used for despatches the name of the writer, not the place from which he writes, is given; for Foreign Office memoranda 'F.O.' is entered in column (vi). The entry in (ix) is brief; that in (x) is more detailed and may run to several lines. The entries in (viii)

---

[1] In 1911 this became the responsibility of the Parliamentary Department (see p.22 above).
[2] Hence they were known as 'green papers'. Not all green papers were secret, nor were all secret papers entered 'green'. The system was essentially a device to control the circulation of papers, so that they were seen only by a limited number of people. Hence otherwise unclassified papers about staffing matters were sometimes entered 'green'.
[3] For General Registers of war-time departments see pp.66–67 below.

and (xi) are to the registry numbers of the last previous and first papers in the file; where the paper is part of a case, the entry in (xi) is 'Case No. . . .'. The entry in (xii) might be to the registry number of the next incoming paper or to the serial number (see p.64) of the related outgoing correspondence: if the former, it is entered in black ink; if the latter, in red and in brackets. Forward and backward references are also entered on the paper's docket sheet. Where a paper is kept under a country other than that from which it has come, it is entered in full in the volume for the country under which it is kept with a briefer entry and a cross reference in the volume for the country of origin. Telegrams are distinguished by entry in red ink.

At the top of each page of the General Register is stamped a code or index number consisting of a one or two figure country code number (e.g. 17 for France), standing on its own in the registers of the political departments and with a one or two figure departmental prefix in those of the other departments (e.g. 217 for France: Consular).[1] This index number is also entered in the compartment of the docket sheet headed 'Index' as a sign of completion of the entry in the General Register.

After entry in the General Register, previous papers on the same subject were located and attached to the new paper. Their location was facilitated by the keeping of the papers for a single year on a single subject in a file in order of their registry numbers, the lowest registry number being also the file or 'kept with' number. As a general rule files were closed at the end of each calendar year, but papers on certain subjects continued to be kept in cases extending over several years. A Case Book was kept in each Sub-Registry, with a duplicate in the Library, in which cases were entered and numbered consecutively; cases were referred to by these case numbers.

After the previous papers had been attached, the paper was sent to the appropriate department for the necessary action to be taken. Minutes were written in the department in the space provided for that purpose on the first and second pages of the docket sheet. Minutes covering more than this space were continued on separate sheets of minute paper, which were attached inside the docket sheet in front of the paper.

It has been maintained that this provision of opportunity for Foreign Office clerks to write extensive minutes gave them for the first time a considerable role in the direction of foreign policy.[2] Certainly Hardinge, the Permanent Under Secretary, encouraged 'the Juniors to take an active interest in their work and to develop political initiative and a sense of responsibility',[3] but, as we have seen, the pressure of increasing business was enforcing the involvement of Junior Clerks in more than routine work before 1906 (see pp.4, 9), and it seems probable that this process would have continued without the 1906 registry reforms and Hardinge's encouragement.

In accordance with directions in the minutes on the docket sheets drafts were prepared either within the departments or, in the case of drafts of a formal or routine nature, in the Sub-Registries, and were then submitted for approval. If a minute contained the exact text of a telegram or directed the employment of a standard printed form, no draft was required and action was taken without further reference back. All drafts were marked with the registry number of the paper to

---

[1] For a list of country code numbers and departmental prefixes see Appendix II(d).
[2] Steiner, *Hist. J.* VI, pp.59–90; Sir H.Nicolson, *Lord Carnock* (1930), pp.325–326. For a contrary view see 7 *B.D.I.L.*, p.176.
[3] F.O.366/761, pp.130–132.

which they related. By this date most drafts for submission were typed. They were initialed by their authors.

After approval drafts of letters and despatches were returned, together with the rest of the file, to the Sub-Registries, which were responsible for checking that the action taken accorded with the directions in the minutes, and for sending the drafts for typing. After typing in duplicate, drafts, papers for signature and duplicates were dated and, in the case of despatches, given their despatch number, except where the papers were to be signed by the Secretary of State himself, when dating and numbering were postponed until the signed paper had been returned to the Sub-Registry. The name of the Secretary or Under Secretary of State signing a paper was added at the end of the draft and duplicate by means of a rubber stamp or in manuscript.

Outgoing correspondence was despatched from the Sub-Registries. As a rule letters to other government departments were delivered by Home Service Messengers; other domestic letters were sent by post. Despatches to diplomatic and consular representatives abroad might be sent by post or by Foreign Office bag.

Telegrams to be sent in cipher were ciphered in the departments[1] on official telegraph forms, which were then passed, together with the drafts, previous papers and minutes, to the Sub-Registries for numbering in the local series and for despatch. Other telegrams were sent in draft to the Sub-Registries for despatch. Drafts or copies of telegrams sent in cipher were returned to departments for paraphrasing. Printing and distribution was the same as for incoming telegrams.

Notices of parliamentary questions continued to originate, as they had before 1906, from the Library. Several copies of each question were affixed to docket sheets stamped 'Parliamentary Question', the file copy being sent direct to the proper Sub-Registry for previous papers on the subject to be located and passed with the notice to the responsible department, while other copies were sent to the Under Secretaries, the Private Secretaries and other departments. After an answer had been given a copy of this from *The Times* was added to the file copy. The paper was only then sent to the Central Registry to receive a registry number and to be entered in the Central Register; it was then passed to the Sub-Registry for entry in the General Register.

Circulation of papers outside the Foreign Office continued to be common. Copies of the more important telegrams were sent to the Prime Minister and, if they were too late for inclusion in that day's telegram sections, to the King. In addition the King and Prime Minister received the daily telegram sections and prints of important despatches, as also did the Prince of Wales (to 1910), such Cabinet Ministers as the Secretary of State might direct and diplomatic missions abroad. These printed sections were periodically put together in consecutive volumes of Confidential Print.[2] Papers continued to be specially printed for the Cabinet.

When action on a paper was completed and all the related papers had been returned to the Sub-Registry, details of the draft were entered on the right-hand page of the General Register. This is ruled into columns for (i) serial number; (ii) registry number; (iii) whether printed; (iv) name; (v) despatch number; (vi) office; (vii) date; (viii) date of despatch; (ix) subject; (x) contents; (xi) form; (xii) forward reference. The serial numbers are entered in red ink and run consecutively through each individual volume or section of a volume. The registry number is that of the

---

[1] After 1911 this became the responsibility of the Parliamentary Department (see p.22 above).
[2] F.O.881/8550, pp.18–23; F.O.371/167, file 25630. There was also an intermediate weekly telegram section (see F.O.366/762, pp. 8A–9). Some series of Confidential Print were suspended and others reduced in volume during the latter part of World War I.

incoming paper to which the draft is a reply; drafts have their own registry number only if they do not arise from an incoming paper. Column (viii) is entered when a paper was not sent off on the day on which it was dated. Code numbers are entered in (xi) to indicate the nature of printed forms used to forward material to other government departments or to posts abroad. Other columns on this side are used in the same way as those on the left-hand side (see p.62).

The draft itself was placed, together with the duplicate typed copy and, in the case of a telegram, the paraphrase, and with any printed copy, in the same docket sheet as and below the paper from which it arose. The sending of a telegram, despatch or letter was noted in the space on the docket sheet headed 'How Disposed of'. In this space was placed the code number if a printed form was used, or a cross if no outgoing correspondence was required. Completion of the entry of the draft in the General Register was indicated by a tick in this same space. The paper or file was then put by in its proper place in the Sub-Registry and was ready for indexing.

Indexing was carried out separately in each Sub-Registry. Entries were made from the papers themselves, both despatches and drafts, on cards which were filed in annual series in alphabetical order, no distinction being made between persons, places and subjects. The main heading appears at the top of the card, followed by any sub-heading; entries on one card are confined to a single subject, person or place, or to a single sub-division of any one of these. The salient facts of each paper indexed under a heading or sub-heading are noted on the card.

The paper's location is indicated from 1906 to 1909 by a numerical reference consisting of (i) index number, indicating country and department; (ii) registry number; and (iii) the last two figures of the year. For example 45/160/06 refers to paper number 160 of 1906 in the United States political correspondence. In general it was considered sufficient to make a subject index card for only the first paper of the file on that subject; in such instances the registry number given in the reference is also the file number. Before 1909, when a later paper in the file is indexed separately, the registry number of that paper only is given and it is, therefore, necessary to consult the appropriate volume of the General Register to discover the file or 'kept with' number.

In June 1909 new instructions to index-makers were issued, which laid down that the file (or case) number as well as the registry number of a paper should be shown,[1] and from that date the reference normally consists of four elements: (i) index number; (ii) registry number; (iii) file number; and (iv) year. Thus the reference 350/9910/43/11 is to paper number 9910 in file 43 of 1911 in the miscellaneous correspondence of the Treaty Department. Three element numbers, however, still appear, indicating either a complete file (when the file number is usually preceded by the letter 'F'), the first paper in the file, or a single paper not part of a file.

Three separate card indexes were prepared each year[2] in the three Sub-Registries and these were transferred to the Library, along with the papers to which they related, after two years. It had originally been intended to amalgamate them into a single alphabetical index covering several years, but difficulties in doing this were experienced from the start due to variations in the conventions employed in the different Sub-Registries and to other defects, particularly the insufficient use of cross-references.[3] The new instructions of June 1909 laid down in more detail

[1] F.O.881/9470, p.iii.
[2] Entries made under the old system in 1920 continue in the 1919 index.
[3] F.O.881/9442*; F.O.366/787, f.170 (p.3); F.O.371/799, file 16051.

how the indexes should be compiled and gave a long list of specimen headings. In order to preserve uniformity Sub-Registries wishing to use additional headings were to agree them with the Librarian.[1] Subsequently the standard and uniformity of indexing improved, although work was frequently in arrears. Work on revising the earliest indexes was started and in the spring of 1914 it was expected that an index for the period 1906–1910 would soon be ready for printing.[2] However, the outbreak of war put a stop to this work and it was not resumed until 1918.[3] The revision then carried out involved the amalgamation of the three indexes for each year, but no attempt was made to amalgamate further the resulting annual indexes. It is in this annual form that the card-indexes for the period 1906–1920 are now kept at the Public Record Office.

As we have seen the papers of the Chief Clerk's Department and the Library did not pass through the normal Sub-Registries and they are not, therefore, included in the index.

The establishment of the various temporary war-time departments of the Foreign Office between 1914 and 1918 (see pp.23–24) required the creation of several new series of General Registers. Those of the political departments were divided into two series: diplomatic, for the normal political correspondence, and 'war', for correspondence dealt with by the War Department. The papers of the Contraband Department, which became the Ministry of Blockade in February 1916, and of the Prisoners of War and Aliens Department passed through the Foreign Office Central Registry and Sub-Registries in the normal way. Their General Registers have been preserved (F.O.566/1678–1836 and 1837–1874 respectively). The contraband registers differ from those of the other departments in that although some volumes cover individual countries, the majority relate to geographical regions, such as America and Scandinavia,[4] while several relate to certain general subjects (e.g. Mails, Relief[5]); even within the country and region series there are often separate volumes for certain subjects (e.g. Jute, Ships).[6] From 1917 to 1920 the Coal and Tonnage volumes have a different prefix in their index numbers (see p.161). The 1914 contraband registers of the Commercial Department have been bound up with later registers of the Contraband Department.[7]

The papers of the Prize Court Department were dealt with in the Registry as papers of the Treaty Department, with which it was linked. There are, however, separate annual General Registers (F.O.566/1602–1607) with cuts for each country concerned. Those for 1914 and 1915 include indexes. Reference to the papers of this Department in the general card index is not by an index number but by 'P' or 'Pr.' followed by the abbreviated name of the country concerned (e.g. 'Pr. Amer.').

The Foreign Trade Department, on the other hand, had its own separate Central Register, kept on exactly the same lines as the main Foreign Office Central Register but with its own series of registry numbers. The Department also kept a General Register divided by countries. The Central Register from January 1916 to May 1919 and the section of the General Register relating to Portugal for the same period are

---

[1] F.O.881/9470.
[2] 5th Rpt. of R. Comm. on Civil Service (1914–16), q.37859.
[3] F.O.366/787, f.170 (p.3).
[4] There are also separate registers for Denmark, Norway and Sweden, but the basic index number for all these is 1130: Contraband, Norway and Scandinavia. See p.162.
[5] Papers relating to the Rhineland, 1919–1920, registered under 'Relief' in F.O.566/1832 are now kept not in the *Contraband* but in the *Political* class (F.O.371/4336–4351). This transfer is noted in the register.
[6] For the supplementary index numbers used for these registers see p.162.
[7] The correspondence itself is, however, in the *Commercial* class (F.O.368).

now in the *Foreign Trade Department* class (F.O.833/4–11 and 12–15 respectively). The rest of the General Register was destroyed under the schedule of 1924 (see p.95).

General Correspondence since 1906: Registration, Action, Indexing since 1920
Defects in the registration and paper keeping system introduced in 1906 were already apparent by 1914, although they were glossed over before the Royal Commission on the Civil Service in that year.[1] The worst defects in the indexes had been remedied to some extent after 1909 (see pp.65–66), but there were also complaints of inadequate dockets and of delays in passing papers to the departments and in producing previous papers. The vast increase in correspondence occasioned by the outbreak of war tried the system even more severely and resulted in a virtual breakdown.[2]

Accordingly in 1917 Alwyn Parker, the Foreign Office Librarian, was instructed to study the filing and registration systems of other government departments and of various commercial undertakings and to make recommendations for reorganizing the Foreign Office system.[3] In September 1918 his recommendations were submitted to an Inter-Departmental Committee, of which Sir Eyre Crowe was chairman and Parker himself a member;[4] the secretary was D. A. Leak, the Assistant Librarian, who had as much to do with the new system as Parker himself. In its Report of 14 November 1918, this Committee endorsed Parker's main recommendation that the existing Central Registry and Sub-Registries be replaced by a single Registry divided into three Branches: Classification, Archive and Despatch. The other major recommendations of the Committee were that the existing filing and registration system be discarded and replaced by an 'Alpha-Numeral' system of 'vertical' filing by subjects with separate précis cards; and that there should be two indexes, a name index and a main index, prepared from the papers themselves and maintained in the Archives Branch 'with unvaried regularity'.[5]

The proposed system was adopted by the British Delegation to the Paris Peace Conference (see p.86) and experience of its application there showed that certain modifications were required to simplify the method and reduce the number of staff needed.[6] As a result the system as finally applied in the Foreign Office was considerably revised. The 'Alpha-Numeral' system was dropped; a fourth branch of the Registry, the Main Index Branch, was added to the three originally envisaged; the proposed Classification Branch became the Opening Branch and most of the work intended for it was assigned to the Archives Branch; and the Archives Branch itself was divided into several divisions, each corresponding to a department of the Office and each in turn sub-divided into country sections.

The revised system received Treasury approval on 12 January 1920,[7] a minute on the organization of the Registry was issued on 16 March[8] and after a period of trial detailed instructions for the new registry procedure were issued in July.[9] The new

[1] For example, *5th Rpt. of R. Comm. on Civil Service* (1914–16), q.37076.
[2] F.O.366/787, ff.165, 170 (pp.3–5); Tilley and Gaselee, *Foreign Office*, pp. 173–174. In 1913 58,811 papers were registered (F.O.662/17); in the busiest war-time year, 1916, 265,159 were registered in the Foreign Office Central Registry (F.O.662/41) and a further 90,595 in the Foreign Trade Department Central Registry (F.O.833/4–7). For the circulation of duplicate despatches to Under Secretaries in an attempt to speed up the work see F.O.371/3087, file 73714.
[3] F.O.366/787, ff.165–167.
[4] *Ibid.*, ff.156, 158–159.
[5] *Ibid.*, ff.170–171.
[6] F.O.366/789, f.86.
[7] *Ibid.*, ff.101–103.
[8] F.O. Confidential Print No.11514 (copy in *F.O. Library: General No.4*).
[9] F.O.370/126, ff.305–312.

system was applied, however, not in a single operation throughout the Office but department by department over a period of several months: in the American and Consular Departments from 1 January 1920; in the Treaty Department from 19 January; in the Eastern Department from 12 February; in the Far Eastern Department from 3 March; in the News Department from 23 March; in the Library from 1 April; in the Central Department from 1 July; in the Western Department from 16 September; and in the Northern Department from 7 October.[1] The dates on which the system was introduced in the Eastern, Central, Western and Northern Departments are those on which the correspondence of these departments was separated from that of the War Department, which ceased to exist on 6 October. The correspondence of the residual Commercial and Contraband Departments continued to be registered in the old manner until 14 February and 20 November respectively.[2]

Official correspondence was opened in the Opening Branch, placed inside docket sheets[3] and sent to the appropriate division of the Archives Branch. There each division had its own separate annual series of registry numbers, each series being distinguished by an initial letter, known as the departmental designation.[4] Upon receipt in the Archives Branch each incoming paper was stamped with the next consecutive number in the appropriate departmental series and summarily entered in order in the appropriate diary (these diaries have not been kept). The registry number and the name of the country to which the paper related were stamped on the docket sheet. The paper, in its docket sheet, was then passed, together with a précis jacket, also stamped with the name of the country, to the Section Clerk dealing with that country.

The précis jacket was the basis of the new registration system, giving a précis of the paper, a record of the action taken on it and a record of its movements from and to the Archives Branch. In combination the précis jackets of a file constituted a synopsis of the whole subject. They remained in the Archives Branch in place of their parent papers while the latter were out of the Branch and were at such times used as a means of reference to both the papers and their contents. When a paper was put by, the précis jacket was placed inside the docket sheet.

The papers of a single year dealing with a particular subject were kept together in a file, the registry number of the first paper constituting the file number. When not in circulation files were kept in the appropriate division of the Archives Branch by countries. To show where they might be found papers were each given a full registry number which consisted of (i) the departmental designation; (ii) the paper number; (iii) the file number; and (iv) the index number.[5] Thus A4567/890/45 is the registry number of American Department paper 4567, kept in file 890 of the United States political correspondence.

The Section Clerk, having located any file of previous correspondence on the subject, wrote on a docket form the registry number, writer, despatch number and date of the paper, together with a concise but complete précis of its contents. He then entered the registry number of the last preceding paper in the file in the backward reference sections of the docket sheet and précis jacket (with a corresponding entry in the forward reference sections of the docket sheet and précis jacket of the

---

[1] F.O.409/1, p.i.
[2] F.O.662/68–69.
[3] See Plate IV.
[4] See Appendix II(e).
[5] The index numbers in use after 1920 were generally those used previously but with some additions and amendments. See Appendix II(d).

previous paper); he also entered the file number on the back of the docket sheet and précis jacket of the new paper. The paper with its docket sheet, précis jacket and docket form then passed to a typist, who made one top copy and three carbon copies of the docket on special forms. The top copy was gummed to the docket sheet, the second copy (Form P.J.) to the précis jacket, the third (Form D.B.) was for the Day Book and the fourth (Form C.F.) for the Chronological File.[1] After its return from typing the paper in its docket sheet, together with the related file, was passed to the appropriate department for the necessary action, this and subsequent movements being recorded on its précis jacket in the Archives Branch.

Within departments minutes were written on the docket sheets and drafts prepared in accordance with directions given in the minutes much as they had been under the pre-1920 system. One temporary innovation was a system introduced in November 1919 by Lord Curzon, who objected to receiving submissions accompanied by a lot of flagged-up files. This system involved the submission of the more important telegrams and papers direct to the Secretary of State on special subject files (known as 'Curzon Files') made up in the departments by removing relevant previous papers from their files. After Curzon had seen the papers they were returned to the files from which they had been taken. This system came to an end when Lord Curzon left office in 1924.[2]

After a draft had been approved, it was returned, together with the parent papers, to the Archives Branch, which then passed them to the typists for the draft to be typed for signature. Draft despatches were dated and numbered in the local series before being sent for typing. On return from typing the name of the person signing the outgoing letter or despatch (normally of the rank of Counsellor or above) was stamped at the end of the draft and of the carbon copies.

After signature despatches to diplomatic and consular posts which received Foreign Office bags were sent to the Despatch Branch to await the next bag. This Branch also prepared and despatched circulars both to diplomatic and consular posts abroad and to foreign representatives in London. All other outgoing correspondence was despatched from the Archives Branch by Home Service Messengers or by post.

Secret correspondence, telegrams and parliamentary questions were dealt with somewhat differently. Letters or despatches marked secret were opened by the Registrar or a person specially authorized by him, placed in the same distinctive 'green' docket sheets as before 1920 (see p.62) and sent direct to the departments; at the same time docket forms containing only sufficient information for purposes of identification were sent to the Archives Branch. The papers themselves were docketed and kept in the departments.

Telegrams were delivered to the Communications Department and passed from there to the Opening Branch of the Registry. There they were put in docket sheets printed in red and passed first to the Archives Branch and then to departments to be dealt with as ordinary urgent papers. Draft telegrams for despatch were sent after approval to the Archives Branch, which passed them to the Communications Department for numbering in the local series and for despatch. When the Archives Branch was closed, urgent telegrams for despatch were sent direct to the Communications Department. All telegrams received and despatched were manifolded in the Distribution Room of the Communications Department and circulated as necessary

---

[1] For the Day Book and Chronological File see p.71 below.
[2] F.O. Confidential Print No.11642* (copy in *F.O. Library: General No.4*).

from there. Paraphrasing was the responsibility of the Cyphering Room of that Department.

Notices of parliamentary questions were pasted in the Library on to special minute sheets stamped 'Parliamentary Question' and sent to the Opening Branch, which passed them to the Archives Branch for submission in the normal way. When questions had been answered, the papers were returned to the Library for the answer, as printed in *Hansard*, to be attached. They were then sent to the Opening Branch to be jacketed in the normal manner and passed to the Archives Branch to be put by or, if further action was required, returned to the department.

When all action on a paper had been completed, the despatch of any outgoing paper arising from it was noted on the docket sheet in the space headed 'How Disposed of'. Where a printed letter was sent its distinctive number was also entered here. As a check that all the directions given in the minutes had been followed, every minute acted upon was ticked. Details of all drafts arising were entered on the précis jacket and a duplicate typed copy placed inside it. As a sign that this had been done, a tick was placed in the 'How Disposed of' space on the docket sheet. Drafts were summarized on docket forms in the same manner as incoming papers, each draft being stamped 'docketed' to indicate that this had been done. Only two typed copies were made from the docket forms for outgoing papers, one (Form D.B. Out) for the Day Book, the other (Form C.F. Out) for the Chronological File. Each draft, together with a duplicate typed copy, was placed inside the docket sheet of the paper on which it arose. When all this had been done, the Section Clerk dealing with the paper placed his initials and the date in the space on the docket sheet headed 'Action completed'. The docket sheet with its contents was then passed to the Main Index Branch.

There the Main Index was made, direct from the original papers and minutes, on cards arranged in separate annual series for the various divisions of the Archives Branch, the cards in each series being filed in alphabetical order with no distinction between subjects, persons and places. The principles on which the index was compiled were much the same as those followed before 1920; that is, the card contained a heading, a sub-heading if necessary, the salient points of the paper and its full registry number. Stress was laid on uniformity and on the judicious use of cross-references. At the end of each year the cards of the several series were amalgamated into a single alphabetical index. Where the new system differed most importantly from the old one was in the great care taken to edit the cards and the entries and in the printing of the index annually. After printing the cards themselves were destroyed. The printed indexes were passed to the Library with the papers to which they related at the end of the second year. Several sets of these indexes have been transferred to the Public Record Office; one set is available on open access; another forms the class of *Indexes* (*Printed Series*) *to General Correspondence* (F.O.409).[1] Also in this class are the separate indexes of confidential ('green') papers (F.O.409/103–104, 109).

As we have seen, the date on which the new system of registration and indexing came into use varied from department to department and a considerable amount of the 1920 correspondence continues in the 1919 card index. When searching in records for 1920, therefore, it may be necessary to consult both the printed index for that year and the card index for 1919. At first the printed indexes do not refer to papers of the Chief Clerk's and Communications Departments.[2] Communications

[1] The indexes from 1920 to 1938 are to be reprinted by the Kraus-Thomson Organisation.
[2] F.O.409/1, p.i.

Department papers are indexed only from 1924 onwards;[1] selected papers of the Chief Clerk's Department are indexed from 1931.[2] At the beginning of each volume of the printed index the index numbers and departmental designations used in that volume are given, together with other notes for the guidance of searchers. It should be borne in mind that the indexes are to the unweeded papers (see p.96).

After indexing had been completed the papers returned to the Archives Branch, where they were put by in their proper place by the Section Clerk dealing with the country concerned.

Meanwhile the C.F. forms for both incoming and outgoing papers were first used in the divisions of the Archives Branch to compile entries for the divisions' separate Name Indexes and were then put into a Chronological File divided into inward and outward sections. The inward section was kept in order of registry numbers in the Opening Branch; the outward section was kept in date order by the several divisions of the Archives Branch. The D.B. forms were similarly filed in the inward and outward Day Books. These were arranged as the Chronological Files but were subdivided by countries; they were kept in the appropriate country sections of the Archives Branch. The Chronological Files have not been preserved; the Day Books are retained in the Foreign Office Library.

The circulation of papers outside the Foreign Office (mostly in print) remained much as it had been before 1920. Circulation to diplomatic posts abroad was the concern of the Despatch Branch; circulation to the King was through the Private Secretary to the Permanent Under Secretary; circulation to the Prime Minister and Cabinet was the responsibility of the Distribution Room of the Communications Department. Certain prints were also circulated to Dominion governments.

General Correspondence since 1906: Make up

From 1906 current papers were no longer kept as hitherto in the several departments of the Foreign Office. Between 1906 and 1920 they were put by in the Sub-Registries when action on them had been completed. There they were kept in boxes in annual series arranged in order of their registry numbers, papers on the same subject being kept in their files and put by under their file numbers. Cases were kept in a separate series. Transfer to the Library continued to take place when the papers were between one and two years old, the corresponding volumes of the Central and General Registers and the card indexes for the year being transferred with them. In the Library the three sets of correspondence were amalgamated into a single annual set arranged by registry and file numbers with cases at the end.[3]

This system of keeping papers was criticized by the Inter-Departmental Committee of 1918[4] and was changed when the new registry procedure was introduced in 1920. Thereafter the papers received in a country section of the Archives Branch remained in the custody of the Section Clerk while they were still current. Within each country series thus created the papers were arranged in order of their file numbers. When they were between one and two years old the papers, together with the corresponding Day Books, Diaries and Main Index, were transferred to the Library, where their country and file number arrangement was maintained.[5] Subsequently the confidential ('green') papers were also put in their proper places in this arrangement.

[1] F.O.409/17, p.i.
[2] F.O.409/45, p.i.
[3] F.O.881/8550, pp.25–29; 5th Rpt. of R. Comm. on Civil Service (1914–16), qq.37848–37853.
[4] F.O.366/787, f.170 (p.5).
[5] F.O. Confidential Print No.11643*, pp.20–21 (in F.O.370/126).

This new system was applied retrospectively to the papers for the period 1906–1920, with the result that all the papers from 1906 onwards are now arranged in a generally uniform manner in eleven classes of *General Correspondence after 1906: Africa, New Series* (F.O.367); *Commercial* (F.O.368); *Communications* (F.O.850); *Consular* (F.O.369); *Contraband* (F.O.382); *Dominions Information* (F.O.627); *Library* (F.O.370); *News* (F.O.395); *Political* (F.O.371); *Prisoners of War and Aliens* (F.O.383); and *Treaty* (F.O.372). Each of these classes contains the papers of the department after which it is named; the *Political* class contains the papers of all the political departments. It should be remembered that in some of these classes the '1919' correspondence ends and the '1920' begins not on 1 January 1920 but on the date in 1920 on which the department adopted the new registry system.[1]

Only the *Consular, Library, Political* and *Treaty* classes cover the whole of the period since 1906. The *Africa, New Series* class ends in 1913 and the *Commercial* class in 1920; the *News* class starts in 1916 and the *Communications* class in 1936; the *Contraband* class covers the period 1915–1920,[2] the *Prisoners* class the period 1915–1919, and the *Dominions Information* class the period 1929–1933.

After 1913 papers relating to Africa will be found in the *Political* class. During the period 1914–1920 the *Political* class includes, in addition to the normal political series, a separate War Department series of correspondence for many countries, and the Political Intelligence Department papers for 1918 and 1919 (F.O.371/4352–4387) (see also p.66, n.5). The *Treaty* class includes the correspondence of the Prize Court Department, bound separately at the end of each year's correspondence from 1914 to 1919; the 1919 correspondence continues into February 1920. For the period 1914–1916 material akin to the later News Department papers will be found in the *Political* class under the headings 'News General (War)' or 'Miscellaneous General (News)'. Until 1926 a certain number of Communications Department papers are to be found among the *Chief Clerk's Department Archives* (F.O.366) (see p.77). After February 1916 the *Contraband* class consists of the papers of the Ministry of Blockade. From 1926 to 1928 papers of the Dominions Information Department are to be found in the *Treaty* class under the heading 'Empire Foreign Policy'; from 1934 to 1938 papers on this subject will again be found in the *Treaty* class under the heading 'Dominions Intelligence'.

Until 1920 the arrangement within each annual series in the *Political* class is alphabetical by countries with a number of general files and cases at the end; from 1920 each annual series is first divided by departments and then sub-divided alphabetically by counties and subjects. Within the *Africa, New Series, Commercial, Consular, Contraband* and *Prisoners* classes the arrangement of each year's papers is by countries in alphabetical order followed by general files and cases. The *Treaty* and *News* classes are also arranged in this way until 1923 and 1925 respectively. From 1924 the *Treaty* class is arranged by subjects, as the *Library* class is throughout. The *News* class is arranged from 1926 in a single 'General' series of file numbers and this same arrangement is also followed in the *Dominions Information* and *Communications* classes.

Papers in these classes of *General Correspondence after 1906* were bound up in volumes in the Library prior to transfer to the Public Record Office. Papers before 1920 continue to be stitched and bound in the traditional way, although in cloth instead of leather covered boards; from 1920 the papers are punched and laced

---

[1] Or was wound up. See p.68 above.
[2] Contraband correspondence for 1914 will be found in the *Commercial* class, although the registers have been bound up with later Contraband Department registers.

between boards by cords, the spine only being covered with cloth. Each paper is accompanied by the first two pages of its docket sheet and any other minute sheets. Before binding, weeding took place. This was fairly extensive from 1915 in the non-political classes. Political files have been extensively weeded only for the period from the mid-1920s to the mid-1930s (see p.96). The General Registers between 1915 and 1920 have been stamped to show which papers have been weeded.

Typescript lists of the classes of *General Correspondence after 1906* are available in the search rooms of the Public Record Office.[1] These list the volumes in each class by year, country or subject and file numbers of first and last files. Where a file is divided between two or more volumes the registry number of the first or last paper of the split file is also shown. From 1938 each file is listed individually and its title is given.

Records of Temporary War-time Departments 1914–1919

The registered papers of the War Department, the Contraband Department and the Ministry of Blockade, the Prize Court Department and the Prisoners of War Department were, as we have seen, dealt with in much the same way as the registered papers of the other departments of the Office. However, in addition to the registered papers a certain amount of unregistered material created in the various divisions of the Contraband Department and the Ministry of Blockade has been preserved.

In the class of *War of 1914–1918: Records of Temporary Departments* (F.O.902) are three volumes of miscellaneous papers of the Finance Section, minutes of the Blockade Committee (1917) and bound copies of the 'Weekly Bulletin of Trade Information' (1915–1919), the 'Contraband Herald' (1915–1918) and the 'Summary of Blockade Information' (1917–1918).

Eleven agreements or proposals for agreements between the Restriction of Enemy Supplies Department and foreign governments or associations (1916–1919) form the class of *Restriction of Enemy Supplies* (F.O.845).

The *Foreign Trade Department* class (F.O.833) includes three volumes of miscellaneous papers relating to the Department's establishment and policy (F.O.833/16–18) in addition to the registers already mentioned (see pp.66–67). The remainder of the Department's records were destroyed under the schedule of 1924 (see p.95).

Certain records of the War Trade Intelligence and War Trade Statistical Departments passed in 1919 into the custody of the Treasury Solicitor's Office for Prize Court purposes and are now among that Office's records in the Public Record Office as the class of *War Trade Intelligence Department Records* (T.S.14). This class consists of minutes of the Contraband Committee (1914–1918), the General Black List Committee and its Sub-Committee (1915–1918) and the Enemy Exports Committee (1915–1918), volumes of the 'Transit Letter Bulletin' (1915–1919)[2] and certain War Trade Statistics.

Papers relating to contraband matters will also be found among the records of other government departments. Among the records of the Cabinet Office are the papers of the *War Trade Advisory Committee* (Cab.39).[3] A few papers of the independent *War Trade Department*[4] have survived among the records of the Board of Trade (B.T.73), which took it over in 1919. But the largest collection outside the Foreign Office of material relating to contraband matters survives in the records of

---

[1] The lists to the end of 1913 have been published in *List of Foreign Office Records* (P.R.O. Supplementary Lists and Indexes XIII), Vol. 5 (*Various Classes, 1879–1913*); see p.94.
[2] Before 13 March 1916 these come from the Trade Clearing House.
[3] *Records of the Cabinet Office to 1922* (P.R.O. Handbook No.11), pp.29–30. See also Cab.15/6/6.
[4] For its history and functions see Cab.15/6/24; also Hall, *Brit. Archives and the Hist. of the World War*, p.100.

F

the Trade Division of the Naval Intelligence Department in the class of *Admiralty,
Historical Section, 1914–1918 War Histories* (Adm. 137/2732–3045). These include
minutes and papers of many inter-departmental committees on which the Foreign
Office was represented.

Records of the Chief Clerk's Department

The records of the Chief Clerk of the Foreign Office reflect both his accounting and
his establishment functions. They go back beyond 1782 and have been kept as a
distinct series from an early date, being retained in the Department and not transferred annually to the Library as the records of other departments of the Office
were.[1] Records in this series down to 1940 are now in the Public Record Office,
where they form the class of *Chief Clerk's Department Archives* (F.O.366).

The *List of Foreign Office Records to 1878* (P.R.O. Lists and Indexes No. LII)
arranged the records in this class under three headings: Accounts, Correspondence
and Ledgers; but the distinction between these categories is not as clear-cut as the
List would suggest and there are some obvious examples of misplacing. A revised
list of the records down to 1905 has, therefore, been made, arranged under the
following main headings: General, Foreign Office, Messengers, Diplomatic and
Consular Services, and Government Departments. There are copies of this list in the
search rooms of the Public Record Office.

The above headings correspond roughly to the divisions of the Department's
registers. These have survived from 1868 to 1905 and are kept in standard form
(F.O.366/641–645, 683–684, 733–738, 768). They follow the Office practice of entering incoming correspondence on the left-hand page; the particulars given are
register number, name, date, date of receipt and subject. Outgoing correspondence
is entered on the right-hand page; the particulars given are register number, name,
date and subject. Each volume covers two or more years. From 1870 volumes are
sub-divided under the headings: Diplomatic Service, Consular Service, Treasury,
Audit Office (to 1896), Miscellaneous (other government departments, institutions
and individuals and Foreign Service Messengers) and Free Deliveries (1878–1890).[2]
Each sub-division has its separate annual series of register numbers for incoming
and outgoing correspondence. Indexes to the registers for the period 1891–1902
have been preserved (F.O.366/739–740). They are arranged by subjects and persons
and give references to the year and page of the registers.

These registers are of only limited use. In the first place their arrangement corre-
sponds only loosely to the arrangement into volumes of the papers to which they
relate and they are, therefore, only an imperfect means of reference. In the second
place they do not record all the papers which passed through the Department, as a
considerable number of incoming papers were sent there from other departments
of the Office, where they had already been entered, while many drafts prepared in
the Department were written out and entered elsewhere.[3]

Only a few of the Chief Clerk's records relating to the overall accounts of the
Foreign Office, the Messengers and the Diplomatic and Consular Services have
been preserved.[4] They include estimates, 1821–1856, ledgers and other accounts of

---

[1] F.O.366/672, p.179; F.O.366/678, p.332.

[2] F.O.366/678, pp.331–332.

[3] *Ibid.*, p.320. Examination of almost any volume of *General Correspondence* or the period will
reveal a substantial number of papers marked as having been seen by the Chief Clerk.

[4] Many were destroyed under the Second and Fourth Foreign Office Schedules (see p.95
below). For details of nineteenth-century accounting procedure in the Chief Clerk's Department
see F.O.366/386: memorandum by T.Bidwell, 23 Aug. 1836; F.O.366/674, pp.50–122; F.O.366/449,
pp.156–157; F.O.881/1367; F.O.366/678, pp.316–337. For Foreign Office accounts preserved
among Treasury and Exchequer and Audit Office records see p.77 below.

detailed expenditure, 1861–1880, and records of the transactions of sub-accountants, 1868–1880. The Annual Estimates and Appropriation Accounts and Reports of the Comptroller and Auditor-General and of the Public Accounts Committee of the House of Commons were printed for Parliament and will be found in the 'Blue Books'.

The Chief Clerk's records relating to the internal affairs of the Foreign Office include several volumes of correspondence, memoranda and minutes on such establishment matters as the distribution of business, Foreign Office Agencies and the appointment and promotion of Foreign Office Clerks. The more important precedents were entered in a series of 'Domestic Entry Books' covering the period 1779–1921 (F.O.366/449,[1] 669–678, 724, 760–762); there is a two volume index to these (F.O.366/685, 769). In addition there are ledgers and other records of payments of salaries to Clerks and of other domestic expenditure from 1795 onwards. These records are an invaluable source of information for the domestic history of the Foreign Office and for the careers of its Clerks; they have been drawn on heavily in the preparation of this Handbook.

The Chief Clerk's miscellaneous correspondence for the period 1824–1905 was bound up separately. It consists mainly of enquiries about appointments in the Foreign Office and in the Diplomatic and Consular Services and of correspondence with tradesmen, although the earlier papers do include some internal minutes and memoranda. A box of miscellaneous papers on establishment matters, mainly devoted to the case of Edward Scheener (see p.154), is in the class of *Miscellanea, Series I* (F.O.95/591). Miscellaneous papers of a similar nature, 1776–1857, are in F.O.95/9/3–5.

Although the Chief Clerk did not assume the superintendence of the Foreign Service Messengers until 1854 (see p.18), he had always kept the Messengers' Fund Account, from which advances for journeys and Messengers' bills were paid.[2] The Chief Clerk's records include, therefore, the Messengers' bills, going back to 1795, and other records relating to Messengers' accounts of an earlier date than 1854. The Chief Clerk's own papers relating to Messengers after 1854 concern establishment as well as accounting matters. The more important precedents are entered in the Domestic Entry Books. For the period 1868–1881 the Memoranda of Service and Certificates of Journeys enable the Messengers' movements to be traced in detail.

In 1854 the Chief Clerk took over the records which Lewis Hertslet had kept as Superintendent of Messengers between 1824 and 1854. With these records Hertslet transferred a register of their contents (F.O.366/277), listing thirty-nine volumes, of which seventeen can be identified, fourteen of them being among the Chief Clerk's records;[3] two other volumes are in *Miscellanea, Series II*,[4] and one is in the class of *Specimens of Classes of Documents Destroyed*.[5] Hertslet's papers as private agent to the Foreign Service Messengers from 1810 to 1824 have also survived in the class of *Private Collections: Hertslet Papers* (F.O.351). This class includes many earlier papers and also some of a later date than 1824. A volume of regulations, circulars and other papers relating to the Foreign Service Messengers started by Hertslet in 1815 and kept up in the Library until 1870 is in the *Great Britain and*

---

[1] F.O.366/449 is Vol. VII in this series. It was formerly thought to be wanting, but had merely been wrongly listed as 'Government Offices. Treasury. Estimates'.
[2] F.O.366/386: memorandum by T.Bidwell, 23 Aug. 1836.
[3] Vols.2, 5, 7, 8, 9, 10, 11, 12, 13, 35, 36, 37, 38 and 39 of Hertslet's register are now F.O.366/276, 473, 474, 494, 495, 490, 491, 492, 493, 485, 486, 521, 501 and 277 respectively.
[4] Vols.1 and 3 are now F.O.96/117 and 115 respectively.
[5] Vol. 4 is now F.O.900/1 (formerly F.O.96/101); vols.14–34, formerly F.O.96/35–54, were destroyed under the Second Foreign Office Schedule.

General class (F.O.83/348). Also in this class are papers from 1893 to 1905 relating to arrangements for Foreign Service Messengers and the conveyance of Foreign Office bags (F.O.83/1424, 1651, 1760, 1883, 1979, 2160). Some Foreign Service Messengers' papers and miscellaneous books for the period 1772–1824 are in *Miscellanea, Series I* (F.O.95/589–590). Many records of Messengers' expenses, formerly in *Miscellanea, Series II* (F.O.96), have been destroyed under schedule (see p.95), specimens only being preserved (F.O.900/1–4). After the establishment of the separate Communications Department in 1921, its records continue to be kept among the *Chief Clerk's Department Archives* until 1926. The separate class of *General Correspondence after 1906, Communications* (F.O.850) does not include any material earlier than 1936.

Records relating to the Chief Clerk's dealings with the Diplomatic and Consular Services, like those relating to the internal affairs of the Office, include a considerable amount of material on establishment matters, particularly on the careers of the members of these Services. In addition there is a considerable correspondence concerning the accounts of the various diplomatic and consular posts abroad, at each of which there was a sub-accountant, usually the secretary of legation or the consul, and of special missions and commissions. This correspondence was largely carried on by the Chief Clerk without reference to the Secretary of State. The bulk of it relates to queries on the extraordinary (that is non-recurring) expenditure of the various posts (particularly of the diplomatic posts), going back to 1825. Correspondence concerning the accounts of consular posts has not been preserved after 1886 and correspondence concerning the accounts of diplomatic posts is extremely scanty between 1893 and 1921.

Correspondence with diplomatic and consular posts on establishment and financial matters which were referred at some stage to the Chief Clerk will also be found in the various classes of *General Correspondence*[1] and also among *Embassy and Consular Archives*. Also among the latter are some accounts of sub-accountants (e.g. F.O.276, F.O.207/1). Some related papers will also be found in the classes of *Miscellanea, Series I* and *Series II*: a volume of memoranda on consular establishments, 1816–1835 (F.O.95/592); a bundle of papers relating to the expenses of the Embassy in Paris, 1828–1833 (F.O.95/562); and accounts of special missions and commissions (F.O.95/502–507; F.O.96/34, 143–146). Some selected files of correspondence on establishment matters affecting senior diplomats, 1904–1942, constitute the class of *Private Office 'Individual' Files* (F.O.794).

Correspondence with government departments before 1905 is bound up by departments in chronological order. Many volumes have summaries of their contents at the front. The most important correspondence is that with the Treasury. This is arranged in several series. There are entry books of correspondence for the period 1761–1881; the main series of bound volumes of original correspondence and drafts commence in 1812 and continues to 1905; a separate volume of original correspondence, 1853–1873, relates to estimates; five volumes from a series of entry books of out-letters on diplomatic and consular allowances, covering the periods 1822–1823, 1826–1832 and 1861–1874, together with indexes to the series from 1719 to 1918, have been preserved; another series of entry books and original correspondence relates to free deliveries (see p.18, n.11), 1845–1890;[2] and two

---

[1] This is particularly true of matters relating to consuls, in which the Consular Department had a considerable interest.

[2] A further volume of correspondence, 1811–1869, is in the *Supplement to General Correspondence* (F.O.97/573); twelve volumes covering the period 1830–1855 were destroyed under schedule (see p.95).

volumes relate to diplomatic salaries and outfits, 1844–1868. The Treasury's own records of correspondence with the Chief Clerk of the Foreign Office in the period before 1920 will be found in the following classes: *Treasury Board Papers* (T.1), *Out Letters, General* (to 1857) (T.27) and (from 1857) *Out Letters, Foreign Office* (T.12). After 1920 this correspondence will be found in the five main classes of *Files* (T.160–164). Civil List and Civil Contingencies Accounts relating to the Foreign Office will be found in *Treasury Accounts, Departmental* (T.38). Some accounts of missions and consulates for the mid-nineteenth century will be found in the series of Foreign and Colonial Stations Accounts in the *Treasury Chest* class (T.39).

Although correspondence with the Exchequer and Audit Office was given a separate section in the register of correspondence, no separate correspondence volumes were made up as they were for other departments. There are, however, two sections of an entry book of correspondence with the Audit Office relating to consular accounts, 1827–1830 and 1840–1844 (F.O.366/350), and original correspondence will be found among various accounting records, such as the Examiners' Queries on Accounts. Accounts relating to extraordinary expenditure on the Diplomatic, Consular and Secret Services will be found among the records of the Exchequer and Audit Office.[1]

When the Foreign Office Registry was established in 1906, the Chief Clerk's correspondence, like that of all departments, passed through the General Registry, where it was given a registry number and entered in the Central Register (see p.61). From there, however, it went direct to the Financial Department, as the Department was known between 1900 and 1913 (see pp.18–19), not to one of the three general Sub-Registries, its destination being marked up under 'Chief Clerk' in the Central Register. The Department had its own Sub-Registry and index, which was not integrated into the annual card indexes of *General Correspondence* now in the Public Record Office; it continued to retain its own papers instead of passing them annually to the Library.[2] Only a few registered papers, now bound in order of year and registry number, have survived for the period 1909–1919 (F.O.366/786–788), together with some unregistered papers for the period bound up in subject files, often with papers of a later date (F.O.366/780–785). Two volumes of out-letters to the Treasury originating in other departments and sent to the Chief Clerk for information, 1908–1909, have been preserved (F.O.366/756–757).

After 1920 the Chief Clerk's papers were registered and filed in much the same way as those of other departments, the registry series being distinguished by the departmental designation X. Papers did not, however, pass to the Main Index Branch for inclusion in the annual printed indexes (see p.70) until 1931, and even thereafter only selected papers were indexed. Files for the period 1920–1940 selected for preservation are arranged in annual series, each divided under three main headings: 'Diplomatic', 'Domestic' and 'General'; under each heading the arrangement is in order of file numbers. Other headings used less frequently are 'Communications' (1924–1926; before 1924 these papers are under 'Domestic'), 'Chief Clerk's Papers' (these are unregistered papers) and 'Claims' (1934–1935 only). There is a typescript list of the post-1906 papers, giving the subject of each, in the search rooms of the Public Record Office.

Records of the Treaty and Royal Letter Department
The records of this Department can be divided into three categories: general correspondence, royal letters and treaties.

[1] Especially in A.O.1, 2, 3 and 19. See also E.404/593.
[2] *5th Rpt. of R. Comm. on Civil Service* (1914–16), qq.37258, 37263–37265.

The general correspondence was concerned not with the conduct of negotiations leading up to the signing of treaties, although the Department would be consulted on matters of precedent and protocol, but with general subjects involving the formalities of international relations.[1] Records of treaty negotiations will be found in the political or commercial correspondence for the country concerned.

Until 1883 correspondence normally reached the Department indirectly through one of the other departments, and it was normally returned after the completion of any necessary action to the originating department to be kept in its proper place in that department's correspondence until such time as it was transferred to the Library. However, much correspondence did remain in the Department and when J.H.G.Bergne became Superintendent in 1881, he found correspondence dating back to 1822, very largely unbound and unindexed. To remedy this situation he commenced binding and to prevent it recurring he secured the issue in 1883 of instructions to diplomatic and consular officers for the writing of a separate treaty series of despatches on matters concerning the Department, which would go there direct and be dealt with, together with the related domestic correspondence, in the same manner as the general correspondence of the other departments.[2]

Treaty Department correspondence before 1906 will be found in the various country classes of *General Correspondence before 1906* so far as it can be assigned to specific countries. From 1883 when the treaty series of correspondence was instituted, it is distinguished from that of the other departments and often bound in separate volumes. Case volumes on general subjects and, from 1883, the Department's miscellaneous correspondence are in the *Great Britain and General* class (F.O. 83). Correspondence since 1906 is in the class of *General Correspondence after 1906, Treaty* (F.O.372). It includes the records of the Prize Court Department, 1914–1919.

Departmental diaries and registers have survived from 1867 to 1919 but appear to have existed at least as early as 1864.[3] Before 1882 they relate to all papers passing through the Department, even when they had originated and been registered already in another department; from 1882 they follow the standard Office pattern. Treaty correspondence is also registered until 1890 in the Library registers. An index to the departmental registers for 1900–1905 has survived (F.O.804/56); after 1906 Treaty Department correspondence is covered by the Card Index to 18 January 1920 and by the printed index (F.O.409) thereafter.

In addition entry books or registers of certain special types of treaty correspondence have survived in the *Miscellanea* and *Great Britain and General* classes. These include letters of introduction addressed to British diplomatic representatives on behalf of travellers abroad, 1820–1858 (F.O.95/473, F.O.96/122–123);[4] presents, 1841–1873 (F.O.96/140–141); foreign ministers' protections, 1782–1846 (F.O. 95/444–445, F.O.91/11);[5] and foreign orders, 1812–1823 (F.O.83/638–639).

Royal letters are of a formal nature and must not be confused with the private correspondence of the Sovereign, which when going abroad would often go by Foreign Office bag but was not recorded in any way in the Office. The royal letters prepared by and received in the Foreign Office are generally of two types: those relating to the affairs of Royal Families and Heads of State, such as accessions or

---

[1] For subjects which were the concern of the Department see pp.19–20 above.
[2] F.O.366/678, pp.428–433.
[3] *Rpt. of Sel. Ctee. on Trade with Foreign Nations* (1864), q.1768.
[4] Applications for and drafts of letters of introduction, 1831–1875 (mainly for the period 1841–1843), are in F.O.83/89–91, 494; others for the period 1836–1851 were destroyed under schedule (see p.94 below).
[5] These continue the series in S.P.104. From 1842 to 1900 lists of the staff of foreign missions in London are to be found in F.O.83. Lists for 1901 are in F.O.97/610.

elections, births, marriages and deaths; and those concerning the formalities of diplomatic relations, such as the issue of credentials, letters of recall, full powers and commissions.

Royal letters received and drafts of those sent from 1781 to 1834, continuing those in *State Papers Foreign, Royal Letters* (S.P.102), are to be found in the class in *Miscellanea, Series I* (F.O.95) arranged by countries with no distinction being made between the two types of royal letter. Those for the period before 1800 are now unbound, but show signs of former binding in a different order.[1] After 1834 royal letters relating to family affairs, etc., continue until 1930[2] in the same class. They are bound up in volumes each covering a year or so, the arrangement within them being alphabetical by countries. Also in this class are two volumes of correspondence of Prince Albert, 1840–1861 (F.O.95/714, 717), a volume of letters of British Princes, 1845–1902 (F.O.95/777), and two volumes of forms, 1882–1883 and 1906 (F.O.95/778 and 782). Certain case volumes relating to the affairs of the British Royal Family will be found in the *Great Britain and General* class (e.g. F.O.83/94, 1034).[3]

From 1834 to 1929 credentials, letters of recall, recredentials and sign manual instructions, including both originals presented by foreign diplomats in London and drafts of those prepared for British diplomats abroad, are bound in chronological order and will be found in the *Great Britain and General* class (F.O.83). Also in this class are drafts of full powers and commissions, 1813–1946, drafts of commissions to Secretaries of Embassies, etc., 1862–1929, and entry books and drafts of consular commissions and exequaturs, 1816–1929.[4] There is also a volume of forms and precedents for the issue and withdrawal of exequaturs, 1837–1905 (F.O. 83/2058).

Some original full powers and commissions, 1791–1852, including those for Secretaries of State, are in the two classes of *Miscellanea* (F.O.95/593–595; F.O. 96/137–139); others will be found among the *Private Collections* (e.g. F.O.705/38–39), as will some sign manual instructions (e.g. F.O.528/19). Three original British full powers and an original exequatur in favour of a British Consul at Funchal are in *Miscellanea, Series II* (F.O.96/203, 213, 217–218; see also F.O.83/2512).

Entry books of royal letters, continuing those in *State Papers Foreign, Entry Books* (S.P.104), were kept until 1834. In this case the dividing date between the State Paper Office and Foreign Office series is about 1710. From that date until 1828 the entry books make up the Foreign Office class of *King's Letter Books* (F.O.90), in which they are arranged largely in country volumes, no distinction being made between the two types of royal letter. From 1828 to 1834 they continue in the class of *Miscellanea, Series I*, where there is one volume of letters on family affairs (F.O.95/501) and another of credentials and letters of recall, etc. (F.O.95/500), each being arranged chronologically. Separate entry books of sign manual instructions start in 1793 and continue to 1834 (F.O.95/449–453); entry books of full powers and commissions start in 1823 and also continue to 1834 (F.O.95/596–597). There is an index to these last two volumes and to full powers and commissions entered in the *King's Letter Books* between 1800 and 1822 (F.O.

---

[1] This former order may be reconstructed from Ind.6845.
[2] There is a gap for 1893–1894.
[3] Some correspondence with Asian rulers, 1835–1897, is in the India Office Records class L/P & S/14 (see p.31, n.4).
[4] See also the Home Office class: *Entry Books, Various, Exequaturs and Recognitions* (H.O.168). For appointments of foreign consuls in India see the India Office Records class L/P & S/16 (see p.31, n.4).

95/598). This index is succeeded by a series of registers of full powers and commissions, 1835–1942 (F.O.95/770–772, 774). A register of royal letters, 1842–1846,
has survived (F.O.96/142) but entries in this are of a very summary nature and give
no indication of contents.

Original treaties are in two classes: *Protocols of Treaties* (F.O.93) and *Ratifications
of Treaties* (F.O.94). Both are listed on a country basis. The protocol is the document
reciting the terms of the treaty as agreed, signed and sealed by the Plenipotentiaries
on both sides; with it is kept the full power or other authorization of the Plenipotentiaries of the other country concerned and any other subsidiary documents.
The ratification is the document recording the formal acceptance of the treaty,
signed and sealed by the Head of State. These are exchanged by the parties to the
treaty, or deposited in an agreed place if there are a number of parties. The ratifications in the F.O.94 class are, therefore, those signed and sealed by foreign Heads
of State. Drafts of British ratifications, 1814–1946, and related correspondence, are
in the *Great Britain and General* class (F.O.83).[1] There are some acceptances of
accessions to treaties, 1816–1841, in *Miscellanea, Series II* (F.O.96/1).

In *Miscellanea, Series I* there are two series of entry books of treaties, together
with related ratifications, full powers, instructions, etc. The first starts in the mid-
seventeenth century and extends to 1800 (F.O.95/523–536); the second continues
from 1800 to 1834, being divided until 1828 into separate North and South volumes
(F.O.95/537–541). The second series also includes a volume of accession to various
international treaties of 1818–1819 (F.O.95/542). There is also a series of entry
books of treaties (including some original treaties) with the Barbary States inherited
from the Colonial Office together with entry books of correspondence (see p.60) in
1836 (F.O.95/510, 518–521; cf. F.O.96/136).

Treaties with native chiefs in Africa will be found in *General Correspondence before
1906, Slave Trade* (e.g. F.O.84/1748) and *Africa* (e.g. F.O.2/167–168).

The class formerly known as *Continent: Treaty Papers* (F.O.92), which appears
under the heading *Treaties* in the *Guide to the Contents of the Public Record Office*,[2]
consists not of records of the Treaty Department but of political correspondence
between the Foreign Office and British representatives at the Congresses of Paris
and Vienna and other international gatherings which followed the Napoleonic
Wars. It is now regarded as a class of *General Correspondence* (see p.113).

Records of the Passport Office

There was no separate Passport Office until 1855 and even thereafter it remained
subordinate first to the Chief Clerk and then, after 1891, to the Treaty Department;
only after World War I did it expand and become virtually independent (see pp.22–
23). With a few exceptions, however, records relating to the issue of passports by
the Secretary of State for Foreign Affairs were always kept in distinct series which
now form the *Passport Office* classes among Foreign Office records.

The class of *Passport Office Correspondence* (F.O.612) covers the period 1815–1905
and there are *Registers of Correspondence* (F.O.613) for 1868–1893 and 1898–1905.
In addition two volumes of replies to circulars on passport questions, 1886 and
1897–1900, form the class of *Passport Office Correspondence with H.M. Embassies, etc.*
(F.O.614).[3] A small selection of representative files for the period 1920–1954 has
also been preserved to illustrate the system of dealing with applications for various

---

[1] For original warrants, countersigned by the Foreign Secretary, for affixing the Great Seal to
treaties, etc., see C.187.
[2] Vol. II, p.129.
[3] See also F.O.83/172 (mentioned below) and 453.

Plate I

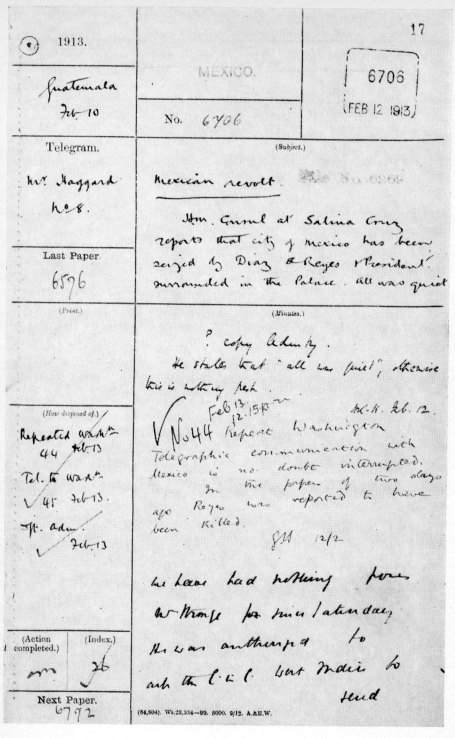

1913.

Guatemala
Feb 10

MEXICO.

No. 6706

6706
(FEB 12 1913)

Telegram.

Mr. Haggard
No 8.

Last Paper.
6576

(Subject.)

Mexican revolt.

H.M. Consul at Salina Cruz
reports that city of Mexico has been
seized by Diaz & Reyes & President
surrounded in the Palace. All was quiet

(Print.)

(Minutes.)

? copy Admy.

He states that "all was quiet", otherwise
this is nothing new.

Feb 13
12.15 p.m.

No 44 Repeat Washington

Telegraphic communication with
Mexico is no doubt interrupted.
In the papers of two days
ago Reyes was reported to have
been killed.

J.M. 12/2

We have had nothing from
Mr. Strange for since Saturday
He was attempting to
ask the C. in C. Great India to
send

(How disposed of.)

Repeated Wash
44 Feb 13

Tel. to Wash
45 Feb 13.

& Adm.
Feb 13

(Action completed.)

(Index.)

Next Paper.
6792

(64,504.) Wt.22,334—99. 5000. 9/12. A.&E.W.

PLATE II

a ship to Vera Cruz, if necessary
on the same day   but a ship
would be of little or no use
an Mexican city is several hundred
miles from the coast.

It is unlikely that the Legation
is in danger   but would you
wish us to ask the Admiralty
to send a ship in any

case?

Repeat to Washington & ask
whether the U.S. Govt. have
any news —   Lll

We might repeat to Washington to
ask if they have any news.
A.N.
And a ship might be sent to Vera
Cruz as probably the Storze cannot
telegraph till he arrives E.G.

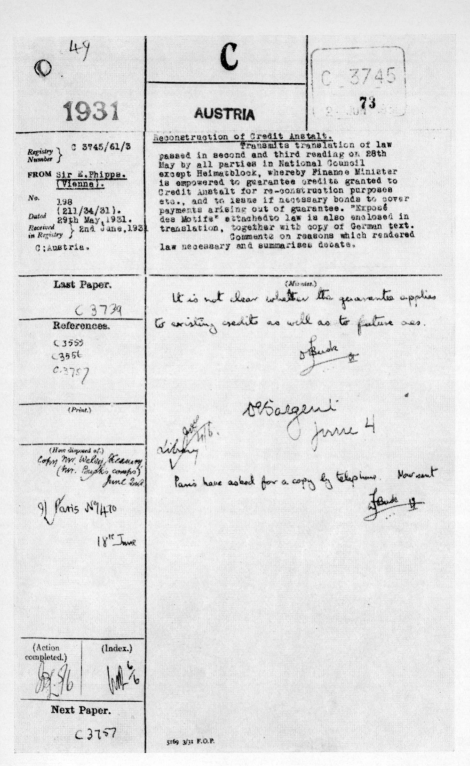

O. 49

1931

C

AUSTRIA

C 3745

73

Registry } C 3745/61/3
Number }

FROM Sir E.Phipps.
(Vienna).

No.   198
Dated (211/34/31).
       29th May,1931.
Received } 2nd June,1931
in Registry }

C:Austria.

Reconstruction of Credit Anstalt.
          Transmits translation of law
passed in second and third reading on 28th
May by all parties in National Council
except Heimatblock, whereby Finance Minister
is empowered to guarantee credits granted to
Credit Anstalt for re-construction purposes
etc., and to issue if necessary bonds to cover
payments arising out of guarantee. "Exposé
des Motifs" attached to law is also enclosed in
translation, together with copy of German text.
          Comments on reasons which rendered
law necessary and summarises debate.

Last Paper.

C 3739

References.

C 3555
C 3556
C 3757

(Print.)

(How disposed of.)
Copy Mr. Welsh, Treasury
(Mr. Bushe compys)
June 2nd

9/ Paris No 1470

18th June

(Action completed.)

(Index.)

Next Paper.

C 3757

(Minute.)

It is not clear whether this guarantee applies
to existing credits as well as to future ones.

Dr Sargent
June 4

Library

Paris have asked for a copy by telephone. Now sent

5169 3/31 F.O.P.

PLATE IV

types of passports, visas and certificates. This forms the class of *Passport Office Representative Case Papers* (F.O.737).

A few records relating to passports are to be found among the *Chief Clerk's Department Archives*. These include two volumes of Passport Fund accounts, 1868–1886 (F.O.366/466, 281), and a volume including papers on Passport Office establishment matters, mainly for the period 1852–1866, but with some as early as 1834 and as late as 1903 (F.O.366/545). References to Passport Office establishment matters will be found elsewhere in this class, especially in the Domestic Entry Books (see p.75) and in papers from 1919 onwards under the heading 'Domestic' (see p.77).

In this same class is an entry book of passes and passports issued by the Secretaries of State for the Southern Department, 1748–1768, by the Secretaries of State for the Northern Department, 1772–1781, and by the Secretaries of State for Foreign Affairs, 1782–1794 (F.O.366/544). It continues the series of entry books of passes and passports in *State Papers Domestic, Entry Books* (S.P.44) and forms a link with the Passport Office class of *Passport Registers* (F.O.610), which continues unbroken from 1795 to 1898.

These *Passport Registers* are all kept in roughly the same manner, with single line entries giving only date, passport number, name, destination, name of person recommending and fee paid. Entries are in numerical order and are generally chronological, although where a block of numbers was assigned to a Passport Agent the entries are retrospective and at this point the chronological order is consequently upset. There is a separate numerical series for each successive Secretary of State. Where a passport has been issued *gratis* to a person going abroad on official business, the nature of this business or a reference to the relevant correspondence is often noted. Until 1858 passports were issued by the Secretary of State to both British and foreign subjects; throughout the period for which registers have been preserved they were normally issued only for a single journey or series of journeys. There are *Indexes of Names* (F.O.611) to the registers for the periods 1851–1862 and 1874–1898.

In addition to those issued in the name of the Secretary of State, passports might be issued at British missions and consulates abroad in the name of the ambassador or minister. Registers of such issues are to be found occasionally among *Embassy and Consular Archives* (e.g. F.O.241/7–8).[1] One such register from Stockholm for the period 1806–1810 is in the class of *Miscellanea, Series I* (F.O.95/454).[2] A case volume in the *Great Britain and General* class (F.O.83/172) consists of replies by consuls to a circular of 1858 enquiring about the issue of passports by them; it includes some lists of persons to whom passports had been issued.

A representative collection of passports issued by various Secretaries of State between 1809 and 1921, by British missions and consulates, by Colonial and Dominion authorities and by foreign missions in London constitutes the class of *Representative Examples of Passports Issued* (F.O.655). A small bundle of British and foreign passports, 1850–1868, with some related correspondence, is among the *Miscellanea, Series II* (in F.O.96/150). Some Messengers' Passports, 1870–1880, are bound up with their Certificates of Journeys (F.O.366/278–279, 475–483).

Related to passports, but not issued by the Passport Office, were letters of introduction addressed to British diplomatic representatives by the Secretary of State on behalf of travellers abroad (see p.78).

[1] Where they exist they are noted in the list on pp.135–144 below.
[2] For the original of this volume see F.O.73/60: A.J.Foster to C.C.Smith, 19 July 1810, and enclosure.

Embassy and Consular Archives

Records or 'archives' from British diplomatic missions abroad surviving in the Public Record Office date from 1568. Until the end of the eighteenth century they are generally in the classes of *State Papers Foreign*, *Archives of British Legations* (S.P. 105) and *Supplementary* (S.P.110), but there is no clear-cut date for the division between these classes and the various Foreign Office classes of *Embassy and Consular Archives*. Some records in the State Paper Office classes continue beyond 1782, notably the archives of the Levant Company, 1606–1866, while several Foreign Office classes go back well into the eighteenth century and earlier (e.g. F.O.227, 335). However the majority of Foreign Office classes start after 1815, when diplomatic and consular posts were re-established in Europe after the Napoleonic Wars.

The correspondence of missions falls into three main categories: with the Foreign Office; with the Foreign Ministry of the country to which the mission is accredited; and with British consular posts within that country. In addition there is a certain amount of miscellaneous correspondence. As the first category consists of original correspondence of which drafts were kept in the Foreign Office and of drafts of which originals went to the Foreign Office, and as much of the correspondence in the other categories would have been copied to the Foreign Office, *Embassy and Consular Archives* duplicate to a large extent the *General Correspondence* of the Office. They do, however, include some material not to be found elsewhere such as minutes, early versions of drafts which might differ from the versions sent out and copies of enclosures of which originals have not been retained or copied in the *General Correspondence*.

In important missions, such as Paris, the series of correspondence with the Foreign Office includes despatches between the Office and other missions, either copied or summarized in transit under flying seal or sent in manuscript or printed copy from the Foreign Office.[1] Ministers were instructed to carry on correspondence on matters of common interest with other British ministers abroad,[2] but this correspondence was regarded as private and does not normally appear in the official archives; it will, however, be found among the classes of *Private Collections* (see p.86–88).

Until about 1814 the language of communications from British ministers to the Foreign Ministries of the countries to which they were accredited was French, but thereafter the use of English gradually became standard; replies were normally in the language of the country.[3]

In the nineteenth century the archives of a mission were bound up periodically,[4] without weeding, in an arrangement maintaining the distinction between the various categories of correspondence. As in the *General Correspondence before 1906*, original correspondence and drafts were kept in their separate numerical or chronological annual series. In the twentieth century the archives have generally been kept in subject files and only the more important of these have been selected for preservation.

Entry books of correspondence were kept up at most missions until the second half of the nineteenth century; in a few instances they persist into the early years of the twentieth century.

Registers of correspondence have survived from some missions from the early years of the nineteenth century and they are general from the 1820s. At first

---

[1] *Rpt. of Sel. Ctee. on Official Salaries* (1850), qq.493, 500–501. See also pp.52, 64, 71 above.
[2] For example, F.O.95/449, p.5.
[3] F.O.83/127; 7 *B.D.I.L.*, pp.961–967.
[4] *Rpt. of Sel. Ctee. on Dipl. and Consular Services* (1870), qq.61, 2962.

separate registers were normally kept for inward and outward correspondence in each of the different categories, but in 1860 instructions were given for missions to keep their registers on the same lines as the departmental diaries of the Foreign Office,[1] a practice which several missions had been following already for a number of years. From some missions indexes to the correspondence or to the registers have also been preserved. The Berlin mission kept separate registers of correspondence passing through under flying seal between 1843 and 1885 (F.O.247).

Most missions also have among their archives some miscellaneous records, such as volumes of Parliamentary Papers, Confidential Print and other printed material, archives of special missions and commissions (see p.85–86), case volumes of correspondence on special subjects, accounts and passport registers. These miscellaneous records tend to be more extensive in the archives of missions in Asiatic countries, a notable example being the class of *Papers in the Chinese Language* (F.O.682) from the archives of the Chinese Secretary's Office at the British Embassy in Peking, which includes not only the records of that Office but also a large number of Chinese official documents. Another unusual series of records is that of the minutes of proceedings of the Council of the Governor General among the archives from the *Anglo-Egyptian Sudan* (F.O.867).

Consular archives were kept on very much the same principles as the archives of missions and included correspondence, entry books, registers of correspondence and, occasionally, indexes of correspondence. A much smaller proportion of these have, however, been preserved; for some consulates only the registers. Instructions to consuls to keep registers of correspondence were first issued in 1836,[2] but for some consulates the surviving registers ante-date these instructions. Consular archives also include a considerable variety of miscellaneous records. Probably the most numerous are the registers of births, marriages (both those performed by consuls under U.K. laws and *lex loci* marriages registered with consuls) and deaths,[3] kept in accordance with instructions issued from time to time by the Foreign Office.[4] Other fairly common types are registers or other records of British subjects, records relating to shipping and deeds or registers of deeds.

Certain consuls in the Levant and Far East exercised magisterial powers over other British subjects within their districts by virtue of capitulations (see p.29), and their archives include, therefore, court registers and other records they were required by the Foreign Office to keep in this connexion.[5] Other consuls, mainly in South America, also kept records of Naval Courts (e.g. F.O.597) (see p.30).

Originally missions and consulates were expected to house their own archives and only to send them home when there was a serious storage problem.[6] Only very recently has there been any regulation laying down the period after which records should be sent home. Moreover in the days before missions and consulates were established on permanent sites, archives passed from house to house, sometimes several times in one year, on a change of minister or consul,[7] and this often resulted in loss or disarrangement. In addition loss might be occasioned by fire, as in Chile,

[1] *Rpt. of Sel. Ctee. on Dipl. Service* (1861), App.2, No.13.
[2] F.O.83/85: draft circular of 1 Oct. 1836 enclosing instruction no.33.
[3] These duplicate the more complete consular returns of births, marriages and deaths preserved at the General Register Office and in the records of the Bishop of London's Registry now at the Guildhall, London, E.C.2.
[4] For example, F.O.83/126: circulars of 6 and 7 Nov. 1849.
[5] For example, F.O.83/110: circular of 2 July 1844.
[6] *Rpt. of Sel. Ctee. on Dipl. and Consular Services* (1870), qq.56–57.
[7] *Rpt. of Sel. Ctee. on Dipl. Service* (1861), qq.1217–1219; *Rpt. of Sel. Ctee. on Dipl. and Consular Services* (1870), qq.55, 2962.

where the correspondence for 1847–1890 was destroyed in 1891, or by deliberate destruction in a dangerous political situation, as in Sweden, where the 1914–1938 correspondence was destroyed in 1940 in anticipation of a German invasion. Variations in the application of destruction schedules (see p.95–96) have also contributed to some extent to the uneven representation of certain posts. Nevertheless, the Foreign Office has always been concerned that missions and consulates should keep their archives in a satisfactory manner and from time to time special instructions have been issued and enquiries made to ensure that this was being done.[1]

The classification of *Embassy and Consular Archives* has not been consistent in the past. At first separate classes of *Correspondence, Registers of Correspondence, Letter Books* and *Miscellanea*, with special classes as required, were created for each mission and consulate. More recently this classification has been used only for archives of missions. The archives of a consulate are now generally regarded as constituting a single class, although the earlier classification has been retained in most cases where it had already been applied. A certain amount of rearrangement and amalgamation, sometimes involving changes in class titles, has, however, taken place for this and other reasons after transfer to the Public Record Office. In some instances the distinction between the archives of diplomatic and consular posts in the same place has become blurred and both may be found together in one class. Some classes of *Correspondence* have been divided into separate *Series* on no very clear basis.

Classes of consular archives are generally grouped under the country exercising sovereignty at the time of their creation.[2] The archives of one consulate may, therefore, appear in different classes (even under different names)[3] at different times. Thus, the archives of the Helsinki consulate are to be found in the class of *Embassy and Consular Archives, Russia, Helsingfors (Helsinki)* (F.O.768) and in the class of *Embassy and Consular Archives, Finland, Helsinki (Helsingfors)* (F.O.753). Here, and in other similar cases, the make up of the records is such that a date overlap between the classes cannot be avoided. Some countries, notably Egypt and the Barbary States, although not formally independent at the time when the records were created, are regarded as such for the grouping of their diplomatic and consular archives. Records of vice-consulates have sometimes been placed among the archives of the consulate to which they are subordinate. For some countries a special class has been created for records from a number of minor consular posts, such as the class of *Embassy and Consular Archives, United States of America, Various Consulates* (F.O.700). In other cases, a single class includes the records of a number of consular posts within a single consular district, such as the class of *Embassy and Consular Archives, Brazil, Sao Paulo Consular District* (F.O.863).

Isolated volumes of records from missions and consulates may occasionally be found among the *General Correspondence before 1906*, especially in the *Supplement* (e.g. F.O.97/33–34, 75). A passport register from Stockholm, 1806–1810, is among the *Miscellanea, Series I* (F.O.95/454) (see p.81).

Archives of Commissions, Conferences, Special Missions, etc.
The commissions whose archives survive among the Foreign Office records are of two main kinds: those established to deal with matters of international importance, on which there were representatives of several countries in addition to Britain; and

---

[1] For example, F.O.83/78, 92–93 (q.33); F.O.83/122–123.
[2] There has been no consistency here, however. See, for example, F.O.226, classified as *Turkey: Beirut* but including material for the period 1942–1945.
[3] No consistent practice has been followed in using new and old names where there has been a change of name between the date of creation of the records in a class and the present.

those established to deal with issues between Britain and one other country, on which there were representatives of only the two countries concerned.

Among those in the first category are the several *Slave Trade Commissions* (F.O. 308, 312–315) established in the nineteenth century to adjudicate on ships detained under the various treaties for the suppression of the Slave Trade; the *Eastern Roumelia Commission 1878–79* (F.O.901), which organized the autonomous state of Eastern Roumelia created by the Treaty of Berlin in 1878; the various *Inter-Allied Commissions* established after World War I (e.g. F.O.894, 896); and the *International Committee for the Application of the Agreement regarding Non-Intervention in Spain* (F.O. 849). Among the second are commissions to settle boundary disputes (e.g. F.O. 302, 303), fishery disputes (F.O.301) and claims by individuals (e.g. F.O.304, 310, 316), and the several *Mixed Arbitral Tribunals*, especially those established under the Peace Treaties of 1919 and 1920 (F.O.324–328).

The archives of these commissions are varied in their content. Some consist of the papers of the British Commissioner only, others of papers of the commission as a whole. Some include only minutes and other formal papers, others have correspondence with the Foreign Office, with other delegations and with local authorities. Commissions dealing with boundaries and claims by individuals usually include among their archives a considerable quantity of supporting papers.

The archives of many commissions form separate classes of *Archives of Commissions* (see List pp.144–148), but some are to be found in the country classes of *General Correspondence before 1906*, alongside the Foreign Office's own correspondence with the commission (e.g. F.O.5/1632–1633), in the *Miscellanea* (e.g. F.O.95/513–514), or in the *Supplement to General Correspondence* (e.g. F.O.97/542–545). The separate class of archives of the *Eastern Roumelia Commission, 1878–79* (F.O.901) is continued for 1880 in the *Supplement* class (F.O.97/527–530). Archives of commissions may also be found among *Embassy and Consular Archives* (e.g. F.O.131/1–2). The archives of the *Archangel High Commission, 1918–1921* (F.O.175, 176) were formerly classified as *Embassy and Consular Archives*. Papers of Commissioners will also be found in various *Private Collections* (e.g. F.O.800/194, 251).

The archives of some conferences have been put into separate classes (see List p.149). These include, under the title *Continent* (F.O.139), the archives of the British delegations to the Congresses of Paris and Vienna, etc., following the Napoleonic Wars, formerly classified as *Embassy and Consular Archives*; the *Peace Conference of 1919–1920* (F.O.373, 374, 608, 893);[1] and the *Lausanne* and *Locarno Conferences* (F.O.839, 840). Archives of delegations to other conferences are to be found alongside the Foreign Office's own correspondence with those delegations in the *General Correspondence*, either in the appropriate country class, as, for example, the archives of the Congress of Berlin, 1878, which are under *Turkey* (F.O.78/2904–2911), or in the *Great Britain and General* class, as, for example, the archives of the Conference on Armaments, 1899 (F.O.83/1702–1704). Papers relating to various conferences during World War I, to the 1919–1920 Peace Conference, and to several conferences of the inter-Wars period, are among the records of the Cabinet Office.[2]

Archives of conferences usually include both formal records and the correspondence of the British delegation with the Foreign Office and with other delegations.

[1] The Peace Conference series of papers of the Political Intelligence Department are F.O. 371/4352–4356.
[2] Cab.25, 28–31. See *Records of the Cabinet Office* (P.R.O. Handbook No. 11), pp.21–23, 34–35. Since this was published the records of several other conferences have been added to Cab.29, which has been re-titled *International Conferences*.

The *Peace Conference of 1919–1920, Correspondence* (F.O.608) was arranged on the 'Alpha-Numeral' system of vertical filing by subjects which had been proposed for the Foreign Office by the 1918 Inter-Departmental Committee (see p.67). A subject index compiled from the précis cards is on the search room shelves at the Public Record Office.

Archives of special missions may be found in various places. In some instances the mission was preparatory to the commencement or resumption of diplomatic relations and its archives will be found among the appropriate *Embassy and Consular Archives* (e.g. F.O.148/1–2; F.O.204/186–187). Archives of other types of special mission may also be found there (e.g. F.O.254/10–12). The archives of the *Milner Mission*, 1919–1920, constitute a separate class of *Embassy and Consular Archives, Egypt* (F.O.848). Archives of some special missions are also to be found in the *Miscellanea* classes (F.O.95/508–509; F.O.96/175–176, 178) and in the *Supplement to General Correspondence* (F.O.97/512). By their very nature archives of special missions were more likely than the other types of archives discussed in this section to escape from official custody. Some are now to be found in the Foreign Office classes of *Private Collections* (e.g. F.O.323/3 and 6) and many more are probably in private hands or in repositories other than the Public Record Office.

The archives of two special para-military organizations operating in the Middle East during World War I may conveniently be mentioned here. They now constitute the classes of *War of 1914–1918: Jedda Agency Papers* (F.O.686) and *Arab Bureau Papers* (F.O.882).

Mention should also be made of the records of the London Office of the League of Nations, which have been deposited by the United Nations Organization in the Public Record Office (P.R.O.30/52) (see p.167).

Private Correspondence

From very early times Secretaries of State conducted a considerable amount of private correspondence on official matters with heads of missions abroad and heads of missions corresponded privately with each other. A similar private correspondence also developed in the nineteenth century between the Under Secretaries and heads of mission and between Foreign Office clerks and junior diplomatic officers.

This private correspondence was defended by Lord Clarendon, a former Foreign Secretary, before the Select Committee on the Diplomatic Service in 1861, on the grounds that:

> . . . it is totally impossible to carry on the business of the Foreign Office with our foreign ministers unless by writing private letters; those private letters never superseding the public instructions, or taking the place of them, or being in any respect a substitute for them. . . . my private letters always were, in fact, either commentaries or explanations of the public despatches, and giving [ministers] all the information that I thought might be useful to them at their posts; . . . if a Foreign Minister came into my room as Secretary of State, he could tell me, and I could tell him, a variety of things, both about countries and about persons also, which would be neither useful nor perhaps proper to make matter of instruction or the subject of a public despatch, and yet which it would be extremely useful, reciprocally, to know; and it was my object, in my private letters, to always keep the Foreign Ministers as much in England as I could, to give them English views and English ideas of all matters that were going on, and to keep them *au fait* as to public opinion, and to let them know everything that I thought was passing in this country and likely to be conducive to the efficient conduct of the business they had to transact.[1]

[1] *Rpt. of Sel. Ctee. on Dipl. Service* (1861), q.988; see also qq.989–992. Compare Lord Grenville writing in 1791: *Manuscripts of J. B. Fortescue at Dropmore*, H.M.C., II (1894), p.142.; also Lord Halifax in 1939: *Docs. on Brit. For. Policy.* 3rd Ser., Vol. VII, App. IV (X).

Lord Wodehouse (later Secretary of State as 1st Earl of Kimberley), Parliamentary Under-Secretary at the time and a former minister at St. Petersburg, looking at private correspondence from the point of view of a head of mission, was more specific:

> ... all matters of public importance should be recorded in despatches, and a private letter should only be supplemental to a public despatch; for instance, in recounting an interview with a minister, there may be some small personal details which it might not be altogether proper to put in a public document, but which might be contained in a private letter, but everything that is of public importance should be recorded. Then, a private letter may contain a good deal of gossip, and many stories which may be more or less worth recounting, but for the precise accuracy of which a minister could not vouch. ...[1]

Other witnesses who defended the practice were clearly influenced to a considerable extent by an awareness that official despatches were liable to publication in the Blue Books (see pp.89–90), notwithstanding that despatches printed there were often subject to considerable editing, while it was not unknown for private letters to be included (with the concurrence of their authors).[2] Private letters were, moreover, as liable as the official correspondence to circulation within the Office and to the Sovereign, the Prime Minister and the Cabinet and might even on occasion be registered and kept with the official correspondence.

Although the printing of despatches in Blue Books became progressively rarer from about 1880, another factor then arose to encourage the private letter, namely the increasing departmentalization of the Foreign Office. A private letter went to its addressee direct, whereas an official despatch had to pass through the Office hierarchy, with consequent delays. Attempts early in the twentieth century to abolish the private letter were not entirely successful, although their volume was reduced, and semi-official correspondence continued to play an important role in relations between the Foreign Office and missions abroad. Since 1906 private letters have been more liable than they were before to eventual registration, although this has not been an invariable rule.[3]

Despite denials before the 1861 Committee that private correspondence was used to conduct 'secret diplomacy',[4] it is clear that at certain periods it did go beyond the strict limits assigned to it by Clarendon and the other witnesses and that important diplomatic matters might figure in private letters without appearing in official despatches.[5] Even when this was not so, the private letters are a valuable complement to the official despatches and when seeking to reconstruct the course of, and even more so the motives for, any particular diplomatic proceeding, it is advisable to consult both the official and the private correspondence of the chief participants.

In the nineteenth century the Secretaries of State, diplomats and Foreign Office officials were permitted to take with them when they resigned or retired their private correspondence,[6] together with précis or copies of official despatches (see p.10) and copies of Confidential Print, etc. Many collections of private papers acquired in this way still remain in private hands, although a number have been deposited for safe keeping in libraries or other institutions, such as the British

---

[1] *Rpt. of Sel. Ctee. on Dipl. Service* (1861), q.897; see also qq.898–902.
[2] *Ibid.*, qq.1772–1778, 2344–2354, 2660–2665, 3499–3502.
[3] Tilley and Gaselee, *Foreign Office*, pp.161–164; Strang, *Foreign Office*, pp.157–158; F.O.371/1463, file 12157, paper 14193: minute by Crowe, 3 April 1912.
[4] For example, *Rpt. of Sel. Ctee. on Dipl. Service* (1861), q.3501.
[5] *Camb. Hist. of Brit. For. Policy* III, pp.569–570.
[6] *1st Rpt. of R. Comm. on Public Records*, Part III, H.C. 1912–13 [Cd.6396] XLIV, q.1572.

Museum; yet others have been deposited in the Public Record Office, or have been transferred there after being returned to the Foreign Office.[1]

In this century, however, the practice has developed of requiring Foreign Secretaries and other senior diplomats and Foreign Office officials to leave behind on their retirement their unregistered papers relating to official affairs. An extensive collection of these, including the Private Office papers of the Secretaries of State from 1900 to 1935 and from 1938 to 1940, have been transferred to the Public Record Office as the class of *Private Collections: Ministers and Officials: Various* (F.O.800) (see pp.150, 163). They continued, however, to take away papers of a personal or political nature, even though these might touch on foreign affairs. Such papers should be sought in private collections elsewhere.[2]

Mention has already been made of the précis and entry books of an earlier period which, although compiled for the private use of Secretaries of State, particularly for Castlereagh, have remained among the Foreign Office records (see pp.57–59).

Printing and Publication

The confidential printing of papers for circulation within the Foreign Office, to the Cabinet, to other government departments and to missions abroad started in 1829,[3] but it was not until 1850 that the regular series of Confidential Print began to assume significant proportions. This confidential printing was carried out on the premises by the Foreign Office's own printers (see p.12 above).

A Confidential Print might consist of a single document, such as a memorandum or report or even a single despatch, or of a substantial volume of correspondence on a particular subject or dealing with the affairs of a particular country. From the latter part of the nineteenth century the 'Correspondence' volumes were based upon printed daily telegram sections and prints of individual despatches, already circulated in the interests of speed but not individually included in the Confidential Print series. In addition to 'Correspondence' volumes, the series includes annual volumes of Law Officers' Reports from 1861 onwards, printed material emanating from other government departments, and a certain amount of non-confidential material, such as Orders in Council also printed in the *London Gazette*, regulations for competitions for clerkships and attachéships and other published material.

At first confidential printing was an extraordinary event and took place only on the express instructions of the Secretary of State or an Under Secretary, but by 1906 virtually every telegram or despatch of importance was printed in the daily sections as a matter of course, a system of priorities being established to ensure that very important material was not held up by that of lesser importance, and the subsequent making up of these sections into periodical 'Correspondence' volumes in the series of Confidential Print was a routine matter for the printers. Similarly a standard procedure for distribution had been developed by that date (see pp. 52, 64, 71).

Confidential Prints are numbered individually, roughly in order of printing. Certain items, mostly extraneous material, have been given numbers followed by asterisks.[4] Occasionally printed papers may be found among Foreign Office

---

[1] For full details of relevant private papers in the Public Record Office see Appendix III. For early attempts to recover or control the places of deposit and conditions of access to private records relating to foreign affairs see F.O.83/276, 299, 460, 909, 1460, 1923, 2034.

[2] For private papers of Secretaries of State, 1782–1939, see Appendix IV below.

[3] 7 *B.D.I.L.*, p.ix.

[4] Much of this extraneous material came from other departments and will be found also in the *Colonial Office, Confidential Print* classes (C.O.879–886), the *War Office, Reports and Miscellaneous Papers* (W.O.33) and in the India Office Records classes *Political and Secret Department: Memoranda* (L/P & S/18) and *Library* (see p.31, n.4).

records which have not been numbered as Confidential Prints.[1] A copy of the Foreign Office Library's numerical register of Confidential Prints 1–11083 (to 1919) is available in the search rooms at the Public Record Office. Prints 1–10600 (to *c.* 1914) will be listed on a country/subject basis in the proposed *List of Foreign Office Confidential Print to 1914.* The Confidential Print series includes an index of Prints, 1815–1876 (F.O.881/3236) and two lists of Prints 1–10000 (*c.*1913), arranged by subjects (F.O.881/10148*) and by countries (F.O.881/10330) respectively.

A virtually complete set of Confidential Prints 1–10600 (those omitted are mainly extraneous or published material) has been transferred to the Public Record Office as the class of *Confidential Print, Numerical Series* (F.O.881). The piece numbers in this class are the same as the original Print numbers. In addition there are several other classes of *Confidential Print* arranged under various country, region, department and subject headings (see pp.127–135) and consisting in the main of the periodical 'Correspondence' volumes. Volumes of Confidential Print and of print sections will also be found in private collections (e.g. P.R.O.39/29/219–384) and in the *Miscellanea* classes of *Embassy and Consular Archives* (e.g. F.O.287). After 1906 Confidential Prints other than the 'Correspondence' volumes, together with print sections, will often be found in the appropriate files in the *General Correspondence* classes.

In addition to Confidential Print from the regular series, special prints were prepared, as in other government departments, for circulation to the Cabinet.[2] Photographic copies of such papers from 1880 to 1916 (Cab.37) and original prints from 1916 (Cab.24) are included among the records of the Cabinet Office.[3] Copies of Foreign Office prints for the Cabinet for the period 1900–1918 are also to be found in a Foreign Office class of *Cabinet Papers* (F.O.899).

The traditional way of making public the contents of documents relating to foreign affairs was to lay them before Parliament and to publish them in the series of Parliamentary Papers.[4] These were of two types: 'Sessional Papers', laid in pursuance of Acts of Parliament, by order of either House or in response to an address from either House; and 'Command Papers' presented by the Crown. The former were laid in original and printed subsequently by the printer to the House on the House's order; the latter were laid already printed by the Foreign Office printer or in 'dummy' for printing by him as soon as possible. Strictly speaking only Sessional Papers were 'Blue Books' but that term is applied generally to both types of Parliamentary Paper.

The systematic employment of Blue Books as an instrument of policy began after the Napoleonic Wars and was much used in the early part of the nineteenth century, especially by Canning and Palmerston. By about 1880, however, publication had become formalized. The distinction between papers presented by command and those laid in response to an address became of no significance. At about the same time it became customary to consult with foreign powers before publishing papers

[1] For example, F.O.366/678, pp.316–337.
[2] F.O.881/8550, p.23.
[3] *Records of the Cabinet Office to 1922* (P.R.O. Handbook No. 11), pp. 1, 6–10, 27–28. Cab.37 is listed in *List of Cabinet Papers, 1880 to 1914* and *List of Cabinet Papers, 1915 to 1916* (P.R.O. Handbooks Nos.4 and 9).
[4] On printing for Parliament see H.Temperley and L.M.Penson, *A Century of Diplomatic Blue Books, 1814–1914* (Cambridge, 1938); R.Vogel, *A Breviate of British Diplomatic Blue Books, 1919–1939* (Montreal, 1963); S.Lambert, 'The Presentation of Parliamentary Papers by the Foreign Office' in *B.I.H.R.* XXIII (1950), pp.76–83, and also *Hist. J.* X (1967), pp.125–131; V.Cromwell, 'The Administrative Background to the Presentation to Parliament of Parliamentary Papers on Foreign Affairs in the Mid-19th Century' in *J. Soc. Archivists* II (1960–64), pp.302–315.
G

affecting their interests.[1] After World War I the use of motions for addresses virtually ceased and the value of the Blue Book diminished with the use of the press conference and the release of documents to the press to give more rapid dissemination, and with the development of question time in the House of Commons as the accepted method of obtaining information from the government.

The authorization of the Foreign Secretary was required before any paper could be included in a Blue Book, although the bulk of many of these was such that in fact decisions as to their composition devolved upon the Under Secretaries or even upon the Senior Clerks.[2] From 1903 to 1920 there was a separate Parliamentary or Blue Book Department in the Office, among the duties of which was the handling of the routine work connected with the publication of Blue Books; after 1920 this work passed to the Library (see p.22). At times the correspondence selected for inclusion in the Blue Books was fairly comprehensive, but extracts or even whole despatches might be omitted or substantially edited, and this might not always be made obvious to the reader.

Regular machinery for the sale of Blue Books was created only in 1835. Before that date copies were made available to Members and were put into circulation by various other means, while individual Parliamentary Papers were published in the appendices to the *Journals* or (until 1829) in *Hansard* and extracts appeared in the *London Gazette* and in the press. Until 1896 Blue Books could be issued only while Parliament was sitting and important papers which it was wished to present during a recess were published in the *London Gazette* and appeared in Blue Books after Parliament had reassembled. Since 1896 Parliamentary Papers have been published in the normal way during a recess and formally laid at the opening of the next session.

Two special series among the Blue Books call for separate mention. The first is the *Treaty Series*, in which treaties and similar documents involving the United Kingdom have been published since 1892.[3] The other is the series of *Commercial Reports*: the reports, originally half yearly, later annual, on industry, trade and general statistics first required of Secretaries of Embassies and Legations and of Consuls by Lord Clarendon in 1857.[4] From 1886 these *Reports*, or extracts from them, might also appear, together with other commercial intelligence supplied by British diplomatic and consular representatives, in the *Board of Trade Journal*.

Two semi-official series of documents relating to foreign affairs were established early in the nineteenth century by Lewis Hertslet, the Foreign Office Librarian. These were *Hertslet's Commercial Treaties*, started in 1820,[5] and *British and Foreign State Papers*, proposed by Hertslet in 1822, the first volume appearing in 1824.[6] These were originally published at Hertslet's own expense and were intended for purchase only by the Foreign Office for distribution to missions and consulates.

[1] From 1893 to 1905 this correspondence is to be found in the F.O.83 class under the title: 'Blue Books. Permission given by Foreign Governments . . .' (e.g. F.O.83/1791); for earlier correspondence see the appropriate country class (e.g. F.O.78/3503). A register of such correspondence, 1886–1900, from the Eastern Department is F.O.566/85.
[2] From 1825 to 1905 authorizations and arrangements for the issue of Blue Books will be found in the F.O.83 class under the title: 'Parliamentary Domestic' (e.g. F.O.83/207).
[3] A list of the *Treaty Series* from 1919 is H.M. Stationery Office's *Sectional List No. 7.*
[4] F.O.83/158: circular of 24 Feb. 1857. For arrangements for publication see F.O.96/25: minutes by Clarendon and others, 9, 10 and 14 Nov. 1857; *Rpt. of Sel. Ctee. on Trade with Foreign Nations* (1864), q.2733; *2nd Rpt. of Sel. Ctee. on Dipl. and Consular Services* (1871), qq.1664–1667; *Rpt. of Sel. Ctee. on Dipl. Services* (1872), qq.235–236; *4th Rpt. of R. Comm. on Civil Estabs.* (1890), qq.27777–27783; *5th Rpt. of R. Comm. on Civil Service* (1914–16), q.37433; Platt, *Econ. Hist. R.*, 2S, XVI, pp.508–509.
[5] F.O.83/636: memorandum [by L.Hertslet], 15 Jan. 1820; circular, Nov. 1820.
[6] F.O.83/181: memorandum [by L.Hertslet], Jan. 1822; circular, 5 July 1824.

The demand, however, was such that they were presently made available for general sale. The series of *British and Foreign State Papers* was not confined to material from the Foreign Office records, and what it did take from that source was normally supplementary to papers published in the Blue Books. Both series normally consisted of material already published elsewhere. They were continued by Hertslet's son and successor, Edward, until his own retirement in 1896. Thereafter they continued to be edited by members of the Foreign Office and printed and published by H.M. Stationery Office, but editorial work was done during non-official time and it was made clear that the Foreign Office assumed no responsibility for their accuracy.[1] With the volume for 1922 the two publications merged into a single series of *British and Foreign State Papers* and the work became an official anonymous publication, the disclaimer of official responsibility disappearing.[2]

Another publication which also began as a private venture was the annual *Foreign Office List*, giving particulars of the staff of the Foreign Office and of the Diplomatic and Consular Corps, including detailed statements of service, and also of foreign missions and consulates in Britain and the British Dominions. This was first published in 1852 by Francis Cavendish, a Foreign Office Clerk, and continued by Edward Hertslet from 1863 (he had assisted Cavendish since 1854) until 1903, when he was succeeded as editor by his son Godfrey,[3] who continued his connection with the work until 1947. Although encouraged, the *List* was never published officially. It was last issued in 1965. In 1966 it was replaced by the *Diplomatic Service List*, published officially.

Two other semi-official works by Edward Hertslet should also be mentioned here: his *Map of Europe by Treaty*, proposed in 1859 and published in 1875; and his *Map of Africa by Treaty*, proposed in 1876 and published in 1895.[4]

In the twentieth century Foreign Office records have been published officially in two great historical collections: *British Documents on the Origins of the War, 1898–1914* and *Documents on British Foreign Policy, 1919–1939*. The former appeared in eleven volumes in thirteen parts between 1926 and 1938. The latter is in three series, starting respectively in 1919, 1929 and 1938, the first series being sub-divided, with series IA starting in 1925; only the third series has so far been completed.[5]

The Public Record Office has published on micro-opaque cards the Foreign Office Confidential Print relating to the American Civil War. A wide range of Foreign Office records is also available on positive microfilm from the Public Record Office.[6]

Custody[7]

As we have seen (seep.53) departments handed their records to the Foreign Office Library after a short period, generally one year from the end of the calendar year in which they were created. There they were arranged and bound (a process

---

[1] F.O.366/760, p.203A.
[2] Records relating to the two publications up to 1905 will be found in the F.O.83 class under the titles: 'State Paper Work' and 'Hertslet's Commercial Treaties'. After 1905 see F.O.370 under the heading 'State Papers'. See also Hertslet, *Recollections*, pp.145–147; F.O.366/392.
[3] Hertslet, *Recollections*, pp.245–248; F.O.366/392.
[4] F.O.83/1655, 1718.
[5] For a list of the volumes in these two collections see H.M. Stationery Office's *Sectional List No. 58.*
[6] A microfilm catalogue is available on request.
[7] What is said in this and the two following sections applies generally to records relating to foreign affairs from the sixteenth century onwards and not just to Foreign Office records in the narrow sense of those created after 1782 (see p.33 above).

that fell seriously into arrears from time to time)[1] and there they remained for a period, originally determined solely by the availability of space in the Library, before being transferred to the State Paper Office or the Public Record Office.[2]

The State Paper Office had existed since at least the early years of the seventeenth century to keep the records of the Secretaries of State, arranging them from an early period in 'Domestic', 'Foreign' and 'Colonial' series and not by the provinces of the respective Secretaries.[3] It remained independent of the new Public Record Office, established in 1838, until 1854, when it was brought under the charge and superintendence of the Master of the Rolls, becoming a Branch Record Office.[4]

Transfers of records in 1793 and 1796 brought those in the State Paper Office down to about 1779;[5] in 1799 Lord Grenville ordered all correspondence before 1793 'to be transmitted to the Paper Office';[6] in 1802 treaties of as recent a date as 1794 were there.[7] After the establishment of the Foreign Office Library in 1801 the transfer of records to the State Paper Office came to be regarded as undesirable,[8] but shortage of space made it a necessity and by 1861 records had been transferred down to 1837. In 1861, however, advantage was taken of the demolition of the State Paper Office and the re-building of the Foreign Office to reclaim the correspondence for the period 1761–1837 and all ratifications of treaties.[9]

At the same time the Public Record Office took over from the State Paper Branch Office all the Foreign Office correspondence of an earlier date than 1760[10] and in 1868 it received its first direct transfer of records from the Foreign Office, the correspondence for the period 1760–1783.[11] This was the situation in 1870, when Hammond, the Permanent Under Secretary, expressed the opinion 'that our librarian would be very glad to have papers 200 years before that time'.[12] Nevertheless only two years later the first transfer to the Public Record Office of Foreign Office records proper had to be made, bringing the correspondence there down to 1810.[13] By 1889 correspondence down to 1847 was at the Public Record Office and transfers were being made about every three years; Edward Hertslet regretted this.[14] Since then periodical transfers have continued to take place.[15] Following the recommendations of the *Grigg Report* in 1954[16] and the enactment of the *Public Records Act 1958*[17] machinery has now been established for regular transfers of records to the Public Record Office when they are between twenty-five and thirty years old.

[1] F.O.366/392: minute by Lord John Russell, 16 March 1862; *4th Rpt. of R. Comm. on Civil Estabs.* (1890), q.26441.
[2] Correspondence with the State Paper Office and Public Record Office, 1811–1905, is in the F.O.83 class under the title 'State Paper Office', with a separate Library register and index (F.O. 802/263); after 1905 the correspondence continues in F.O.370.
[3] *Guide to the Contents of the Public Record Office* (1963) II, pp.1–3.
[4] *Sixteenth Report of the Deputy Keeper of Public Records*, pp.3–4.
[5] F.O.95/599.
[6] F.O.366/671, p.127.
[7] F.O.95/635.
[8] For example, F.O.366/392: minutes of Aug.–Sept. 1839.
[9] F.O.83/234: draft to Master of the Rolls, 27 Jan. 1862; *23 D.K. Rpt.*, pp.6, 35; *24 D.K. Rpt.*, p.viii; *Rpt. of Sel. Ctee. on Dipl. and Consular Services* (1870), q.1669.
[10] *23 D.K. Rpt.*, pp.6, 35.
[11] *30 D.K. Rpt.*, p.22.
[12] *Rpt. of Sel. Ctee. on Dipl. and Consular Services* (1870), q.60; see also qq.59, 1668.
[13] F.O.83/439: A. Kingston to E.Hertslet, 9 Aug. 1872, and enclosure.
[14] *4th Rpt. of R. Comm. on Civil Estabs.* (1890), qq.27590–27593.In his evidence Hertslet still referred to the Public Record Office as the 'State Paper Office'.
[15] For details of transfers see the *D.K. Rpts.* and *Keeper's Reports*, the Foreign Office correspondence cited on in n.2 above, and the Public Record Office's own *Correspondence* (P.R.O.1) and *Transfer Registers* (P.R.O.40).
[16] *Rpt. of Ctee. on Departmental Records* (Cmd.9163).
[17] 6 and 7 Eliz.II, c.51.

Access

Until 1858 access to Foreign Office records was given only by special permission of the Secretary of State, but in that year Lord Malmesbury decided that papers prior to 1688 should be open to public inspection without special permission.[1] With the special permission of the Secretary of State 'Strangers' might be allowed to inspect records between 1688 and 1760, this latter date being advanced to 1783 in 1868.[2] In 1872 Lord Granville extended the general open date to 1760 and that to which access might be allowed by special permission to 1802;[3] the latter date was extended to 1815 in 1879. In 1891 the records were opened, subject to certain conditions, to 1802 with an extension to 1830 by special permission; at the same time papers relating to Newfoundland Fisheries were withheld from the general opening.[4] The conditions of access to records between 1761 and 1802 were, however, such that in practice the general open date continued to be 1760 until 1903, when it was brought forward to 1780, the date of opening by special permission being brought forward at the same time to 1850.[5] By 1903 various other subjects had, like Newfoundland Fisheries, been excluded from the general opening: Treaties, Embassy and Consular Archives, Great Britain, Slave Trade, Frontiers of Holland, Foreign Various, Confidential Miscellaneous, Continent and Continent Archives and Domestic Letters. After 1903 only Newfoundland Fisheries and Frontiers of Holland (because it contained material relating to secret service agents) remained outside the general arrangement.[6]

In 1908 an Inter-Departmental Committee to consider 'what, if any, relaxations can now be permitted in the restrictions hitherto maintained on public access to departmental records' recommended that the general open date be brought forward to 1837[7] and this recommendation was accepted by the Foreign Office in 1909, Law Officers' Reports only being excepted.[8] The Committee also recommended that the open date be advanced by a decade every ten years. In the event the open date was reviewed again in 1919, when it was brought forward more than a decade to 1860, except for correspondence relating to Newfoundland, the Falkland Islands, Malta and Gibraltar.[9] In 1925 it was brought forward further to 1878,[10] Law Officers' Reports now being no longer excluded and other exceptions being presently ended; in 1930 it was brought forward again to 1885.[11] This last open date remained in force until 1948, when it was extended to 1902.[12]

When the *Public Records Act 1958* came into effect in January 1959, the 'fifty-year rule' laid down in Section 5 opened records to the end of 1908 and thereafter a further year's records became open each January until 1966, when the Lord Chancellor made use of special powers under the Act to open records to the end of 1922.[13] Access is now governed by the *Public Records Act 1967*,[14] which introduced from

[1] F.O.83/232: draft, Malmesbury to Treasury, 28 May 1858.
[2] F.O.83/439: minute by E.Hertslet, 30 Aug. 1872.
[3] *Ibid.*: draft, Granville to P.R.O., 13 Nov. 1872.
[4] F.O.83/1158: draft, Sanderson to P.R.O., 28 March 1891, and enclosure; draft, Sanderson to Deputy Keeper, 14 July 1891; F.O.83/1249: minute by Hertslet, 30 May 1892.
[5] *1st Rpt. of R. Comm. on Public Records*, Part II, H.C.1912–13 [Cd.6395] XLIV, App.V.5, Schedule I. A.7; Schedule III.
[6] *Ibid.*, Schedule II.2.
[7] *Ibid.*, App.V.6.
[8] F.O.370/23, file 7526; *1st Rpt. of R. Comm. on Public Records*, Pt.III, qq.1562–1563.
[9] F.O.370/88, ff.54–55.
[10] F.O.370/203, file 1399.
[11] F.O.370/344, file 43.
[12] *110 D.K. Rpt.*, p.7.
[13] Instrument No.11 of 10 Feb. 1966.
[14] 15 & 16 Eliz.II, c.44.

1 January 1968 a 'thirty-year rule', opening the records then to the end of 1937 and making provision thereafter for the annual advancement of the open date on 1 January of each year. A few papers are closed for fifty years by Lord Chancellor's Instruments under Section 5(i) of the 1958 Act.

Listing

The first printed list of Foreign Office records was made in 1868 and included all the records in the Public Record Office at that time; that is to about 1783 (now *State Papers Foreign*).[1] This list was brought up to date in 1872 and again in 1883;[2] in 1886 a list of records open to general inspection, that is down to 1760, was printed.[3] These lists were not available for general sale. The numeration of pieces in them does not always correspond to that now in use.

The first published list was the *List of State Papers, Foreign, 1577–1781* (P.R.O. Lists and Indexes XIX) of 1904. This was followed in 1914 by the *List of Foreign Office Records, 1781–1837* (P.R.O. Lists and Indexes XLI), which was superseded in 1929 by the *List of Foreign Office Records to 1878* (P.R.O. Lists and Indexes LII). The first and third of these have now been reissued, with corrections and additions, by the Kraus Reprint Corporation, who have also issued a supplementary *List of Foreign Office Records* (P.R.O. Supplementary Lists and Indexes XIII) in eight volumes: *General Correspondence, 1879–1905* (Vols. 1–4), *Various Classes, 1879–1913* (Vol. 5) and *Embassy and Consular Archives, 1879–1913* (Vols. 6–8).

These and typescript lists of open records of a later date, together with various special means of reference, are available for consultation in the search rooms of the Public Record Office.

Elimination

The elimination of valueless Foreign Office records was long regarded as impracticable, one of the obstacles being the early stage at which they were bound up,[4] and not until 1895 did the Foreign Office subscribe to the Rules made under Section 1 of the *Public Record Office Act 1877*.[5] The Office's first two schedules under these Rules were further delayed until 1910 and even then related only to records already in the Public Record Office.[6] The *First Foreign Office Schedule* authorized the weeding of three classes of *Archives of Commissions: Slave Trade, Sierra Leone* (F.O.315); *British and Buenos Airean Claims, 1830* (F.O.307); and *British and Portuguese Claims, 1840* (F.O.309). It also authorized the destruction of some 'so-called' Registers of Correspondence, 1781–1796, compiled at a later date in the State Paper Office and said not to be an exhaustive means of reference; requests for letters of introduction, 1836–1857 (see p.78); postcards against the War with Greece, 1897; and illegible and irreparable fragments. The *Foreign Office (Paris Exhibition 1900) Schedule* authorized the weeding of the archives of the *Royal Commission for the Paris Exhibition of 1900* (F.O.311).

---

[1] P.R.O. Obsolete Indexes: OBS 710.
[2] OBS 710; OBS 886/7.
[3] OBS 877.
[4] *4th Rpt. of R. Comm. on Civil Estabs.* (1890), qq.27532, 27594–27595.
[5] *Statutes, Rules and Schedules governing the disposal of Public Records, 1877–1913* (1914), p.14.
[6] *Ibid.*, pp.304–308; *1st Rpt. of R. Comm. on Public Records*, Pt.III, qq.1615, 1622–1632; but see also q.1614.

The *Second Foreign Office Schedule* (No. 29)[1] of 1923 was the first to apply to records in the Foreign Office itself. It authorized the elimination of duplicates, minor and routine correspondence, documents relating to Messengers' expenses, formal letters authorizing free deliveries, consuls' life certificates,[2] and minor accounting records. To these the *Third Schedule* (No.117) of 1938 added copies of printed papers emanating from other government departments, records relating to the details of consular accounts, and papers (other than those of the Establishment and Finance Department) relating to the appointment, etc., of individual consular officers and to leave arrangements of members of the Diplomatic Service. The *Fourth Schedule* (No.202) of 1946 extended the elimination of records to the Establishment and Finance Department, providing for the destruction of records relating to accounts and to such establishment matters as accommodation, equipment and stationery unless they constituted precedents, were of political, legal or historical use or interest, contained important information not available from other sources or were otherwise specially ordered to be kept.

In addition there were special schedules for various departments of the Office. The *Foreign Office (Foreign Trade Department Archives) Schedule* (No.31) of 1924 provided for the elimination of correspondence, reports on individual firms, the 'country' registers and the indexes of the Foreign Trade Department. The *Foreign Office (Passport Office) Schedule* (No.211) of 1947 authorized the destruction of application forms for passports and visas, impounded and expired passports, minor or ephemeral correspondence and papers, and establishment and accounting records. Two schedules, the *Foreign Office (Control Office) Schedule* (No.205) of 1946 and the *Foreign Office (German Section) Schedule* (No.254) of 1950, regulated the elimination of valueless records of the Control Commissions established in Germany and Austria after World War II.

The elimination of material among consular archives was authorized by the *Foreign Office (Consular Archives) First Schedule* (No.30) of 1920, which provided for the destruction of duplicates, minor correspondence, marine protests, etc., applications for passports and visas, accounting records, and returns and other papers of minor or ephemeral importance. This was the first Foreign Office schedule to apply to records still accruing as opposed to those already in the Public Record Office. It was superseded by a *Second Schedule* (No.280) in 1953, which added to the categories of 1920 a wider range of shipping documents, and copies of notices of and caveats against marriages.[3] The *Foreign Office (Consular Archives: Tahiti) Schedule* (No.105) of 1936 authorized the transfer of certain correspondence and miscellaneous records of the Papeete Consulate, 1826–1888, which would otherwise have been destroyed, to the Mitchell Library, Sydney.[4]

With one exception archives of diplomatic missions were not subject to a schedule until 1946, when the *Foreign Office (Archives of H.M. Missions) Schedule* (No.200) was issued, authorizing the elimination of correspondence not of political

---

[1] The numbers in brackets following the titles of the schedules mentioned hereafter are those assigned to them in the collection of schedules from 1914 onwards kept in the search rooms of the Public Record Office. Where material in the classes of *General Correspondence* between 1915 and 1920 was weeded under this and the succeeding schedules an appropriate entry was made in the General Register (see p.73 above).

[2] For surviving specimens of records relating to Messengers' expenses and free deliveries see pp.75–76 above; for a specimen volume of consuls' life certificates see F.O.83/204. Other records in these three categories which were already in the P.R.O. in F.O.96 were destroyed (see OBS 1049/15).

[3] For specimens of records destroyed under this schedule see F.O.900/5–7.

[4] See also F.O.687/19.

or historical interest, duplicates, accounting records and minor or ephemeral documents. The exception was the Vienna Legation, closed in April 1938 on the annexa-
tion of Austria by Germany. The *Foreign Office (Vienna Mission Archives) Schedule*
(No.118) of December 1938 provided for the elimination of duplicates, minor
correspondence and minor accounting records of this legation.

The weeding of Foreign Office records under these schedules was quite extensive
so far as the non-political departments and embassy and consular archives were
concerned. The files of the political departments were, however, left largely complete until those for the period from the mid-1920s to the mid-1930s were extensively weeded by the stripping of individual papers during the transitional period
before the introduction of the present selection procedure. This is governed by the
Public Records Act 1958 and puts into practice the recommendations of the *Grigg
Report*. Under this procedure, where the subject of the file is considered of sufficient
importance to justify preservation, all the papers on it are preserved.[1]

Withdrawal of Records

Certain records created in the Foreign Office will now be found elsewhere than in
the *Foreign Office* group of records in the Public Record Office. Some passed for
administrative reasons to other government departments and have subsequently
come to the Public Record Office among the successor departments' records. Thus
when responsibility for the administration of Cyprus passed in 1880 from the
Foreign Office to the Colonial Office (see p.22) the records of the Cyprus Department, 1878–1880, passed with it and are now among the *Colonial Office* group of
records.[2] Similarly after World War I certain records of the War Trade Intelligence
and Statistical Departments passed to the Treasury Solicitor for Prize Court purposes and are now among the records of his Office at the Public Record Office (see
p.73).

The transfer of certain records of the Papeete Consulate direct to the Mitchell
Library, Sydney, has been mentioned in the preceding section.

In addition to records withdrawn for destruction under the schedules mentioned
above others have been withdrawn from the *Foreign Office* group after transfer to
the Public Record Office. In 1957 three classes of copies of *German Foreign Ministry
Documents* (F.O.520, 553, 584) were transferred to the *Captured Enemy Documents*
group (G.F.M.); they remain at the Public Record Office.[3] Four other classes of
copies of documents, the *War Crimes Trials, 1945–1951* (F.O.645–648), were transferred in 1966 to the Imperial War Museum.

The division of records between the *Foreign Office* group and *State Papers Foreign*
is, as we have seen, artificial (see p.33). It is not clear cut at 1782 and in some
classes of *State Papers Foreign* records of a considerably later date will be found (e.g.
S.P.81, 105, 110). In addition a stray Foreign Office record has been noted among
Home Office records (see p.59), probably as a result of misplacement in the State
Paper Office.

Extraneous Records

Similarly records relating to foreign affairs of an earlier date than 1782 will be found
in the *Foreign Office* group. In addition to individual strays from *State Papers Foreign*,
many of the country classes of *General Correspondence* go back to 1780 or 1781 and a
number go back even further (e.g. F.O.28, 41, 42, 57, 81; also F.O.83, 90, 366).

---

[1] *Documents on Brit. Foreign Policy*, Series IA, Vol.I, pp.x–xiii.
[2] The original correspondence is C.O.67/1–12, 14–15; the departmental diary is C.O.512/1.
[3] One class: *Series M* (G.F.M.2) was returned to the Foreign Office in 1968.

Moreover, as the Foreign Office on occasion handed over records to other government departments, so it received records when it in its turn took over functions formerly exercised by others. The most notable records taken over in this way are those relating to the Barbary consulates inherited in 1836 from the Colonial Office, which had in its turn inherited some from the Home Office. They go back beyond 1782. They are now among the *General Correspondence before 1906* in the following classes: *Algiers* (F.O.3), *Barbary States* (F.O.8), *Morocco, Series I* (F.O.52), *Tripoli, Series I* (F.O.76) and *Tunis, Series I* (F.O.77); and also in *Miscellanea, Series I* (F.O.95/164-167, 510, 518-521; cf. F.O.96/136) (see pp.30, 60, 80). Some related records have, however, remained among the records of the Colonial Office.[1]

Another class of Foreign Office records which originated elsewhere, in this case in the Home Office, is that of *General Correspondence before 1906, Corsica* (F.O.20). There appears to be no reason why this class should be in the Foreign Office group; it may be the result of rationalization in the State Paper Office. Two volumes of entry books related to these records are among Colonial Office records.[2]

Certain extraneous papers of various dates will be found in the class of *Miscellanea, Series I*. These include the D'Avaux papers, 1672-1701 (F.O.95/543-578), the *Mémoires Historiques* of the Marquis de Dangeau (F.O.95/579-588) and portions of the Bouillon papers, 1793-1812 (F.O.95/602-629), and Calonne papers, 1789-1792 (F.O.95/630-635). Other portions of the Bouillon papers will be found among the records of the Home Office, Privy Council Office and War Office and of the Calonne papers in the Privy Council Office records.[3]

---

[1] C.O.2/3-4, 6, 10; C.O.173/5. See Pugh, *Records of Col. and Dom. Offices*, pp.47-48.
[2] C.O.65. See Pugh, *Records of Col. and Dom. Offices*, p.74.
[3] The Bouillon papers are in H.O.69, P.C.1 and W.O.1 and the Calonne papers in P.C.1. See *Guide to the Contents of the Public Record Office* II, pp.183, 233-234, 305. There are typescript lists in the search rooms of the Public Record Office.

III. Specimen Searches

Coup d'état *of Louis Napoleon 1851*

By a *coup d'état* on the night of 1–2 December 1851 Louis Napoleon Bonaparte, President of the French Republic since 1848, instituted personal rule and perpetuated his powers beyond the four years permitted to the President by the constitution. A plebiscite of 14 December 1851 endorsed the *coup* and gave Louis Napoleon powers to promulgate a new constitution, which he did on 14 January 1852. On 2 December 1852, after a further plebiscite, he proclaimed himself Emperor as Napoleon III.

Meanwhile in London Viscount Palmerston, the Secretary of State for Foreign Affairs, had met Count Walewski, the French Ambassador, on 3 December 1851 and expressed his approval of the *coup*. However, the instructions given by the Queen and Cabinet on 4 December and embodied in Palmerston's official despatch to the Marquis of Normanby, the British Ambassador in Paris, was that Normanby should take a passive attitude. In communicating the contents of this despatch to Turgot, the French Foreign Minister, Normanby interpreted it as implying British disapproval of the *coup*, but he was thereupon informed of Palmerston's private expression of approval. Relations between Palmerston and both Court and Cabinet were already strained, and when his conversation with Walewski became known, it provided a suitable opportunity to replace him. Accordingly on 19 December, Lord John Russell, the Prime Minister, dismissed him and appointed Earl Granville in his place. The formal changeover occurred a week later. Further changes followed, for on 3 February 1852 Lord Cowley replaced Normanby as Ambassador to France and on 27 February the Earl of Malmesbury succeeded Granville as Secretary of State on a change of ministry.

This general outline is given in the standard histories[1] and can be filled out from the published biographies and correspondence of those involved in events,[2] but anyone wishing to compile a fuller account of the British reaction to Louis Napoleon's *coup* will need to go behind the printed sources and to consult the Foreign Office records in the Public Record Office.

There the starting point will be the official despatches between Palmerston and Normanby in the class of *General Correspondence before 1906, France* (F.O.27). Reference to the *List of Foreign Office records to 1878* (P.R.O. Lists and Indexes LII), p.79, gives F.O.27/897 as the volume containing drafts of despatches to Normanby, November–December 1851, and F.O.27/905 as the volume containing his despatches to the Foreign Office for the same period. Most of the contents of these two volumes from 2 December 1851 onwards are concerned with the *coup* and in this particular case the searcher will probably not hesitate to work through the volumes themselves, although if he prefers he can discover in advance precisely which despatches are relevant, thus restricting his search somewhat, by first consulting the *Library Register* for France, 1850–1851 (F.O.802/177 [Ind.28864]).[3]

---

[1] For example, *New Cambridge Modern History* X (1960), pp.442–446; *Camb. Hist. of Brit. For. Policy*, II, pp.325–340, III, pp.575–576.

[2] For example, E.Ashley, *Life of Viscount Palmerston*, I (1876); *Letters of Queen Victoria*, II (1908); G.P.Gooch, *Later Correspondence of Lord John Russell*, II (1925); Lord Edmond Fitzmaurice, *Life of Earl Granville*, I (1905). In this case no relevant material was published in the Blue Books (see H.Temperley and L.M.Penson, *A Century of Diplomatic Blue Books, 1814–1914* (1938)), but in other cases these may be a valuable published source.

[3] For an explanation of this double reference see p.109, n.2.

There under the heading 'Foreign 1851' will be found listed first the drafts to Normanby (pp.548–556), then the despatches from him (pp.628–640).

Whichever way is chosen, the searcher will find his attention directed to Normanby's despatch no.360 of 2 December announcing the *coup* and enclosing copies of proclamations, followed by nos.361 and 363 of the same date (no.362 concerns another subject) and nos.364 and 366 of 3 December giving further details. A third despatch of 3 December, no.365, asks for instructions on the line he should take in his relations with the French government. All these are in F.O.27/905. Bound with no.365 in that volume are minutes by Palmerston of 4 December giving instructions for drafting a reply, for its submission to the Queen for approval and for its despatch on 5 December.[1] The draft itself, no.600 of 5 December, accompanied by a minute by Palmerston of the same date recording the Queen's approval, is in F.O.27/897. A considerable amount of further correspondence on the subject follows in the two volumes, including Normanby's despatch no.372 of 6 December, recounting his interview with Turgot.[2] It will be noticed that with the succession of Granville on 26 December a new numbered series of both drafts and despatches commences.

Having consulted the main diplomatic correspondence, the searcher will then wish to see what relevant material there is in the other correspondence for 1851 in F.O.27. Of this nine volumes might be relevant: six of consular correspondence (F.O.27/906–911), one of correspondence with various attachés, etc. (F.O.27/912), one of correspondence with Count Walewski, September–December 1851 (F.O. 27/917), and one of domestic various correspondence, November–December 1851 (F.O.27/923). Much of this can be expected to be routine and the searcher will certainly save time at this stage by first consulting the *Library Register* (F.O. 802/177). There under the heading 'Consuls 1851', he will find that of the consuls in France only Bonham at Calais recorded for the Foreign Office any account of local reactions to the *coup* and its aftermath (pp.649–650). Bonham's correspondence, including the despatches in which he did this (no.31 of 3 December, no.33 of 12 December and no.34 of 22 December), will be found by reference to the *List* to be in F.O.27/906. Also in the *Register*, under the heading 'Foreign (Attaché) 1851', the searcher will find a note of a despatch from R.Edwardes of 8 December enclosing a report on the state of affairs in France (p.749); this despatch will be found in F.O. 27/912. There is no reference under the heading 'Domestic 1851' to any correspondence with Walewski on the subject, but under 'Domestic Various 1851' (pp.901, 903, 905) will be found references to a letter from C.Corbett of 12 December enclosing a memorial from Sheffield asking for the recall of the Ambassador from Paris in protest at the *coup* (acknowledged 17 December), a letter from A.Rae of 29 December enclosing a similar memorial from Hamilton and a Foreign Office memorandum of 31 December on the agreement of 1815 for the permanent exclusion of the Bonaparte family from France. These will be found in F.O.27/923.

As a check that all the relevant material in the *General Correspondence* has been traced, the searcher should examine the entries for December 1851 in the *Departmental Diaries* for France: political, 1850–1852 (F.O.566/159 [Ind.22848]), and consular, 1848–1857 (F.O.566/158 [Ind.22847]). These show that the only relevant material not in the volumes of F.O.27 already consulted are circulars of 26 and 27

---

[1] Minutes might also be sought in the loose minutes in *Miscellanea, Series II*. None of these for 1851 (F.O.96/23) appear to be relevant to this particular enquiry.

[2] Palmerston's despatch no.600, Normanby's no.372 and two further despatches (Normanby's no.406 of 15 December and Palmerston's no.617 of 16 December) were printed in the *Confidential Print* (F.O.881/253).

December to Normanby from Palmerston and Granville respectively and of 27 December to Walewski from Granville announcing the change of Secretary of State. Such circulars, which are purely formal, will be found in the class of *General Correspondence, Great Britain and General* (F.O.83); reference to the *List*, p.260, shows that these particular ones are among Circulars to Ministers and Consuls Abroad, 1849–1851 (F.O.83/126), and Circulars to Foreign Ministers in London, Volume 2, 1843–1855 (F.O.83/144).

The next step will be to examine the archives of the British Embassy in Paris. These will be found in the classes of *Embassy and Consular Archives, France, Correspondence* (F.O.146) and *Registers* (F.O.147). As most *Embassy and Consular Archives* (apart from *Registers*) are kept at Ashridge and require advance notice for production in London, the searcher will probably find it advisable to check first the relevant *Register* (kept in London) to discover whether the *Correspondence* contains any material not in the *Foreign Office General Correspondence*. The *Register* for 1851, which is shown by the *List*, p.365, to be F.O.147/34 [Ind.13556], reveals no additional correspondence with the Foreign Office and nothing relevant among the correspondence with the French Foreign Ministry. The correspondence with consuls does, however, include three despatches (of 5, 8 and 24 December) from the consul at Marseilles, commenting on reaction there to the *coup* and plebiscite. These will be found from the *List*, p.355, to be in F.O.146/430.

Although the *Register* shows that the *Correspondence* with the Foreign Office contains no new material, the searcher may nevertheless decide to examine it to discover whether there are any minutes or memoranda or any significant amendments to drafts. Despatches from the Foreign Office, November–December 1851, are in F.O. 146/420–421, and drafts to the Foreign Office, October–December 1851, in F.O. 146/426. Examination of these shows that, as is common at this period, they include only unminuted despatches and fair copies of drafts.

The searcher may next wish to take his research further by studying how far British reactions were influenced by those of other countries. Starting, for example, with Prussia, he will first consult the *Library Register* for Prussia, 1849–1851 (F.O.802/434 [Ind. 29121]). Here in the 'Foreign' section will be found references to relevant despatches from Henry Francis Howard, Secretary of Legation and Chargé d'Affaires in Berlin (pp.476–483).[1] This *Register* describes the class of *General Correspondence before 1906, Prussia and Germany* (F.O.64) and reference to the *List*, p.161, shows that Howard's despatches, November–December 1851, are in F.O.64/334. The enquiry could be further extended to *Embassy and Consular Archives, Germany: Prussia and Germany* (F.O.244–246) and to the *General Correspondence before 1906* and the *Embassy and Consular Archives* for other countries.

Having exhausted the official records, the searcher should next turn to the private correspondence of those involved in the events. Here it will be very largely necessary to go outside the Public Record Office and to track down the relevant private collections with the aid of the National Register of Archives. But within the Public Record Office will be found two private collections of considerable importance to the study of this particular subject: the *Russell Papers* (P.R.O.30/22) and the *Granville Papers* (P.R.O.30/29).[2] In the former will be found correspondence of Lord John

[1] The *Library Index* for Prussia and Germany, 1810–1890 (F.O.802/442 [Ind.29129]), might in some similar cases restrict the search in the *Register* itself, but in this case it would be misleading as there are references in it to only three of the relevant despatches: to no.136 under the heading 'France, President, Powers of', and to nos.148 and 141 under 'France, recognition of Emperor'; but not to nos.127 and 132.

[2] See pp.166,169. These classes are listed in *Gifts and Deposits*, Pt.2 (List and Index Society, 11), pp.19–33, and Pt.1 (L. & I. Soc.10), pp.169–212, respectively.

Russell with Palmerston and Normanby in December 1851 and copies of letters to him from Queen Victoria and Prince Albert on the subject of the *coup* (P.R.O. 30/22/9J); in the latter is a certain amount of correspondence relating to Granville's first brief period at the Foreign Office (P.R.O.30/29/18 and 20).

Each of the above enquiries will need to be extended if they are to cover the British government's reactions to events in France in 1852. One further source in the Public Record Office, the *Cowley Papers* (F.O.519),[1] will also prove of value if such an extension is undertaken.

The Kruger Telegram 1896

An invasion by a secretly recruited military force led by Dr. Jameson (hence known as the 'Jameson Raid'), launched on 29 December 1895 to coincide with an abortive insurrection aimed at obtaining from the Transvaal government a recognition of equality for *Uitlanders*, i.e. non-Boer settlers, ended in failure with Jameson's surrender on 2 January 1896. A telegram from the Emperor William II of Germany congratulating President Kruger of the Transvaal on his success in defeating the invaders was regarded in Britain as a provocative intervention in a purely British affair and for a while Anglo-German relations became strained.

A study of the effect of the telegram on British foreign policy will start with the African Department's *Register*, 1896, and the *Index* to it, 1891–1896 (F.O.566/1645 [Ind.28399] and F.O.804/1 [Ind.29366] respectively).[2] In this case the searcher will probably wish to work through the whole of the section of the *Register* tagged 'Berlin', but to use the *Index* to pick out relevant material in other sections.

In the 'Berlin' section of the *Register* (pp.23–41) are registered all the 1896 Africa series despatches and telegrams from and to Sir Frank Lascelles, the British Ambassador in Berlin, or the Chargé d'Affaires in his absence. News of the Kaiser's telegram is contained in Lascelles' telegram no.2 of 3 January, followed by despatches nos.3 and 5 of 4 January giving details of reactions in the German press. Over the next few days more telegrams and despatches concerning the telegram follow and correspondence concerning the Transvaal continues spasmodically throughout the year.

At this particular period the Africa series of correspondence with each British diplomatic or consular representative is to be found in the appropriate country class of *General Correspondence before 1906*;[3] in this case in *General Correspondence before 1906, Prussia and Germany* (F.O.64). Reference to the *List of Foreign Office Records* (P.R.O. Supplementary Lists and Indexes XIII), Vol. 3 (*General Correspondence, 1879–1905, Japan–Saxony*), pp.186–187, shows that the Africa series drafts to Lascelles for 1896 are in F.O.64/1385, despatches from him in F.O.64/1386–1388 and telegrams to and from him in F.O.64/1389.

References in the African Department *Register* to further correspondence on the general subject of the Transvaal and on the Emperor's telegram in particular may be most readily discovered by using the *Index*. There under 'Transvaal, Incursion of Dr. Jameson, Emperor of Germany's congratulatory telegram to President Kruger'

---

[1] See p.165. There is a list in *List of Foreign Office Records to 1878* (1963 reprint only), pp.442–472.

[2] To fill in the background it will also be necessary to work back using the 1895 *Register* (F.O. 566/1644 [Ind.28398]) and the corresponding records. German reactions may also be studied in the photocopies of *Captured Enemy Documents* (G.F.M.) (see p.96 above). A copy of the *Catalogue of German Foreign Ministry Files and Microfilms 1867–1920* (1959) and other finding aids are kept in the search rooms of the Public Record Office.

[3] Before 1893 such correspondence is in the class of *General Correspondence before 1906, Slave Trade* (F.O.84); from 1901 to 1905 it is in *General Correspondence before 1906, Africa* (F.O.2) (see pp.55-56).

are references to pp.95, 328 and 330 of the *Register*, as well as to pages within the 'Berlin' section already consulted. On p.95 of the *Register* is an entry of a despatch (no.8 political of 24 January) from Mr. Strachey, the British Minister to Saxony, reporting comments by the King of Saxony on the Emperor's telegram; reference to the supplementary *List of Foreign Office Records*, Vol. 3, p.268, for *General Correspondence before 1906, Saxony* (F.O.68) will locate this despatch in F.O.68/181. On pp.328 and 330 of the *Register* are entries in the 'South of Zambezi' section[1] of drafts to the Colonial Office transmitting copies of despatches and telegrams from Lascelles. These are marked 'O', which indicates that no drafts were kept.[2] Had drafts been kept they would have to be sought under the heading 'Miscellaneous: Africa' in the *Great Britain and General* class (correspondence for 1896 being in F.O. 83/1440–1452).[3]

Entries in other sections of the *Register* may also be found by following up cross-references from entries in the 'Berlin' section. For example, the entry of Lascelles' telegram no.2 has the cross-reference '10SZ' in red ink: this refers to entry no.10 in the out-letters of the 'South of Zambezi', section, which relates to one of the drafts to the Colonial Office already discovered by use of the *Index*. (Although in this case the following up of a cross-reference provides no new material, it need not always be so).

Having exhausted the African Department correspondence, the searcher will be advised to consult the main political (diplomatic) correspondence relating to Germany. Here again the starting point will be the *Register*, this time the Germany sections of the Western Department's *Register*, 1896–1900, and the Germany *Index*, 1891–1905 (F.O.566/758 [Ind.24941] and F.O.804/24 [Ind.29389] respectively). In the *Index* under 'Transvaal, Kaiser's telegrams to Kruger' is a reference to p.11 of the *Register*,[4] where it relates to Lascelles' despatch no.59 of 4 March. Under 'Transvaal Affairs' and 'Transvaal and Germany' will be found further references to pp.5, 16 and 18 of the *Register*. On p.5 the relevant entries are of Lascelles' despatches nos.19 and 25 and telegram no.10, the last two of which are marked '(African Dept.)'.[5] On pp.16 and 18 the relevant entries are of drafts nos.88, 89 and 118 to Lascelles and a draft of 13 May to the Colonial Office. The entry of draft no.89 could also be discovered by following up the cross-references from the entry of Lascelles' despatch no.59; the other three entries are all of transmitting drafts and are marked 'O'.

The records themselves (including despatch no.25 and telegrams no.10) are among the political correspondence for 1896 in the *General Correspondence before 1906, Prussia and Germany* (F.O.64), the despatches from Lascelles in F.O.64/1376, telegram no.10 in F.O.64/1380 and draft no.89 in F.O.64/1375.

Much of the correspondence with Lascelles concerning the Transvaal will be found in the Confidential Print, 'Affairs South of the Zambezi, Part XIII, January–June 1896' (F.O.881/6910).[6]

---

[1] In this section is registered the African Department's correspondence relating to southern Africa with (i) foreign ministers in London ('domestic'), (ii) other government departments and (iii) institutions and individuals; the two latter categories are known as 'domestic various'.
[2] See Appendix II(b).
[3] Before 1893 the Slave Trade and Africa series of domestic various correspondence is in F.O.84; from 1899 to 1905 the Africa series is in F.O.2 (see pp.55-56).
[4] References to this page are also given under the headings 'Kruger' and 'Transvaal and Germany'.
[5] Despatch no.25 is also entered in the African Department *Register* (F.O.566/1645, p.23).
[6] There is another copy in F.O.403/231. There is no Foreign Office Blue Book on the Transvaal or on relations with Germany at this date (see Temperley and Penson, *Century of Dipl. Blue Books*), and, with a few minor exceptions, Foreign Office correspondence is omitted from the Colonial Office Blue Books: H.C.1896 (C.7933 and C.8063) LIX, 445 and 559.

Examination of the archives of the Berlin Embassy, which are in *Embassy and Consular Archives, Germany: Prussia and Germany, Correspondence* (F.O.244) and *Registers of Correspondence* (F.O.246), will be the next step, starting with the *Register* for 1896 (F.O.246/27 [Ind.14306]). This suggests that the *Correspondence* itself includes no material additional to that in the *General Correspondence* of the Foreign Office. A check of the Embassy's Africa series of Correspondence of 1896, which the *List of Foreign Office Records* (Supplementary), Vol. 7 (*Embassy and Consular Archives, 1879–1913, Colombia–Portugal*), pp.164–165, shows to be in F.O.244/541–543, will reveal no unregistered minutes or memoranda and only fair copies of drafts.

Turning to private papers, those of Sir Frank Lascelles are in the class of *Private Collections: Ministers and Officials: Various* (F.O.800/6–20), which the search room list will show contains material for this period in F.O.800/9, a volume of correspondence relating to Germany addressed to Lascelles, 1895–1900, and F.O.800/17, an entry book of correspondence written by him, 1894–1900. A valuable collection of private letters from Cecil Spring-Rice, at that time Second Secretary in Berlin, will also be found in this class in the papers of Francis Villiers (F.O.800/23). There are also papers of Sir Thomas Sanderson, the Permanent Under Secretary, including in F.O.800/1 an important minute of 5 January 1896 on Anglo-German relations; and of G.N.Curzon, the Parliamentary Under-Secretary (F.O.800/28, 147), which, however, contain nothing on this particular subject (see pp.165, 167, 169).

The Foreign Office was not the only government department with an interest in the Kruger telegram and its aftermath. Mention has already been made of the transmission of copies of despatches to the Colonial Office. These will be found, together with accompanying Colonial Office minutes and other Colonial Office correspondence in the Colonial Office class of *Africa, South, Original Correspondence* (C.O.417), where correspondence with the Foreign Office for 1896 occupies six volumes (C.O. 417/189–194). The matter, as might be expected, also came before the Cabinet. Reference to the search room list of the Cabinet Office class of *Photographic Copies of Cabinet Letters in the Royal Archives* (Cab.41),[1] shows that South African affairs were discussed on 11 January 1896, and examination of Lord Salisbury's letter reporting this meeting (Cab.41/23, no.42) shows that the telegram was included in the discussion.

General Huerta and Anglo-Mexican Relations 1913

The Mexican revolution of 1910–1911, which ended the rule of President Profirio Diaz, was followed by ten years of almost continuous civil war, including periods of intervention by the United States in 1914 and 1916. The first President after the 1910–1911 revolution, Francisco Madero, was deposed on 19 February 1913 (he was subsequently assassinated) by General Victoriano Huerta, who became Provisional President until he was in turn ousted in the middle of 1914.

A searcher wishing to see how the events of 1913 affected Anglo-Mexican relations in general will probably not think it impracticable to work through the whole of the Foreign Office political correspondence relating to Mexico for the year. This will be found in the class of *General Correspondence after 1906, Political* (F.O.371), which the *List of Foreign Office Records* (Supplementary), Vol. 5 (*Various Classes, 1879–1913*), p.174, will show to contain twelve volumes relating to Mexico: F.O. 371/1670–1681. The card index will indicate any relevant papers not among the Mexico political correspondence for the year and may limit the search by showing

---

[1] Published as *Cabinet Letters at Windsor, 1868–1916* (List and Index Society 5).

which papers within the Mexico political correspondence are likely to be of most importance; it would be essential to consult it if the subject were more limited or the bulk of the correspondence greater.

In the card index under the general heading 'Mexico' will be found several sub-headings, of which 'Revolution in' is the largest. The first entry under this sub-heading is   26/6706/6269/13: British ship to go to Mexico

which is a reference to the Mexico political correspondence (index number 26),[1] paper 6706 in file 6269[2] of 1913. The *List* shows that file 6269 occupies nine volumes (F.O.371/1671–1679), and that of these F.O.371/1671 contains papers ('pp') 6269 to 13384. Hence it is in this volume that the searcher will look for paper 6706. (It is to be found on ff.17–21). The registered paper itself is a telegram from the British Minister to Guatemala conveying a report of the consul at Salina Cruz of events in Mexico City (f.18); it is in the accompanying draft of a letter to the Admiralty that the reference to sending a ship to Mexico occurs (f.21) (See Plates II and III).

Most of the references under the general heading 'Mexico' and its various sub-headings are to papers in the Mexico political correspondence (index number 26) and particularly to file 6269, but there are some with different references and of these three appear to be of some significance.[3]

Under 'Mexico: Revolution' will be found the entries:

    51/50003/13: U.S. allegation that Huerta was recognised by H.M.G.
         in return for oil contracts denied by Pearsons; and
    8/53975/13: U.S. force Honduras to endorse their policy.

The index numbers show that both are among the political correspondence, the former under 'America: General', the latter under 'Central America'. That both are single papers and not part of files is shown by the single registry number. References to the *List*, pp.183 and 170, will show that the papers are in F.O.371/1873 and F.O. 371/1587 respectively.

Under 'Mexico: Ruling family' will be found a reference to the correspondence relating to the formal recognition of Huerta as President: '326/F11196/13'. The index number 326 indicates Treaty Department correspondence relating to Mexico, which is in *General Correspondence after 1906, Treaty* (F.O.372); F11196/13 indicates file 11196 in that correspondence for 1913. The *List*, p.208, shows that this file is in F.O.372/448. The file originally included Huerta's autograph letter announcing his accession and a draft of King George V's reply (papers 13809 and 15282 respectively), but although the docket sheets and the accompanying minutes, translations and covering letters are still there, the letter and draft themselves are not. This is because royal letters were removed from the *General Correspondence* and bound up separately; they are in the class of *Miscellanea, Series I* (F.O.95). Reference to the search room list of this class will show that royal letters for 1913–1914 are in F.O. 95/766 and Huerta's letter and the draft reply will be found in the 'Mexico' section of this volume.

In addition to the heading 'Mexico' other possible headings in the card index

---

[1] See Appendix II(d).

[2] Before the middle of 1909 the file number would not be given and would have to be discovered from the appropriate volume of the *General Register* (F.O.566).

[3] Other references are to papers of minor importance in the *General Correspondence after 1906, Commercial* (F.O.368), *Consular* (F.O.369) and *Treaty* (F.O.372) classes. All these papers appear to have been preserved, but in a search for similar papers between 1915 and 1919–1920, which are more extensively weeded, it would be advisable to consult the *General Registers* (F.O.566) before the *Correspondence* itself to make sure the papers have not been destroyed (where they have been the *Registers* are marked 'Not Kept').

might be tried. For example, under 'Huerta' there are a number of references to papers in the Mexico political correspondence.

Before 1906, as we have seen from the two previous specimen searches, when a third country was involved in events it was necessary to look in the *General Correspondence* for that country as well as in that for the country primarily concerned. But from 1906 the country arrangement of papers in the *General Correspondence* classes is according to the countries to which papers relate, not to those from which they have come. Thus reference to the card index under 'Mexico: Revolution in' reveals an entry

26/11957/6269/13: German Gt. will not recognise President until formally elected.

When the paper (in F.O.371/1671) is examined, it proves to be a telegram from the British Ambassador in Berlin. Similarly reference to the card index under 'United States' reveals that papers dealing with U.S.–Mexican relations have the index number 26 and will be found, therefore, in the Mexico political correspondence.

As a final check the *General Register*, especially the political volume (F.O.566/1157 [Ind.27908]), might be consulted.[1]

The more important papers from the *General Correspondence* are confidentially printed in 'Further Correspondence respecting the Affairs of North America, Part VIII, 1913' (F.O.881/10472).[2] In this and other Confidential Prints of the period register numbers are given but not full references. Hence a searcher starting with the Confidential Print and wishing to compare any of its contents with the original papers will find it necessary to refer first to the *Central (Numerical) Register* for 1913 (F.O.662/15–17 [Ind.28633–28635]) to discover which department dealt with each paper and under which country it is kept (this stage may be omitted if the paper's origin is self evident) and then to the appropriate volume of the *General Register* (in F.O.566) to discover the 'kept with' or file number.

The *Embassy and Consular Archives, Mexico,* include two series of *Correspondence;* at this period *Series I* (F.O.203) contains the records of the Consulate-General and *SeriesII* (F.O.204) those of the Legation. There is also a class of *Registers* (F.O.206). The *Series II* correspondence for 1913 (omitting the commercial correspondence) is in F.O.204/417–430; the corresponding *Register* is F.O.206/25 [Ind.20285].[3] The *Register* will indicate any relevant material additional to that already seen in the Foreign Office *General Correspondence*. This will be found to be mainly correspondence with consuls and miscellaneous correspondence, which includes some with the United States Ambassador to Mexico. The correspondence with the Foreign Office duplicates the *General Correspondence*, although the drafts may be of some interest since they are originals, showing the various stages of drafting, not fair copies.

Relations with Mexico do not appear to have been discussed in the Cabinet. There is no mention of Mexico in the 1913 sections of the search room list of *Photographic Copies of Cabinet Letters in the Royal Archives* (Cab.41) or of the *List of Cabinet Papers, 1880–1914* (P.R.O. Handbook no.4).

Turning to private papers, the searcher will find those of the Secretary of State at the time, Sir Edward Grey, in the Public Record Office in the class of *Private Collections: Ministers and Officials: Various* (F.O.800/35–113). F.O.800/113 [Ind.

---

[1] Papers are entered in the *General Register* for both the county of origin and the country to which they relate and under which they are kept. Cross-references should enable every relevant document to be traced.
[2] There is another copy in F.O.414/235.
[3] See *List of Foreign Office Records* (Supplementary), Vol.7, pp.306–307, 311.

H

29436] is a contents list of these papers and reference to it shows that there is material for 1913 relating to Mexico in the volumes for Central America (F.O. 800/43) and the United States (F.O.800/83) and in the Foreign Office memoranda, 1912–1914 (F.O.800/94). Relevant material might also be found in the papers of Sir Arthur Nicolson, the Permanent Under-Secretary; those for 1913 are in F.O. 800/362–371. The papers of Lord Bryce, Ambassador in Washington until April 1913, (F.O.800/331–335) contain nothing for 1913, but there are some papers of Sir Cecil Spring-Rice, his successor (F.O.800/241) (see pp.164, 166, 168, 169).

Kreditanstalt *and the 1931 Financial Crisis*

The failure of the Austrian bank *Kreditanstalt für Handel und Gewerbe* in May 1931 is generally taken to be the event which precipitated the severe financial crisis which affected first Austria, then Germany, and subsequently spread throughout Europe. International efforts to save the situation were mounted, involving considerable diplomatic activity in which the British Government was a major participant. *Documents on British Foreign Policy, 1919–1939*, Second Series, Vol. II (1947), prints only a selection of the Foreign Office records resulting from this activity and those that are printed are not accompanied by the related minutes. Consequently for full details of Britain's part it is necessary to consult the records themselves.

The starting point for such a search will be the *Indexes (Printed Series) to General Correspondence* (F.O.409), those for 1931 being F.O.409/45 and 46 [Ind.24245 and 24246].[1]

Looking first under 'Kredit Anstalt' (p.876) the searcher is referred to 'Banks and Banking: Austria (Credit Anstalt)'. There (p.166) he will find a number of references, the first, for example, being

> Proposed appointment of M.Rist as Comptroller of the Credit Anstalt. C3738/61/3.

This is Central Department paper 3738 on file 61 of the Austria political correspondence.[2] The paper itself will be in the class of *General Correspondence after 1906, Political* (F.O.371) and reference to the Central Department, 1931, section of the search room list will show that file 61 of the Austria correspondence occupies six volumes (F.O.371/15150–15155), paper 3738 being in F.O.371/15150.

There is reference is only to one paper, but some are to a series of papers, not necessarily all in the same file, as, for example:

> Govt. guarantee of credits for reconstruction purposes: text of bills. C3745/C3761/61/3/C3686/3126/3/C4759/61/3.

This refers to Central Department papers 3745 and 3761 on file 61, paper 3686 on file 3126 and paper 4759 on file 61, all in the Austria political correspondence. The first two papers should be found in F.O.371/15150,[3] the third in F.O.371/15165 and the fourth in F.O.371/15151.

All the references under 'Banks and Banking: Austria (Credit Anstalt)' are to file 61 of the Austria political correspondence, except that to file 3126 just cited and one other:

> Bankruptcy of Credit Anstalt: effect in Poland. N4864/4864/55.

This refers to Northern Department paper 4864 on file 4864 of the Poland political correspondence; the paper will be found, by looking under Poland in the Northern Department, 1931, section of the search room list, to be in F.O.371/15585.

---

[1] There is also a set on open access at the Public Record Office.
[2] See Appendix II(d) and (e).
[3] For the docket sheet of paper C3745 see Plate IV. Paper C3761 has not been preserved.

The *Index* gives a cross-reference from 'Banks and Banking: Austria (Credit Anstalt)' to the sub-heading which precedes it, 'Banks and Banking: Austria'. Here again the references are mainly to file 61 of the Austria political correspondence with one reference to another file (150) of the same correspondence. A further cross-reference leads to 'Austria (Financial and Economic Crisis)' (p.134), which in turn leads to 'Austria: Finances' (p.135). Again the references are to files (mainly file 61) of the Austria political correspondence, but under the last heading there is the reference

> Appointment of M.Rost as financial adviser to Government.
> C8992/8992/62.

This refers to Central Department paper 8992 on file 8992 of the Central: General political correspondence. The paper itself is in F.O.371/15208.

The search may be extended to other countries by looking under other country sub-headings of the general heading 'Banks and Banking' and under the sub-headings 'Financial and Economic Crisis' and 'Finances' of various country headings. For example, under 'Banks and Banking: Hungary' (p.170), 'Hungary (Financial and Economic Crisis)' (p.766) and 'Hungary: Finances' (pp.766–767) are references to many relevant Central Department papers in file 2307 of the Hungary political correspondence, which is in F.O.371/15244–15245.

Other general headings, such as 'Finance' (pp.603–604) and 'Europe' (pp.567–568), will produce reference to further papers, particularly to file 172 of the Central: General political correspondence, which is in F.O.371/15181–15203. As the search progresses, further headings, such as the names of persons involved, will suggest themselves.

Search should also be made in the index to 'green' (secret) papers for 1931 in F.O. 409/103 [Ind.29859]. Here under 'Austria' will be found the reference

> Financial situation and French policy. C.4017/73/18/C.4037/4037/62.

This refers to Central Department paper 4017 on file 73 of the Germany political correspondence and to Central Department paper and file 4037 of the Central: General political correspondence. These 'green' papers, although originally kept separately, have now been filed in their proper places and are to be found in F.O. 371/15219 and 15208 respectively. A similar search under other relevant headings will produce further references.

Much of the correspondence is printed in the *Confidential Print*, mainly in the series *Europe, Central* (F.O.404) and *Germany* (F.O.408), the 1931 volumes being F.O.404/22–23 and F.O.408/57–58 respectively. Here papers are printed with their full references, which can be used to locate the originals and related papers. Full references are also given for papers printed in *Documents on British Foreign Policy*.

The records of the British Legation at Vienna are in the classes *Embassy and Consular Archives, Austria, Correspondence* (F.O.120) and *Registers* (F.O.122). By this date the *Correspondence* is arranged in annual subject files, the key to which is the series of annual indexes of correspondence in the class of *Registers*.[1] The index for 1931 is F.O.122/33 [Ind.19058], which is made up of three sections: (i) an index of correspondents; (ii) an index of subjects and persons; (iii) an index of file titles with a

---

[1] It cannot be stated that these are fully typical of *Embassy and Consular Archives* at this period, as each post had its own system of record keeping, registration and indexes; it was, however, general practice to keep records in subject files. At the same time the uneven application of destruction schedules and the varying effects of World War II mean that fewer records survive from some posts than from others. Users of *Embassy and Consular Archives* must be left to discover for themselves precisely how the means of reference to the archives of any particular post work and to what extent the records themselves survive.

contents list of each file. Subjects which are also file titles appear in section (ii) only when they are mentioned in files other than the main one. Reference to section (iii) shows that 'Credit Anstalt' is the title of file 211; reference under the same heading to section (ii) reveals a number of relevant papers in other files. One such entry in section (ii) reads

> 108/8/31   Dr. Schürff on urgency of reconstruction. Banks in Germany etc. shaky.

This refers to paper 8 on file 108 of 1931, the subject of which is given in the register of file numbers, 1928–1937 (F.O.122/45 [Ind.19070]), as 'Internal General'. From the search room list it will be found that the main 'Credit Anstalt' file, file 211, is in F.O.120/1054; file 108 is in F.O.120/1050.

The files are much more informative than earlier correspondence in *Embassy and Consular Archives*. They include original drafts showing amendments and additions, and also minutes and memoranda. Files on subjects of minor importance have not been kept; dummy sheets giving the file numbers and subjects are bound in their place. There is no notation for weeded files in the index or register of file numbers. Details of the contents of weeded files may be discovered from section (iii) of the index.

Additional material will be found in the papers of Arthur Henderson, the Secretary of State, and Orme Sargent, Counsellor in the Central Department at the time, in the class of *Private Collections: Ministers and Officials: Various* (F.O.800/280–284 and 272–279 respectively) (see pp.166, 169). Henderson's papers for 1931 are in F.O.800/283–284; Sargent's papers are arranged on a country basis with an index of countries at the beginning of F.O.800/272. This indicates that material relating to Austria is in that same volume.

The financial crisis was not, of course, an affair confined to the Foreign Office. It occupied the attention of the Cabinet and is represented therefore in the Cabinet Office records. For example, the index to the class of *Cabinet Minutes* for 1928–1932 (Cab.23/74 [Ind.30106]) mentions under 'Austria' a discussion of the financial situation there. The reference given, 34(31)1, indicates minute 1 of the 34th meeting of 1931, which will be found in Cab.23/67. Other Cabinet Office classes which should be consulted are *Cabinet Papers* (Cab.24), *Committees: General Series* (Cab.27) and *International Conferences* (Cab.29). The last class includes papers of the international conference on financial matters held in London in July 1931 (Cab.29/136–137).

The crisis also concerned the Treasury, where records relating to it may be found in the class of *Finance Files* (T.160). At this period there are annual subject indexes to this class on the search room shelves and a search in these will produce references to relevant material. Thus, for example, under '*FINANCE* Loans: General' in 1931[1] is the entry 'German financial crisis. Position of Bank of England in connection with credit'; the file number is F12505/013, the period covered by it 22 July to 18 August 1931 and the box no.401. The file will, therefore, be found in T.160/401.

Other records in the Public Record Office which might be consulted on this topic are the *League of Nations Assembly and Council Documents* (P.R.O.30/52) (see pp.86, 167) and the various classes of *Captured Enemy Documents* (G.F.M.).

---

[1] The date of each annual index is that in which the relevant files closed; as files often cover several years, the indexes for quite a period must be consulted.

IV. Annotated List of Record Classes[1]

GENERAL CORRESPONDENCE
Registers and Indexes[2]
Registers of General Correspondence (F.O.566)   1817–1920

These include departmental diaries, 1817–1890 (see p.34–39), departmental registers, 1891–1905 (see pp.42–43), and general registers, 1906–1920 (see pp.62–65).

For registers and departmental diaries, 1782–1817, see *Miscellanea, Series I* (F.O. 95) (p.125) and pp.33–34; for general registers of the Foreign Trade Department, 1916–1919, see WAR OF 1914 TO 1918: *Foreign Trade Department* (F.O.833) (p.126) and pp. 66–67.

Registers (Library Series) and Indexes of General Correspondence (F.O.802)   1808–1890
Registers (Library Series) and Indexes of General Correspondence: Microfilm Copies (F.O. 605)   1808–1890
See pp.39–42.

Registers of the General Correspondence compiled in the Library after the records had been arranged and bound. They include registers for the U.S.A. from 1793 and for France, 1761–1768.

Indexes to General Correspondence (F.O.804)   1891–1905
Indexes to General Correspondence: Photographic Copies (F.O.738)   1891–1905
See pp.43–44.

These are indexes to the departmental registers of the period.

Numerical (Central) Registers of General Correspondence (F.O.662)   1906–1920
See pp.61–62.

For similar central registers of the Foreign Trade Department, 1916–1919, see WAR OF 1914 TO 1918: *Foreign Trade Department* (F.O.833) (p.126) and p.66.

Card Index to General Correspondence   1906–1920
See pp.65–66.

Annual indexes of subjects, persons and places.

Indexes (Printed Series) to General Correspondence (F.O.409)[3]   1920–1951
See pp.70–71.

Annual indexes of subjects, persons and places. They include indexes to 'green' papers.

Before 1906
Abyssinia (Ethiopia) (F.O.1)   1808–1905

Relations with Abyssinia were first established 1808–1813, but thereafter were spasmodic until 1897.

---

[1] This covers classes of records transferred to the Public Record Office up to 31 December 1968.
[2] With the exception of F.O.605 and the Card Index the records under this heading are kept in Index Rooms and are produced by their Index Room press numbers [Ind.], which are given in the search room class lists. It is customary, however, to cite them by their class and piece numbers in the normal way; the Ind. numbers may be added in parentheses.
[3] A reference set of these indexes (including those to 'green' papers) is on open access at the Public Record Office.

GENERAL CORRESPONDENCE (continued)
Before 1906 (continued)
Africa (F.O.2)   1825–1905
See pp. 55–56.
The earliest correspondence in this class is domestic various. Consuls were first appointed to the West Coast of Africa in 1849, all their correspondence for that year being in the *Slave Trade* class (F.O.84/775). Between 1850 and 1866 and in 1872 their consular correspondence was separated from their Slave Trade correspondence and put in this class. There is also correspondence relating to various expeditions of exploration, 1850–1874. After 1874 there is a gap until 1893, after which the class continues for records of the African (East and West) Department, relating to West Africa, Uganda, Central Africa and (from 1899) East Africa, except the Africa series of correspondence with missions and consulates and with foreign ministers in London, 1893–1900, which are in the appropriate country classes, and domestic various correspondence, 1893–1898, which is in the *Great Britain and General* class (F.O.83).

See also *Abyssinia* (F.O.1), *Comoro* (F.O.19), *Liberia* (F.O.47), *Madagascar* (F.O. 48), *Muscat* (F.O.54), *Slave Trade* (F.O.84), *Zanzibar* (F.O.107), many *Colonial Office* record classes,[1] and *Treasury, Expired Commissions, etc., African Companies* (T.70), 1660–1833.

Algiers (F.O.3)   1760–1850
See pp. 30, 60, 80, 97.
Before 1836 this is correspondence of the Secretary of State for the Southern Department (to 1782), the Home Office (1782–1803) and the Colonial Office (1804–1836). For entry books, 1801–1836, see *Barbary States* (F.O.8). From 1851 see *France* (F.O.27).

For correspondence 1595–1780 see *State Papers Foreign, Barbary States* (S.P.71).

America, Central, and Guatemala (F.O.15)   1824–1905
[*Central America* to 1848; *Guatemala* from 1849][2]
The Central American provinces of the Spanish Empire, Guatemala (a name also used for them collectively), Honduras, Salvador, Nicaragua and Costa Rica, revolted in 1821 and from 1822 to 1823 formed part of the Mexican Empire. From 1823 to 1839, and again from 1842 to 1845 (except Costa Rica), they formed the Republic of the United States of Central America. After 1845 they became separate independent republics. However, a single British diplomatic representative, normally resident in Guatemala, continued to be accredited to all five republics. His correspondence will be found in this class.

There are separate classes for correspondence with consuls and domestic correspondence from 1848 for *Costa Rica* (F.O.21) and *Nicaragua* (F.O.56); from 1856 for *Salvador* (F.O.66); and from 1857 for *Honduras* (F.O.39). Until 1857 there is some overlap of F.O.21 and F.O.56 with F.O.15.

See also *Cuba* (F.O.108), *Dominican Republic* (F.O.23), *Hayti* (F.O.35), *Mexico* (F.O.50), *Mosquito* (F.O.53) and *Panama* (F.O.110).

[1] See Pugh, *Records of Colonial and Dominions Offices*, pp. 57–119.
[2] This and subsequent entries in square brackets appearing under class titles refer to the labelling of the bound volumes in a class where it differs from the class title.

GENERAL CORRESPONDENCE (continued)
Before 1906 (continued)

America, United States of, Series I (F.O.4)   1782–1792
America, United States of Series II (F.O.5)   1793–1905

The division into two series appears to have originated from separate transfers to the State Paper Office.[1]

For correspondence relating to the U.S.A. – Canada boundary see also *Colonial Office, America, British North, Original Correspondence* (C.O.6), etc.[2] See also *Texas* (F.O.75).

Argentine Republic (F.O.6)   1823–1905
   [*Buenos Ayres* to 1855; *Argentine Confederation* from 1856]

The United Provinces of Rio de la Plata (the modern Argentina, Bolivia, Paraguay and Uruguay) declared their independence in 1816. By the time the Spanish forces were finally defeated in 1824 the United Provinces had broken up. The Argentine Republic was declared independent in 1825.

For correspondence before 1823 relating to Spanish America see *Spain* (F.O.72).

Asia, Central (F.O.106)   1899–1905

Mostly correspondence with the India Office concerning the North-West Frontier of India.

It continues a series of case volumes entitled 'Proceedings in Central Asia', 1858–1898, under *Russia* (F.O.65).[3]

Austria (F.O.7)   1781–1905

Until 6 August 1806 known officially as the Holy Roman Empire. Includes Hungary throughout this period.

See also *Flanders* (F.O.26) and *Venice* (F.O.81). Before 1781 see *State Papers Foreign, Germany (Empire) and Hungary* (S.P.80).

Baden, see *Württemberg* (F.O.82) to 1871 and *Germany* (F.O.30) from 1871.

Barbary States (F.O.8)   1801–1836
   See pp. 30, 60, 80, 97.

This class includes foreign and domestic correspondence of the Foreign Office, 1809–1830, and entry books, 1801–1836 (from 1825 relating to Algiers only), and consular bonds, 1826–1833, inherited from the Colonial Office in 1836.

See also *Algiers* (F.O.3), *Morocco, Series I* (F.O.52), *Tripoli, Series I* (F.O.76), *Tunis, Series I* (F.O.77); also *Colonial Office, Africa, Explorations* (C.O.2) and *Mediterranean* (C.O.173).[4] Before 1780 see *State Papers Foreign, Barbary States* (S.P.71).

Bavaria (F.O.9)   1781–1897

After 1897 see *Germany* (F.O.30). Before 1781 see *State Papers Foreign, Germany (States)* (S.P.81).

Belgium (F.O.10)   1830–1905

Before 1830 see *Flanders* (F.O.26), *Holland, Frontiers of, etc.* (F.O.38) and *Holland and Netherlands* (F.O.37).

---

[1] The original labelling of F.O.4 is 'New Series: America: State Paper Office'. When a transfer of Foreign Office correspondence was made to the State Paper Office in 1825, for most countries it covered the period 1781–1810, but for America it dated only from 1793 (F.O.83/221: draft to S.P.O., 23 July 1825, and enclosure). See also OBS 710: *List of F.O. Records* (1872), p.2.

[2] See Pugh, *Records of Col. and Dom. Offices*, p.62.

[3] The departmental diaries, 1882–1889, are listed as 'Russia and Central Asia' (F.O.566/382–383); the 1890 diary and the departmental registers, 1891–1905, are listed as 'Russia (Central Asia)' (F.O.566/935).

[4] See Pugh, *Records of Col. and Dom. Offices*, pp.20, 48, 59, 90.

GENERAL CORRESPONDENCE (continued)
Before 1906 (continued)

Bolivia (F.O.11)   1843–1905
  Originally known as Upper Peru. Became the independent state of Bolivia in
1825. From 1837 to 1839 with Peru made up the Peru-Bolivian Federation.
  Before 1843 see *Peru* (F.O.61).

Borneo (F.O.12)   1842–1905
  Concerning dealings with independent and protected chiefs in Borneo.
  See also *Sulu* (F.O.71) and *Colonial Office* classes.[1]

Brazil (F.O.13)   1825–1905
  Brazil's independence of Portugal, proclaimed in 1822, was acknowledged by
Portugal in 1825.
  Before 1825 see under *Portugal* (F.O.63).

Brunswick (F.O.14)   1785–1830
  There was no regular diplomatic representative at Brunswick until 1847; there-
after the minister was simultaneously accredited to Hanover, where he resided.
  This class consists of foreign and domestic correspondence, 1785–1814, and
correspondence between King William IV, Lord Aberdeen and the Duke of
Brunswick, Sept.–Nov. 1830.
  See also *Hanover* (F.O.34). For correspondence 1748–1770 see *State Papers
Foreign, Germany (States)* (S.P.81).

Buenos Ayres, see *Argentine Republic* (F.O.6)
Bulgaria, see *Turkey* (F.O.18)
Central America, see *America, Central, and Guatemala* (F.O.15)
Central Asia, see *Asia, Central* (F.O.106)

Chile (F.O.16)   1823–1905
  Proclaimed its independence of Spain 1817.

China (F.O.17)   1815–1905
  See pp.13, 37–38, 42, 44–45.
  The main series of correspondence in this class commences with Lord Napier's
mission in 1834, but there is earlier correspondence with Lord Amherst's mission of
1816–1817 and some miscellaneous material for the intervening period. For Lord
Macartney's mission of 1793–1794 see *Colonial Office, East Indies* (C.O.77/29).[2]
  The class includes despatches from the consul general at Seoul, Korea, from
1890.[3]

Coburg, see *Saxony* (F.O.68) to 1867 and *Germany* (F.O.30) from 1868.
Cologne, see *Germany, States* (F.O.31) to 1806 and *Prussia and Germany* (F.O.64) from
1815.

Colombia (F.O.18)   1823–1834
Colombia and New Granada (F.O.55)   1835–1905
  [*New Granada* 1835–1861; *Colombia (New Granada)* 1862–1886; *Colombia* 1887–
1905]
  The Spanish presidency of New Granada consisted of the provinces of Colombia,

---

[1] See Pugh, *Records of Col. and Dom. Offices*, pp. 68–69, 87, 106–107.
[2] For correspondence relating to China, 1596–1835, see India Office Records, Class G (see p. 31,
n.4).
[3] There is a separate Korea (diplomatic) register, 1901–1905 (F.O.566/682).

GENERAL CORRESPONDENCE (continued)
Before 1906 (continued)
Colombia and New Granada (continued)
Venezuela and Ecuador. During the war of independence against Spain these were
united by Bolivar in the Republic of Colombia. Venezuela seceded in 1829 and
Ecuador in 1830. The remainder became the Republic of New Granada in 1831.
This title was changed to the Granadine Confederation in 1853 and to the United
States of Colombia in 1861.
See also *Ecuador* (F.O.25), *Panama* (F.O.110) and *Venezuela* (F.O.80).

Comoro (F.O.19)   1848–1867
Four islands midway between Madagascar and the African coast. Originally
independent sultanates, one (Mayotte) was ceded to France in 1843 and the rest were
placed under French protection in 1886.
Before 1848 and after 1867 see *Madagascar* (F.O.48).

Continent, Conferences (F.O.92)   1814–1822
Correspondence with plenipotentiaries at the Conferences of Paris, 1814 and
1815, Congress of Vienna, 1814–1815, Conferences of Aix-la-Chapelle, 1818, and
Verona, 1822, etc.
Formerly classified as *Treaty: Continent: Treaty Papers.*

Corsica (F.O.20)   1783–1798
See p.97.
Occupied by Britain in 1794, but retaken by the French in 1796.
Correspondence of the commissioners and civil administrator with the Home
Office, 1793–1796, a survey of the island, 1795–1796, papers relating to the Toulon
Expedition, 1794–1796, and supplementary papers, 1783–1798.
See also *Colonial Office, Corsica, Entry Books* (C.O.65).[1]
For consular correspondence from 1818 see *France* (F.O.27).

Costa Rica (F.O.21)   1848–1905
Proclaimed independent 1848.
This class consists mainly of consular and domestic correspondence.
Before 1848, for diplomatic correspondence, 1848–1905, and for consular corre-
spondence, 1848–1852, see *America, Central, and Guatemala* (F.O.15).

Cuba (F.O.108)   1902–1905
Spanish rule in Cuba ceased in 1899 and from then until 1902 the island was
under the military rule of the U.S.A.
Before 1902 see *Spain* (F.O.72) to 1898 and *America, United States of, Series II*
(F.O.5) from 1899.

Cyprus
See pp.22, 96.
Foreign Office records relating to Cyprus, 1878–1880, are now in *Colonial Office,
Cyprus, Original Correspondence* (C.O.67/1–12, 14–15) and *Registers of Correspondence*
(C.O.512/1)[2]
Before 1878 see *Turkey* (F.O.78).

---

[1] See Pugh, *Records of Col. and Dom. Offices*, p.74.
[2] See *Ibid.*, p.74.

GENERAL CORRESPONDENCE (continued)

Before 1906 (continued)

Denmark (F.O.22) 1781–1905
   Including Norway to 1814.
   Correspondence before 1781 is in *State Papers Foreign, Denmark* (S.P.75).
   See also *Iceland* (F.O.40).

Dominican Republic (F.O.23) 1848–1905
   The island of Santo Domingo, Saint Dominique or Hispaniola had been French
since 1697 (apart from the period 1793–1798, when it was occupied by the British)
until 1804, when the French evacuated the island. The eastern part of the island was
then occupied by Spain, the western part becoming the independent republic of
Hayti. The eastern part became independent of Spain in 1821 and joined Hayti
until 1844 when it became the independent Dominican Republic.
   See also *Hayti* (F.O.35) and *Colonial Office, Santo Domingo* (C.O.245)[1]

Eastern Roumelia, see *Turkey* (F.O.78)
East Indies, see *Indies, East* (F.O.41)

Ecuador (F.O.25) 1835–1905
   Part of the Republic of Colombia until 1830 when it seceded to become an
independent republic.
   Before 1835 see under *Colombia* (F.O.18).

Egypt (F.O.24) 1785–1818
   This class consists of correspondence with the Consul-General at Alexandria,
1785–1796 and 1803–1816, with some domestic correspondence of 1818.
   After 1816 see *Turkey* (F.O.78).[2]

Empire, Holy Roman, see *Austria* (F.O.7)
Ethiopia, see *Abyssinia* (F.O.1)

Flanders (F.O.26) 1781–1794
   The Southern Netherlands or Flanders formed an autonomous province of the
Holy Roman Empire until 1794, when they were annexed to France. From 1814
to 1830 they formed part of the Kingdom of the United Netherlands. In 1830 they
became independent as Belgium.
   After 1794 see *Holland, Frontiers of, etc.* (F.O.38), *Holland and Netherlands* (F.O.
37) and *Belgium* (F.O.10). Before 1781 see *State Papers Foreign, Flanders* (S.P.77) and
Holland and Flanders (S.P.83).

France (F.O.27) 1781–1905
   Before 1781 see *State Papers Foreign, France* (S.P.78).
   See also *Algiers* (F.O.3), *Corsica* (F.O.20), *Holland, Frontiers of, etc.* (F.O.38),
Madagascar (F.O.48), *Nice* (F.O.57), *Pacific Islands* (F.O.58) and *Tunis* (F.O.77 and
F.O.102).

Frankfort, see *Germany* (F.O.30)

Genoa (F.O.28) 1776–1803
   The Genoese Republic passed under French control in 1797 and was annexed
to the French Empire in 1805. In 1814 Genoa passed to Sardinia.

---

[1] See Pugh. *Records of Col. and Dom. Offices*, p.106.
[2] The departmental diaries and registers in F.O.566 appear indiscriminately under 'Egypt' or
'Turkey (Egypt)'.

GENERAL CORRESPONDENCE (continued)
Before 1906 (continued)
Genoa (continued)

From 1814 see *Sardinia* (F.O.67) and *Italy* (F.O.45). Before 1776 see *State Papers Foreign, Genoa* (S.P.79).

German Empire, see *Prussia and Germany* (F.O.64)

Germany (F.O.30)   1811–1905
This class relates to the Territorial Commission of Frankfort, 1815–1819, the Germanic Confederation (Diet of Frankfort), 1820–1866, and the German National Assembly, 1848–1849. The minister to the Germanic Confederation was also accredited to Hesse-Cassel (from 1826), Hesse-Darmstadt and Nassau (from 1847). After the dissolution of the Confederation in 1866 the class continues for correspondence for Hesse-Darmstadt, and subsequently for Coburg (from 1868), Baden (from 1871), and Bavaria, Saxony and Württemberg (from 1897). There is a volume of domestic various correspondence, 1811–1816.

Before 1897 there are separate classes for *Bavaria* (F.O.9), *Saxony* (F.O.68) and *Württemberg* (F.O.82); for Coburg before 1868 see *Saxony* (F.O.68); for Baden before 1871 see *Württemberg* (F.O.82).

See also *Brunswick* (F.O.14), *Germany, Army in* (F.O.29), *Germany, States* (F.O.31), *Hamburg and Hanse Towns* (F.O.33), *Hanover* (F.O.34), and *Prussia and Germany* (F.O.64). Before 1784 see *State Papers Foreign, Germany (States)* (S.P.81).

Germany, Army in (F.O.29)   1793–1802
Correspondence with special missions to the armies of Prussia, Austria and other German States.

Germany, States (F.O.31)   1781–1819
Correspondence relating to Cologne (to 1806) and Hesse-Cassel (to 1815), with a volume of foreign and domestic correspondence, 1815–1819.

Cologne was an independent city state until occupied by France in 1794 and annexed in 1801. In 1815 it became part of Prussia. See also *Prussia and Germany* (F.O.64).

Hesse-Cassel was occupied by the French, 1801–1813. Diplomatic relations were not restored until 1826, after which date ministers accredited to Hesse-Cassel were also accredited to the Germanic Confederation and resided at Frankfort. See also *Germany* (F.O.30).

Before 1781 see *State Papers Foreign, Germany (States)* (S.P.81).

Granada, New, see *Colombia and New Granada* (F.O.55).

Greece (F.O.32)   1827–1905
The Turks were expelled from Greece during the War of Independence, 1821–1827, and Greek independence was recognized at the Conferences of London, 1827–1828.

Before 1827 see *Turkey* (F.O.78). See also *Ionian Islands* (F.O.42).

Guatemala, see *America, Central, and Guatemala* (F.O.15).

Hamburg and Hanse Towns (F.O.33)   1781–1870
This class relates to the free city states of Hamburg, Bremen and Lübeck. These became part of the German Empire in 1871.

After 1870 see *Prussia and Germany* (F.O.64). Before 1781 see *State Papers Foreign, Hamburg and Hanse Towns* (S.P.82).

GENERAL CORRESPONDENCE (continued)

Before 1906 (continued)

Hanover (F.O.34)   1807–1866

Until 1837 the Kings of England were also Kings of Hanover. Hanover was annexed to Prussia in 1866.

Before 1838 the correspondence is mainly with the Hanoverian ministers in London. For correspondence 1780–1806 see *Supplement to General Correspondence* (F.O.97/243). After 1866 see *Prussia and Germany* (F.O 64). Before 1780 see *State Papers Foreign, Foreign Ministers* (*in England*) (S.P.100) under 'Germany (States)'. See also *Brunswick* (F.O.14).

Hanse Towns, see *Hamburg and Hanse Towns* (F.O.33)

Hayti (F.O.35)   1825–1905

The western half of the island of Santo Domingo. Became independent of France in 1804. Included the whole of the island 1821–1844.

See also *Dominican Republic* (F.O.23).

Heligoland (F.O.36)   1808–1817

Captured by the British from the Danes in 1807 and formally ceded to Britain in 1814. It was ceded to Germany in 1890.

The correspondence in this class is mainly with Edward Nicholas, the Political Agent, 1808–1813, but there is also correspondence with William Hamilton, the Lieutenant Governor, 1812–1814, and with others. The domestic various correspondence continues to 1817.

There is a parallel series of correspondence from 1807 between Hamilton and the Secretary of State for War and the Colonies, to whom sole responsibility for Heligoland passed in 1815. See *Colonial Office, Heligoland, Original Correspondence* (C.O. 118), *Entry Books* (C.O.119), etc.[1]

Hesse-Cassel, see *Germany, States* (F.O.31) to 1815 and *Germany* (F.O.30) from 1826. *Hesse-Darmstadt*, see *Germany* (F.O.30)

Holland and Netherlands (F.O.37)   1781–1905

[*Holland* to 1822; *Netherlands* from 1823]

Includes the Southern Netherlands 1814–1830. See also *Flanders* (F.O.26) and *Belgium* (F.O.10). Before 1781 see *State Papers Foreign, Holland and Flanders* (S.P.83) and *Holland* (S.P.84).

Holland, Frontiers of, etc. (F.O.38)   1795–1815

Correspondence with British Secret Service agents on the Continent of Europe during the wars with France. Originally consisted of correspondence with agents on the frontiers of Holland (hence the title) in communication with disaffected elements in the Southern Netherlands (Flanders), at that time under French occupation. Later the centre of activity moved to northern Germany, and then to Sweden, and the interests became more general. From 1800 most of the correspondence is with Sir Charles Gordon (between 1803 and 1814 it is unsigned).

For more correspondence with British Secret Service agents operating against France in this period see *Switzerland, Series I* (F.O.74) and *Miscellanea, Series I* (F.O. 95/2–4).

Holy Roman Empire, see *Austria* (F.O.7)

---

[1] See Pugh, *Records of Col. and Dom. Offices*, pp.81–82.

GENERAL CORRESPONDENCE (continued)
Before 1906 (continued)

Honduras (F.O.39)   1857–1905
Became independent on the dissolution of the Republic of the United States of Central America in 1845.

This class consists mainly of consular and domestic correspondence.

Before 1857 and for diplomatic correspondence, 1857–1905, see *America, Central, and Guatemala* (F.O.15).

Hungary, see *Austria* (F.O.7)

Iceland (F.O.40)   1809–1815
Iceland was a dependency of Denmark until 1918.

There was a British consul at Reykjavik, 1811–1815, when special measures had to be taken to prevent the blockade of Denmark (on which Iceland relied for supplies) leading to the starvation of the island's inhabitants. The earlier correspondence is mainly domestic.

From 1882, when the consulate was re-established, see *Denmark* (F.O.22).

Indies, East (F.O.41)   1776–1797
Correspondence with the East India Company.

See also *China* (F.O.17) and *Colonial Office, East Indies* (C.O.77).[1]

Ionian Islands (F.O.42)   1778–1820
The Ionian or Seven Islands were held by Venice until captured by France in 1797. In 1799 they were captured by Russia and became a Russo-Turkish protectorate until 1807, when they were restored to France. They were occupied by the British in 1809–1810 and made a protectorate in 1814. In 1864 they were ceded to Greece.

Diplomatic representation in the Islands ended in 1813 and correspondence after this date is mainly with the Civil Commissioner, 1814–1816, with some foreign and domestic various correspondence, 1816–1820. From 1816 the High Commissioner was responsible solely to the Colonial Office.

For consular correspondence after 1864 see *Greece* (F.O.32). See also *Colonial Office, Ionian Islands, Original Correspondence, etc.* (C.O.136) and *Register of Correspondence* (C.O.350).[2]

Italian States and Rome (F.O.43)   1795–1874
[Rome]
Britain had no formal diplomatic representation at the Vatican until 1887, but there were a number of special missions to Rome and from 1832 an attaché from the Legation at Florence was usually resident there. There was consular representation in the Papal States from 1815.

For correspondence with consuls at Ancona from 1861, with consuls and vice-consuls at Rome and Civita Vecchia from 1871 and with diplomatic representatives after 1874 see *Italy* (F.O.45).

For correspondence concerning other Italian states see *Genoa* (F.O.28), *Nice* (F.O.57), *Sardinia* (F.O.67), *Sicily and Naples* (F.O.70), *Tuscany* (F.O.79) and *Venice* (F.O.81); also *Italy, Earl of Minto's Mission* (F.O.44). Before 1773 see *State Papers Foreign, Italian States and Rome* (S.P.85)

---

[1] See Pugh, *Records of Col. and Dom. Offices*, p.76.
[2] See *Ibid.*, p.84.

GENERAL CORRESPONDENCE (continued)
Before 1906 (continued)
Italy (F.O.45)   1861–1905
  With the exception of Venice and Rome, Italy became a united kingdom in 1861.
Venice was ceded by Austria in 1866; Rome became incorporated in the Italian
kingdom, as its capital, in 1870.
  For earlier correspondence see the previous entry.

Italy, Earl of Minto's Mission (F.O.44)   1847–1848
  Correspondence with the Earl of Minto on a special mission to Italy.

Japan (F.O.46)   1856–1905
  See pp.38, 42, 44–45.
  The main series of correspondence starts with the appointment of the first Consul-
General in 1859. There is a volume of correspondence with the Admiralty for 1856
concerning naval contacts with Japan.

Korea, see *China* (F.O.17)
Kuria Muria Islands, see *Muscat* (F.O.54)
Levant, see *Turkey* (F.O.78)

Liberia (F.O.47)   1848–1905
  Declared an independent republic in 1847.
  The class contains correspondence for the periods 1848–1860 and 1893–1905,
with one case volume concerning a wreck for the period 1873–1888. For the period
1861–1892 (intermittently only to 1883) see *Slave Trade* (F.O.84).

Madagascar (F.O.48)   1836–1895
  A French protectorate, 1885–1895, and a colony from 1896.
  There is a gap in the correspondence between 1854 and 1862. Before 1847 and
again from 1868 the correspondence relates also to the Comoro Islands.
  After 1895 see *France* (F.O.27). See also *Comoro* (F.O.19) and *Slave Trade* (F.O.
84)

Malta (F.O.49)   1781–1816
  Malta was governed by the Knights of St. John of Jerusalem until captured by
the French in 1798. It was surrendered to Britain in 1800 and ceded to her in 1814.
Between 1801 and 1813 the government of the islands was in the hands of a Civil
Commissioner; from 1813 it was in the hands of a Governor.
  Parallel and later correspondence with the Secretary of State for War and the
Colonies is in *Colonial Office, Malta, Original Correspondence* (C.O.158) and *Entry
Books* (C.O.159), etc.[1] For correspondence 1577–1773 see *State Papers Foreign,
Malta* (S.P.86).

Mexico (F.O.50)   1822–1905
  Proclaimed its independence of Spain in 1821 and included all Central America
until 1823.
  See also *Texas* (F.O.75).

Montenegro (F.O.103)   1879–1905
  A principality under the suzerainty of Turkey until 1878 when it became an
independent kingdom.
  Before 1879 see *Turkey* (F.O.78).

[1] See Pugh, *Records of Col. and Dom. Offices*, p.89.

GENERAL CORRESPONDENCE (continued)
Before 1906 (continued)
Monte Video (Uruguay) (F.O.51)   1823–1905

The province of Monte Video was in dispute between the Argentine Confederation and Brazil until 1828. Its independence as the Republic of Uruguay was formally proclaimed in 1829.

Morocco, Series I (F.O.52)   1761–1837
Morocco, Series II (F.O.99)   1836–1905

See pp.30, 60, 80, 97.

The division into series at 1837–1838 here and in the correspondence for *Tripoli* (F.O.76 and F.O.101) and *Tunis* (F.O.77 and F.O.102) appears to have been dictated by the 1837 open date in force when the 1914 *List of Foreign Office Records* was published (see pp.93–94).[1]

Series I is correspondence of the Secretary of State for the Southern Department (to 1782), the Home Office (1782–1803), the Colonial Office (1804–1836) and the Foreign Office (1837). Apart from one case volume extending back to 1836, *Series II* commences in 1838.

Entry Books for Morocco, 1825–1836, are in *Miscellanea, Series I* (F.O.95/164–167). See also *Barbary States* (F.O.8). Correspondence for the period 1577–1774 is in *State Papers Foreign, Barbary States* (S.P.71).

Mosquito (F.O.53)   1844–1895

Between 1655 and 1850 Britain claimed a protectorate over Mosquito. In 1860 suzerainty was transferred to Nicaragua, into which country it was formally incorporated in 1894.

Consular correspondence in the class ends in 1859 and thereafter the class consists mainly of case volumes on the subject of duties at Greytown. For consular correspondence from 1860 and the remaining correspondence from 1896 see *Nicaragua* (F.O.56).

Muscat (F.O.54)   1834–1905

The independent Imamate of Muscat held wide possessions in Arabia and in East Africa, including Zanzibar, which had been occupied in 1730. In 1832 Zanzibar became the capital of the Imamate and there the first British consul to the Imamate was established in 1832. In 1856 the Imamate was divided into African and Arabian sections and in 1863 the first consul at Muscat itself (paid by the India Office) was appointed.

The correspondence in this class falls into two parts: that from 1834 to 1867, which is mostly concerned with Zanzibar; and that from 1883 to 1905, which is mainly with the consuls at Muscat. Correspondence with the consuls at Muscat before 1883 will be found under *Slave Trade* (F.O.84). See also *Zanzibar* (F.O.107).[2]

The class also includes a volume of correspondence relating to the Kuria Muria Islands in the Arabian Sea, 1853–1857. These were ceded to Britain by the Sultan of Muscat in 1854 and became part of the colony of Aden, which was the responsibility of the India Office until 1937 and then of the Colonial Office. See also *Colonial Office, Kuria Muria Islands, Original Correspondence* (C.O.143).[3]

---

[1] For an earlier numeration of these classes see OBS 886/7.
[2] Correspondence with the India Office is in the India Office Records class L/P & S/9 (see p.31, n.4).
[3] See Pugh, *Records of Col. and Dom. Offices*, pp.58, 87.

GENERAL CORRESPONDENCE (continued)
Before 1906 (continued)
Naples, see *Sicily and Naples* (F.O.70)
Netherlands, see *Holland and Netherlands* (F.O.37)
Netherlands, Southern, see *Belgium* (F.O.10) and *Flanders* (F.O.26).
New Granada, see *Colombia and New Granada* (F.O.55)

Nicaragua (F.O.56)   1848–1905
Became independent on the dissolution of the Republic of the United States of Central America in 1845.
This class consists mainly of consular and domestic correspondence.
Before 1848, for diplomatic correspondence, 1848–1905, and for some consular and domestic correspondence, 1848–1857, see *America, Central, and Guatemala* (F.O.15).
See also *Mosquito* (F.O.53).

Nice (F.O.57)   1777–1800
Nice was part of the Kingdom of Sardinia until 1860, apart from a period of French occupation, 1792–1814. It was ceded to France in 1860.
The one volume in this class consists of correspondence with British consuls at Nice, 1777–1792, and claims by the last consul and his widow, 1795–1800.
See also *Sardinia* (F.O.67) to 1859 and *France* (F.O.27) from 1860.

Norway (F.O.109)   1905
Part of the Kingdom of Denmark until 1814, when it became an independent kingdom united with Sweden under one king. It became a fully independent kingdom in 1905.
The one volume in this class commences on 29 October 1905.
Before 1905 see *Denmark* (F.O.22) to 1814 and *Sweden* (F.O.73) from 1814.

Ottoman Empire, see *Turkey* (F.O.78)

Pacific Islands (F.O.58)   1822–1905
Includes Tahiti (Society or Georgian Islands), Hawaii (Sandwich Islands), Samoa (Navigator Islands), Fiji, Tonga and Rarotonga (Cook or Hervey Islands); also New Zealand (1838–1841).
For Tahiti from 1880 see *France* (F.O.27); for Hawaii (Honolulu) from 1899 see *America, United States of, Series II* (F.O.5); for Samoa (Apia) from 1900 see *Prussia and Germany* (F.O.64). See also case volumes on 'Western Pacific Islands', 1880–1905, under *France* (F.O.27). See also *Colonial Office, Fiji, Original Correspondence* (C.O.83), etc., and *Pacific, Western, Original Correspondence* (C.O.225), etc.[1]

Panama (F.O.110)   1904–1905
Part of Colombia until 1903 when it became an independent republic.
Before 1904 see *Colombia* (F.O.18) and *Colombia and New Granada* (F.O.55).

Paraguay (F.O.59)   1852–1905
Declared independent 1811 but diplomatic relations with Britain were not established until 1852. The minister accredited to Paraguay was also accredited to the Argentine Republic and resided in Buenos Ayres. Between 1859 and 1862 and between 1868 and 1882 there was no British diplomatic representative in Paraguay.
See also *Argentine Republic* (F.O.6), *Brazil* (F.O.13) and *Monte Video* (F.O.51).

[1] See Pugh, *Records of Col. and Dom. Offices*, pp.78, 99.

GENERAL CORRESPONDENCE (continued)
Before 1906 (continued)

Persia (F.O.60)   1807–1905
Diplomatic relations between Persia and Britain were first established in 1809. Between 1826 and 1835 they were the responsibility of the East India Company and Board of Control, and in 1858 and 1859 of the India Office.[1]
See also *Colonial Office, East Indies, Original Correspondence, etc.* (C.O.77).[2]

Peru (F.O.61)   1823–1905
Proclaimed independent 1821.

Peru, Upper, see *Bolivia* (F.O.11)

Poland (F.O.62)   1782–1796
The Kingdom of Poland was extinguished in 1795.
For later correspondence with British consuls at Warsaw see *Russia* (F.O.65). Before 1782 see *State Papers Foreign, Poland* (S.P.88).

Portugal (F.O.63)   1781–1905
Before 1781 see *State Papers Foreign, Portugal* (S.P.89).

Prussia and Germany (F.O.64)   1781–1905.
[*Prussia* to 1870; *Germany* (*Prussia*) from 1871]
Before 1870 the correspondence relates to Prussia; after 1870 to the German Empire. After 1870 several German states retained the right to have their own diplomatic representation and separate series of correspondence continue: see *Bavaria* (F.O.9), *Germany* (F.O.30), *Saxony* (F.O.68) and *Württemberg* (F.O.82).
Before 1781 see *State Papers Foreign, Prussia* (S.P.90).

Rome, see *Italian States and Rome* (F.O.43)

Roumania (F.O.104)   1878–1905
Moldavia and Wallachia, principalities under the suzerainty of Turkey, united as Roumania in 1859 and became independent in 1878.
Before 1878 see *Turkey* (F.O.78).

Roumelia, Eastern, see *Turkey* (F.O.78)

Russia (F.O.65)   1781–1905
See also *Asia, Central* (F.O.106). Before 1781 see *State Papers Foreign, Russia* (S.P.91).

Salvador, El (F.O.66)   1856–1905
Became independent on the dissolution of the Republic of the United States of Central America in 1845.
This class consists mainly of consular and domestic correspondence.
Before 1856 and for diplomatic correspondence, 1856–1905, see *America, Central, and Guatemala* (F.O.15).

Santo Domingo, see *Dominican Republic* (F.O.23) and *Hayti* (F.O.35).

Sardinia (F.O.67)   1781–1860
See also *Genoa* (F.O.28) and *Nice* (F.O.57). After 1860 see *Italy* (F.O.45). Before 1781 see *State Papers Foreign, Savoy and Sardinia* (S.P.92).

[1] See Factory Records, 1620–1822, and Political and Secret Department correspondence, 1814–1888, in India Office Records classes G and L/P & S/9 respectively (see p.31, n.4).
[2] See Pugh, *Records of Col. and Dom. Offices*, p.76.

I

GENERAL CORRESPONDENCE (continued)
Before 1906 (continued)
Saxony (F.O.68)   1780–1897
   Includes Coburg to 1867.
   After 1897 see *Germany* (F.O.30). Before 1780 see *State Papers Foreign, Poland* (S.P.88).

Serbia (F.O.105)   1878–1905
   A Turkish pashalik until 1817, when it became autonomous under Turkish suzerainty. Became independent in 1878.
   Before 1878 see *Turkey* (F.O.78).

Seven Islands, see *Ionian Islands* (F.O.42).

Siam (F.O.69)   1849–1905
   See pp.38, 42, 44–45.
   Diplomatic relations between Britain and Siam were first established in 1850.

Sicily and Naples (F.O.70)   1780–1860
   After 1860 see *Italy* (F.O.45). Before 1780 see *State Papers Foreign, Sicily and Naples* (S.P.93).

Slave Trade (F.O.84)   1816–1892
   [*Slave Trade* to 1884; *Africa (Slave Trade)* from 1885]
   See pp.38–39, 55.
   Correspondence of the Slave Trade Department (to 1872), the Slave Trade correspondence of the Consular and Slave Trade Department (1872–1880) and of the Slave Trade and Sanitary Department (1880–1882), and the Africa correspondence of the Consular and African (East and West) Department (1883–1892). It consists of correspondence with Slave Trade Commissioners, with British diplomatic and consular representatives in countries interested in the Slave Trade or in Africa, with the representatives of those counties in London, with consular and other British representatives in Africa, and with other government departments, institutions and individuals.
   See also *Africa* (F.O.2), *Comoro* (F.O.19), *Liberia* (F.O.47), *Madagascar* (F.O.48), *Muscat* (F.O.54) and *Zanzibar* (F.O.107).

Southern Netherlands, see *Belgium* (F.O.10) and *Flanders* (F.O.26).

Spain (F.O.72)   1781–1905
   Includes Central and South America (excluding Brazil) to 1823.
   See also *Sulu* (F.O.71). Before 1781 see *State Papers Foreign, Spain* (S.P.94).

Sulu (F.O.71)   1849–1888
   Nineteen case volumes relating to the Sulu Islands (between Borneo and the Philippines) removed from the correspondence relating to Spain and made into a separate class.
   See also *Spain* (F.O.72) and *Borneo* (F.O.12).

Sweden (F.O.73)   1781–1905
   [*Sweden* to 1895, *Sweden and Norway* from 1896]
   Includes Norway from 1814 to October 1905.
   See also *Norway* (F.O.109).   Before 1781 see *State Papers Foreign, Sweden* (S.P.95).

GENERAL CORRESPONDENCE (continued)
Before 1906 (continued)
Switzerland, Series I (F.O.74)   1781–1837
Switzerland, Series II (F.O.100)   1838–1905
   The reason for the division into two *Series* appears to be the same as that for the division of the *Morocco* correspondence (F.O.52 and F.O.99).[1]
   Before 1781 see *State Papers Foreign, Switzerland* (S.P.96).

Texas (F.O.75)   1840–1846
   Texas proclaimed its independence of Mexico in 1836; it was admitted to the United States of America in 1845.
   The class includes *Embassy and Consular Archives*, 1842–1845.
   After 1846 see *America, United States of, Series II* (F.O.5).

Tripoli, Series I (F.O.76)   1756–1837
Tripoli, Series II (F.O.101)   1824–1905
   See pp.30, 60, 80, 97.
   For the distinction between the two *Series* and the origin of *Series I* see *Morocco* (F.O.52 and F.O.99). Apart from a case volume for the period 1824–1841, *Series II* starts in 1838.
   Series I includes Entry Books, 1825–1836.
   See also *Barbary States* (F.O.8). For the period 1590–1766 see *State Papers Foreign, Barbary States* (S.P.71).

Tunis, Series I (F.O.77)   1770–1837
Tunis, Series II (F.O.102)   1838–1891
   See pp.30, 60, 80, 97.
   Tunis became a French protectorate in 1881 and this position was recognized by Britain abandoning her consular jurisdiction in 1883 and withdrawing her diplomatic representation in 1885.
   For the distinction between the two *Series* and the origin of *Series I* see *Morocco* (F.O.52 and F.O.99). *Series II* ends in 1887 except for one case volume which continues to 1891; from 1885 to 1887 the correspondence is with consuls only.
   Series I includes Entry Books, 1825–1836.
   See also *Barbary States* (F.O.8). After 1887 see *France* (F.O.27). For the period 1622–1769 see *State Papers Foreign, Barbary States* (S.P.71).

Turkey (F.O.78)   1780–1905
   This class includes Egypt (except 1785–1796 and 1803–1816) and the Levant, Bulgaria, Eastern Roumelia (1878–1885),[2] Montenegro (to 1878), Roumania (to 1877), Serbia (to 1877) and Cyprus (to 1877).
   See also *Egypt* (F.O.24), *Montenegro* (F.O.103), *Roumania* (F.O.104) and *Serbia* (F.O.105). Before 1780 see *State Papers Foreign, Turkey* (S.P.97). For correspondence between the Levant Company and its consuls to 1825 see *State Papers Foreign, Archives of British Legations* (S.P.105).

Tuscany (F.O.79)   1780–1860
   After 1860 see *Italy* (F.O.45). Before 1780 see *State Papers Foreign, Tuscany* (S.P.98).

---

[1] For an earlier numeration of these classes see OBS 886/7.
[2] Egypt (from 1817) and Bulgaria and Eastern Roumelia (from 1881) have separate sections in the departmental diaries and registers.

GENERAL CORRESPONDENCE (continued)
Before 1906 (continued)
United States of America, see *America, United States of* (F.O.4 and F.O.5).
Uruguay, see *Monte Video* (F.O.51)

Venezuela (F.O.80) 1835–1905
Seceded from the Republic of Colombia in 1829.
Before 1835 see *Colombia* (F.O.18).

Venice (F.O.81) 1778–1805
An independent republic until 1797. Between 1798 and 1814 occupied at various times by France and Austria. Became part of the Austrian Empire in 1814 and of the Kingdom of Italy in 1866.
See *Austria* (F.O.7), 1814–1866, and *Italy* (F.O.45) from 1867. Before 1778 see *State Papers Foreign, Venice* (S.P.99).

Württemberg (F.O.82) 1795–1897
Diplomatic relations with Württemberg were irregular until 1814.
Includes Baden to 1871.
After 1897 see *Germany* (F.O.30).

Zanzibar (F.O.107) 1893–1905
Capital of the Imamate of Muscat from 1832 and of the African part of the Imamate after its division in 1856. Became a British protectorate in 1890.
This class relates not only to Zanzibar but to the whole of East Africa. From 1899 the Africa series of correspondence continues in the *Africa* (F.O.2) class, F.O.107 continuing for consular, commercial and treaty correspondence and a few case volumes.
Before 1893 see *Muscat* (F.O.54) to 1867 and *Slave Trade* (F.O.84).

Supplement to General Correspondence (F.O.97) 1780–1905
See pp.54–55.
Case volumes, etc., arranged by countries. Also includes some *Embassy and Consular Archives* and *Archives of Commissions.*

After 1906
From 1906 the country classes of General Correspondence are replaced by departmental classes. See pp.71–73.

Africa, New Series (F.O.367) 1906–1913

Commercial (F.O.368) 1906–1920

Communications (F.O.850) 1936–1941
For the period 1921–1926 see CHIEF CLERK'S DEPARTMENT: *Archives* (F.O.366) (p.127). See also pp.75–76.

Consular (F.O.369) 1906–1941

Contraband (F.O.382) 1915–1920
Correspondence of the Contraband Department, 1915–1916, and of the Ministry of Blockade from 1916. See pp.67, 72. See also WAR OF 1914 TO 1918: *Records of Temporary Departments* (F.O.902) (p.126).

Dominions Information (F.O.627) 1929–1933
Before 1929 and 1933–1938 see *Treaty* (F.O.372). See p.72.

GENERAL CORRESPONDENCE (continued)
After 1906 (continued)
Library (F.O.370) 1906–1941

News (F.O.395) 1916–1938

Political (F.O.371) 1906–1941
Before 1920 there is a single alphabetical arrangement of countries and subjects. From 1920 the records for each political department are arranged separately for each year.
Includes the records of the Political Intelligence Department, 1918–1920.

Prisoners of War and Aliens (F.O.383) 1915–1919

Treaty (F.O.372) 1906–1941
Includes Prize Court Department correspondence, 1914–1920; also includes Dominions Information Department correspondence, 1926–1928, and similar correspondence, 1934–1938.

Various
Great Britain and General (F.O.83) 1745–1946
See pp.20 (n.6), 56, 78–80.
Includes correspondence with other government departments, 1745–1806; miscellaneous domestic various correspondence; circulars; case volumes on general subjects; Library correspondence; Treaty Department correspondence on general subjects, and certain formal records of that Department; Law Officers' Reports, 1781–1876. After 1905 the class contains only formal records of the Treaty Department and printed Consular Instructions.

King's Letter Books (F.O.90) 1710–1828
See p.79.
Entry books of royal letters arranged under countries. They are continued to 1834 in *Miscellanea, Series I* (F.O.95). Before 1710 see *State Papers Foreign, Entry Books* (S.P.104).

Letter Books, Public Offices (F.O.91) 1822–1846
See pp.60, 78.
Apart from an entry book of foreign ministers' privileges, 1822–1846, the class ends in 1839. It continues entry books in *Miscellanea, Series I* (F.O.95).

Miscellanea, Series I (F.O.95) 1639–1942
See pp.56–60, 78–80, 97.
Includes registers and departmental diaries (to 1817); Secretary of State's entry and précis books (to 1822); domestic entry books (to 1821); supplementary correspondence (to 1847); treaty papers (1639–1834); royal letters; extraneous records, including D'Avaux, Bouillon and Calonne Papers.

Miscellanea, Series II (F.O.96) 1816–1937
See pp.56–57, 78–80.
Includes drafts, minutes and memoranda (1820–1884); petitions and addresses; A.J.Toynbee's papers on the treatment of Armenian and Assyrian Christians by the Turks (1915–1916).

WAR OF 1914 TO 1918

Arab Bureau Papers (F.O.882)   1911–1920
  See p.86.
  See also *Jedda Agency Papers* (F.O.686).

Blockade, Ministry of, see *Records of Temporary Departments* (F.O.902) and
  GENERAL CORRESPONDENCE AFTER 1906: *Contraband* (F.O.382)
  (p.124).
Contraband Department, see GENERAL CORRESPONDENCE AFTER 1906:
  Contraband (F.O.382) (p.124).

Foreign Trade Department (F.O.833)   1916–1919
  See pp.24, 66–67, 73.
  The class consists of the central register and the general register for Portugal,
and of papers relating to the formation of the Department, the Statutory Black List
and other policy matters.
  Formerly classified as *Commercial Department and Foreign Trade Department:
Registers and Indexes*. The Commercial Department indexes, 1891–1905, have been
transferred to GENERAL CORRESPONDENCE, REGISTERS AND IN-
DEXES, *Indexes to General Correspondence* (F.O.804) (p.109).

Jedda Agency Papers (F.O.686)   1913–1925
  See p.86.
  See also *Arab Bureau Papers* (F.O.882) and EMBASSY AND CONSULAR
ARCHIVES: *TURKEY: Jedda* (F.O.695) (p.144).

Political Intelligence Department, see GENERAL CORRESPONDENCE AFTER
  1906: *Political* (F.O.371) (p.125).
Prisoners of War and Aliens Department, see GENERAL CORRESPONDENCE
  AFTER 1906: *Prisoners of War and Aliens* (F.O.383) (p.125).

Records of Temporary Departments (F.O.902)   1915–1919
  See pp.24, 73.
  Includes miscellaneous papers of the Finance Section of the Ministry of Blockade
and duplicated and printed information bulletins, etc.

Restriction of Enemy Supplies Department (F.O.845)   1916–1919
  See pp.24, 73.
  Files relating to agreements with foreign governments and associations concern-
ing exports.

War Trade Intelligence Department Records (TREASURY SOLICITOR) (T.S.14)
  1914–1919
  See pp.24, 73, 96.

WAR OF 1939 TO 1945

British Mission to the French National Committee (F.O.892)   1940–1943
Consular (War) Department: Prisoners of War and Internees (F.O.916)   1940–1946
Ministers Resident, etc. (F.O.660)   1942–1945
Ministry of Economic Warfare (F.O.837)   1931–1951
Political Warfare Executive (F.O.898)   1938–1946

CHIEF CLERK'S DEPARTMENT
Archives (F.O.366)   1719–1940
See pp.17–19, 74–77.

PRIVATE OFFICE
Correspondence, see PRIVATE COLLECTIONS, especially *Ministers and Officials: Various* (F.O.800) (p.150); for précis books see GENERAL CORRESPON- DENCE, VARIOUS, *Miscellanea, Series I* (F.O.95) (p.125). See also Appendices III and IV.

'Individual' Files (F.O.794)   1904–1942
Selected correspondence relating to senior diplomatic and Foreign Office officials.

TREATIES
See p.80.
Protocols of Treaties (F.O.93)   1778–1962
Ratifications of Treaties (F.O.94)   1782–1966
Both classes are arranged by countries or geographical areas.
They continue the class of *State Papers Foreign, Treaties* (S.P.108).

PASSPORT OFFICE
See pp.22–23, 80–81.
Correspondence (F.O.612)   1815–1905

Correspondence, Registers of (F.O.613)   1868–1893; 1898–1905
One volume has been used also as a passport register for March–May 1915.

Correspondence with H.M. Embassies, etc. (F.O.614)   1886; 1897–1900
Replies to circulars inquiring into the issue of passports by consuls and of the passport requirements of foreign countries.

Passport Registers (F.O.610)   1795–1898

Passport Registers, Indexes of Names to (F.O.611)   1851–1862; 1874–1898

Representative Case Papers (F.O.737)   1920–1954

Representative Examples of Passports Issued (F.O.655)   1809–1921

CABINET PAPERS (F.O.899)   1900–1918
See pp.51–52, 64, 71, 89.

CONFIDENTIAL PRINT
See pp.52, 64, 71, 88–89.
The Public Record Office does not have copies of all Foreign Office Confidential Prints, although the *Numerical Series* (F.O.881) is virtually complete to about 1914 (no.10600). The various country, etc., classes, which overlap and continue the *Numerical Series*, contain in general only the regular series of 'Correspondence' and other Prints of some substance.

Numerical Series (F.O.881)   1829–c.1914
Prints 1–10600 arranged in order of their Print Numbers.

CONFIDENTIAL PRINT (continued)

Abyssinia (Ethiopia) (F.O.401)   1846–1910; 1914; 1924–1939; 1947–1956
    For 1911–1913, 1919–1923, 1942–1946 see *Africa* (F.O.403).

Afghanistan (F.O.402)   1922–1941; 1947–1957
    Before 1911 see *Asia, Central* (F.O.539); for 1942–1946 see *Eastern Affairs* (F.O.
406).

Africa (F.O.403)   1834–1957
    The countries of Africa, including Madagascar; Liberia (to 1946); Libya (to
1950); Algeria and Tunisia (to 1951); Abyssinia (1911–1913, 1919–1923, 1942–
1946); Morocco (1919–1920 and 1942–1946); Egypt and Suez Canal (1942–1946).

Albania, see *Europe, South-Eastern* (F.O.421) to 1933 and 1942–1946, *Europe,
Southern* (F.O.434) 1934–1941, *Yugoslavia and Albania* (F.O.504) from 1947.
Algeria, see *Africa* (F.O.403) to 1951, *Morocco and North-West Africa* (F.O.413)
    from 1952.

America (F.O.461)   1942–1956
    United States, Canada and South and Central America; from 1947 general corre-
spondence only.

America, Central, and the Caribbean (F.O.533)   1947–1957
    Costa Rica, Dominican Republic, Guatemala, Hayti, Honduras, Nicaragua,
Panama, El Salvador.

America, North (F.O.414)   1711–1941
    United States and Canada; Mexico (to 1919).

America, South and Central (F.O.420)   1833–1941
    Countries of South and Central America; Mexico (from 1920).

America, South, Other Countries (F.O.497)   1947–1956
    Bolivia, Chile, Colombia, Ecuador, Peru, Venezuela.

America, United States of (F.O.462)   1947–1956
    Before 1947 see *America, North* (F.O.414) to 1941, *America* (F.O.461) 1942–1946.

Antarctica (F.O.463)   1947–1957.
    See also *Polar Territorial Claims* (F.O.429)

Arabia (F.O.464)   1947–1957
    Before 1947 see *Eastern Affairs* (F.O.406) to 1898 and 1905–1946, *Persia* (F.O.
416) 1899–1904.

Argentina, see *America, South and Central* (F.O.420) to 1941, *America* (F.O.461)
    1942–1946, *River Plate Countries* (F.O.495) from 1947.

Asia, Central (F.O.539)   1834–1911
    Afghanistan, Persia and Turkestan.
    See also *Afghanistan* (F.O.402), *Persia* (F.O.416).

Asia, South-East, see *Siam and South-East Asia* (F.O.422) and *Far-Eastern Affairs*
    (F.O.436).

CONFIDENTIAL PRINT (continued)

Austria (F.O.465)   1947–1957
 Before 1947 see *Europe, Western* (F.O.425) to 1919, *Europe, Central* (F.O.404) 1920–1933 and 1942–1946, *Europe, Southern* (F.O.434) 1934–1938, *Germany* (F.O. 408) 1938–1941.

Baltic States, see *Scandinavia and Baltic States* (F.O.419) to 1941, *Northern Affairs* (F.O.490) 1942–1946.

Belgium and Luxembourg (F.O.466)   1947–1956
 Before 1947 see *Europe Western* (F.O.425) to 1933 and 1942–1946, *France* (F.O. 432) 1934–1941.

Bolivia, see *America, South and Central* (F.O.420) to 1941, *America* (F.O.461) 1942– 1946, *America, South, Other Countries* (F.O.497) from 1947.

Borneo and Sulu (F.O.572)   1844–1905

Brazil (F.O.467)   1947–1951
 Before 1947 see *America, South and Central* (F.O.420) to 1941, *America* (F.O.461) 1942–1946.

British Commonwealth (F.O.468)   1945–1949
 See also *Inter-Imperial Relations* (F.O.426).

Bulgaria (F.O.469)   1947–1957
 Before 1947 see *Europe, South-Eastern* (F.O.421) to 1933 and 1942–1946, *Europe, Southern* (F.O.434) 1934–1941.

Burma (F.O.435)   1947–1957
 See also *Siam and South-East Asia* (F.O.422).

Canada, see *America, North* (F.O.414) to 1941, *America* (F.O.461) 1942–1946.
Caribbean, see *America, South and Central* (F.O.420) to 1941, *America* (F.O.461) 1942–1946, *America, Central, and Caribbean* (F.O.533) from 1947.
Ceylon, see *India, Pakistan and Ceylon* (F.O. 479).
Chile, see *America, South and Central* (F.O.420) to 1941, *America* (F.O.461) 1942– 1946, *America, South, Other Countries* (F.O.497) from 1947.

China (F.O.405)   1848–1937; 1947–1957
 For the period 1937–1946 see *Far-Eastern Affairs* (F.O.436); from 1954 relates also to Formosa.

Colombia, see *America, South and Central* (F.O.420) to 1941, *America* (F.O.461) 1942– 1946, *America, South, Other Countries* (F.O.497) from 1947.

Contraband and Trading with the Enemy (F.O.551)   1915–1918

Costa Rica, see *America, South and Central* (F.O.420) to 1941, *America* (F.O.461) 1942–1946, *America, Central, and the Caribbean* (F.O.533) from 1947.

Crete, see *Europe, South-Eastern* (F.O.421).

Cultural Propaganda (F.O.431)   1919–1938

Cyprus, see *Europe, South-Eastern* (F.O.421).

CONFIDENTIAL PRINT (continued)

Czechoslovakia (F.O.470)   1947–1957

   Before 1947 see *Europe, Western* (F.O.425) to 1919, *Europe, Central* (F.O.404) 1920–1933 and 1942–1946, *Europe, Southern* (F.O.474) 1934–1938, *Poland* (F.O.417) 1939–1941.

Denmark (F.O.471)   1947–1957

   Before 1947 see *Europe, Western* (F.O.425) to 1919, *Scandinavia and Baltic States* (F.O.419) 1920–1941, *Northern Affairs* (F.O.490) 1942–1946.

Dominican Republic, see *America, South and Central* (F.O.420) to 1941, *America* (F.O. 461) 1942–1946, *America, Central, and the Caribbean* (F.O.533) from 1947.

Eastern Affairs (F.O.406)   1812–1946

   Arabia (except 1899–1904), Iraq, Palestine, Syria and the Levant; Turkey (1918–1922); Afghanistan and Persia (1942–1946).

Eastern Sanitary Reforms (F.O.542)   1899–1914

Economic Affairs, General (F.O.433)   1932–1939

Ecuador, see *America, South and Central* (F.O.420) to 1941, *America* (F.O.461) 1942–1946, *America, South, Other Countries* (F.O.497) from 1947.

Egypt and the Sudan (F.O.407)   1839–1941; 1947–1957

   For 1942–1946 see *Africa* (F.O.403); after 1957 see *United Arab Republic* (*Egypt and Syria*) (F.O.552); see also *Suez Canal* (F.O.423).

Estonia, see *Scandinavia and the Baltic States* (F.O.419) to 1941, *Northern Affairs* (F.O.490) 1942–1946.

Ethiopia, see *Abyssinia* (*Ethiopia*) (F.O.401).

European Affairs, General (F.O.430)   1932–1933

   Correspondence relating to war debts and to pacts between countries.

Europe, Central (F.O.404)   1920–1933; 1938; 1942–1947

   Austria, Czechoslovakia, Hungary (to 1933 and 1942–1946); Germany, Poland (1942–1946). The volumes for 1938 and 1947 contain general correspondence only, which is continued in *Europe, Eastern* (*General*) (F.O.472).

Europe, Eastern (*General*) (F.O.472)   1948–1956

   Continues the general correspondence previously in *Europe, Central* (F.O.404) and *Europe, South-Eastern* (F.O.421).

Europe, South-Eastern (F.O.421)   1812–1933; 1942–1947

   Albania, Bulgaria, Crete, Cyprus, Greece, Montenegro, Roumania, Serbia and Yugoslavia; Italy and the Vatican (from 1919); Turkey (from 1942). The volumes for 1947 contain general correspondence only, which is continued in *Europe, Eastern* (*General*) (F.O.472).

Europe, Southern (F.O.434)   1934–1941

   Albania, Bulgaria, Greece, Italy, Roumania, the Vatican and Yugoslavia; Austria, Czechoslovakia and Hungary (to 1938).

Europe, Western (F.O.425)   1769–1956

   Gibraltar, Portugal, Spain, Switzerland; Finland, Italy and the Vatican (to 1918); Austria, Czechoslovakia, Denmark, Germany, Hungary, Norway and Sweden (to

CONFIDENTIAL PRINT (continued)

Europe, Western (continued)

1919); Belgium, France and Luxembourg (to 1933 and 1942–1946); the Netherlands (to 1936 and 1942–1946). The volumes from 1947 onwards contain general correspondence only.

Far Eastern Affairs (F.O.436)   1937–1956
China, Japan, Nepal, Siam, South-East Asia. The volumes from 1947 onwards contain general correspondence only.

Finland (F.O.473)   1947–1956
Before 1947 see *Europe, Western* (F.O.425) to 1918, *Scandinavia and the Baltic States* (F.O.419) 1919–1941, *Northern Affairs* (F.O.490) 1942–1946.

France (F.O.432)   1934–1941; 1947–1956
Includes Belgium and Luxembourg (to 1941); and the Netherlands (1937–1941). Before 1934 and 1942–1946 see *Europe, Western* (F.O.425).

General Affairs (F.O.475)   1942–1956
Economic and financial questions, fishing limits, telecommunications, the United Nations, the world situation, etc.
See also *Miscellaneous* (F.O.412).

Germany (F.O.408)   1920–1941; 1947–1957
Includes Austria (1938–1941).
Before 1920 see *Europe, Western* (F.O.425); for the period 1942–1946 see *Europe, Central* (F.O.404).

Gibraltar, see *Europe, Western* (F.O.425).

Greece (F.O.476)   1947–1957
Before 1947 see *Europe, South-Eastern* (F.O.421) to 1933 and 1942–1946, *Europe, Southern* (F.O.434) 1934–1941.

Guatemala, see *America, South and Central* (F.O.420) to 1941, *America* (F.O.461) 1942–1946, *America, Central, and the Caribbean* (F.O.533) from 1947.
Hayti, see *America, South and Central* (F.O.420) to 1941, *America* (F.O.461) 1942–1946, *America, Central, and the Caribbean* (F.O.533) from 1947.
Honduras, see *America, South and Central* (F.O.420) to 1941, *America* (F.O.461) 1942–1946, *America, Central, and the Caribbean* (F.O.533) from 1947.

Hungary (F.O.477)   1947–1957
Before 1947 see *Europe, Western* (F.O.425) to 1919, *Europe, Central* (F.O.404) 1920–1933 and 1942–1946, *Europe, Southern* (F.O.434) 1934–1938, *Poland* (F.O.417) 1939–1941.

Iceland (F.O.478)   1947–1956
Before 1947 see *Scandinavia and the Baltic States* (F.O.419) to 1941, *Northern Affairs* (F.O.490) 1942–1946.

India, Pakistan and Ceylon (F.O.479)   1947–1949

Indo-China (F.O.474)   1947–1956
Before 1947 see *Siam and South-East Asia* (F.O.422) to 1888 and 1928–1937, *Far Eastern Affairs* (F.O.436) 1937–1946.

CONFIDENTIAL PRINT (continued)

Indonesia (F.O.480)   1947–1957
  See also *Siam and South-East Asia* (F.O.422).

Inter-Imperial Relations (F.O.426)   1926–1941
  See also *British Commonwealth* (F.O.468).

International Copyright (F.O.544)   1883–1914

Iraq (F.O.481)   1947–1957
  Before 1947 see *Eastern Affairs* (F.O.406).

Israel (Palestine) (F.O.492)   1947–1957
  Before 1947 see *Eastern Affairs* (F.O.406).

Italy (F.O.482)   1947–1957
  Before 1947 see *Europe, Western* (F.O.425) to 1918, *Europe, South-Eastern* (F.O.
  421) 1919–1933 and 1942–1946, *Europe, Southern* (F.O.434) 1934–1941.

Japan (F.O.410)   1859–1937; 1947–1956
  For 1937–1946 see *Far Eastern Affairs* (F.O.436).

Jordan (F.O.437)   1949–1957

Korea (F.O.483)   1947–1956

Latvia, see *Scandinavia and the Baltic States* (F.O.419) to 1941, *Northern Affairs* (F.O.
  490) 1942–1946.

Law Officers' Opinions (F.O.834)   1835–1939

League of Nations (F.O.411)   1924–1941

Lebanon (F.O.484)   1947–1957
  Before 1947 see *Eastern Affairs* (F.O.406).

Levant, see *Eastern Affairs* (F.O.406).

Liberia (F.O.485)   1947–1949
  Before 1947 see *Africa* (F.O.403).

Libya (F.O.540)   1951–1956
  Before 1951 see *Africa* (F.O.403).

Lithuania, see *Scandinavia and the Baltic States* (F.O.419) to 1941, *Northern Affairs*
  (F.O.490) 1942–1946.
Luxembourg, see *Europe, Western* (F.O.425) to 1933 and 1942–1946, *France* (F.O.432)
  1934–1941, *Belgium and Luxembourg* (F.O.466) from 1947.
Madagascar, see *Africa* (F.O.403).
Malaya, see *Siam and South-East Asia* (F.O.422).

Mexico (F.O.486)   1947–1956
  Before 1947 see *America, North* (F.O.414) to 1919, *America, South and Central*
  (F.O.420) 1920–1941, *America* (F.O.461) 1942–1946.

Middle East (General) (F.O.487)   1947–1957

Miscellaneous (F.O.412)   1836–1927
  Quarantine regulations, foreign refugees, international maritime law, limitation
  of armaments, etc.
  See also *General Affairs* (F.O.475).

CONFIDENTIAL PRINT (continued)

Mongolia, see *Tibet and Mongolia* (F.O.535).

Montenegro, see *Europe, South-Eastern* (F.O.421).

Morocco and North-West Africa (F.O.413)   1839–1915; 1921–1941; 1947–1957
For 1919–1920 and 1942–1946 see *Africa* (F.O.403).
Includes Algeria and Tunisia from 1952.

Nepal (F.O.488)   1947–1956
Before 1947 see *Far-Eastern Affairs* (F.O.436).

Netherlands (F.O.489)   1947–1956
Before 1947 see *Europe, Western* (F.O.425) to 1936 and 1942–1946, *France* (F.O.
432) 1937–1941.

Nicaragua, see *America, South and Central* (F.O.420) to 1941, *America* (F.O.461)
1942–1946, *America, Central, and the Caribbean* (F.O.533) from 1947.

Northern Affairs (F.O.490)   1942–1946
Baltic States, Denmark, Finland, Iceland, Norway, Russia, Sweden.

Norway (F.O.491)   1947–1956
Before 1947 see *Europe, Western* (F.O.425) to 1919, *Scandinavia and the Baltic
States* (F.O.419) 1920–1941, *Northern Affairs* (F.O.490) 1942–1946.

Opium (F.O.415)   1910–1941

Pacific Islands (F.O.534)   1822–1923

Pakistan, see *India, Pakistan and Ceylon* (F.O.479).

Palestine, see *Israel (Palestine)* (F.O.492).

Panama, see *America, South and Central* (F.O.420) to 1941, *America* (F.O.461)
1942–1946, *America, Central, and the Caribbean* (F.O.533) from 1947.

Paraguay, see *America, South and Central* (F.O.420) to 1941, *America* (F.O.461) 1942–
1946, *River Plate Countries* (F.O.495) from 1947.

Persia (F.O.416)   1899–1941; 1947–1957
For 1942–1946 see *Eastern Affairs* (F.O.406); see also *Asia, Central* (F.O.539).
Includes Arabia (1899–1904).

Peru, see *America, South and Central* (F.O.420) to 1941, *America* (F.O.461) 1942–
1946, *America, South, Other Countries* (F.O.497) from 1947.

Philippines (F.O.493)   1947–1956

Poland (F.O.417)   1814–1941; 1947–1956
For 1942–1946 see *Europe, Central* (F.O.404).
Includes Czechoslovakia and Hungary (1939–1941).

Polar Territorial Claims (F.O.429)   1930–1941
See also *Antarctica* (F.O.463).

Portugal (F.O.494)   1947–1956
Before 1947 see *Europe, Western* (F.O.425).

River Plate Countries (F.O.495)   1947–1956
Argentina, Paraguay, Uruguay.

CONFIDENTIAL PRINT (continued)

Roumania (F.O.496)   1947–1956
   Before 1947 see *Europe, South-Eastern* (F.O.421) to 1933 and 1942–1946, *Europe, Southern* (F.O.434) 1934–1941.

Russia and Soviet Union (F.O.418)   1821–1941; 1947–1956.
   For 1942–1946 see *Northern Affairs* (F.O.490).

Salvador, El, see *America, South and Central* (F.O.420) to 1941, *America* (F.O.461) 1942–1946, *America, Central, and the Caribbean* (F.O.533) from 1947.

Scandinavia and the Baltic States (F.O.419)   1919–1941; 1948–1949
   Estonia, Finland, Latvia, Lithuania; Denmark, Iceland, Norway, Sweden (from 1920); from 1948 general correspondence relating to Scandinavia only.

Serbia, see *Europe, South-Eastern* (F.O.421).

Siam and South-East Asia (F.O.422)   1882–1937; 1947–1956
   Siam; Indo-China (to 1888); Indonesia, Malayan Peninsula (to 1892); Burma (to 1894); South-East Asia (1928–1937).
   For 1937–1946 see *Far-Eastern Affairs* (F.O.436).

Slave Trade (F.O.541)   1858–1892

Soviet Union, see *Russia and Soviet Union* (F.O.418).

Spain (F.O.498)   1947–1956
   Before 1947 see *Europe, Western* (F.O.425).

Sudan, see *Egypt and the Sudan* (F.O.407).

Suez Canal (F.O.423)   1859–1941; 1947
   For 1942–1946 see *Africa* (F.O.403).

Sugar Bounties (F.O.549)   1877–1915

Sulu, see *Borneo and Sulu* (F.O.572).

Sweden (F.O.499)   1947–1956
   Before 1947 see *Europe, Western* (F.O.425) to 1919, *Scandinavia and the Baltic States* (F.O.419) 1920–1941, *Northern Affairs* (F.O.490) 1942–1946.

Switzerland (F.O.500)   1947–1956
   Before 1947 see *Europe, Western* (F.O.425).

Syria (F.O.501)   1947–1956
   Before 1947 see *Eastern Affairs* (F.O.406), from 1958 see *United Arab Republic (Egypt and Syria)* (F.O.552).

Territorial Waters (F.O.427)   1910–1931

Tibet and Mongolia (F.O.535)   1903–1923

Traffic in Arms (F.O.428)   1907–1928

Tunisia, see *Africa* (F.O.403) to 1951, *Morocco and North-West Africa* (F.O.413) from 1952.
Turkestan, see *Asia, Central* (F.O.539).

CONFIDENTIAL PRINT (continued)

Turkey (F.O.424)   1841–1914; 1922–1941; 1947–1957
  For 1918–1922 see *Eastern Affairs* (F.O.406), for 1942–1946 see *Europe, South-Eastern* (F.O.421).

Union of Soviet Socialist Republics, see *Russia and Soviet Union* (F.O.418).

United Arab Republic (*Egypt and Syria*) (F.O.552)   1958–1960

United Nations (F.O.502)   1947–1956
  See also *General Affairs* (F.O.475).

United States of America, see *America, United States of* (F.O.462).
Uruguay, see *America, South and Central* (F.O.420) to 1941, *America* (F.O.461) 1942–1946, *River Plate Countries* (F.O.495) from 1947.

Vatican (F.O.503)   1947–1956
  Before 1947 see *Europe, Western* (F.O.425) to 1918; *Europe, South-Eastern* (F.O.421) 1919–1933 and 1942–1946, *Europe, Southern* (F.O.434) 1934–1941.

Venezuela, see *America, South and Central* (F.O.420) to 1941, *America* (F.O.461) 1942–1946, *America, South, Other Countries* (F.O.497) from 1947.

War (*General*)   (F.O.438) 1914–1941

Yugoslavia and Albania (F.O.504)   1947–1956
  Before 1947 see *Europe, South-Eastern* (F.O.421) to 1933 and 1942–1946, *Europe, Southern* (F.O.434) 1934–1941.

EMBASSY AND CONSULAR ARCHIVES

  See pp.82–84.
  In the list which follows where no additional place-name appears after the name of the country, the reference is to the archives of the diplomatic mission to that country; where the name of the country is followed by a further place-name, the reference is to the consulate at that place. Where records from a single mission or consulate have been arranged in several classes, these have been reduced to a single entry; in these cases the covering dates given may not apply to each of the individual classes. Records of vice-consulates have normally been placed with the records of the consulates to which they are subordinated and are not noted individually here.
  The general nature of the records from each post is indicated by the following abbreviations:

C	Correspondence
Court	Records of Consular or other Courts
IC	Indexes to correspondence[1]
LB	Letter books
M	Miscellanea
RB	Registers of births
RBS	Registers, etc., of British subjects
RC	Registers of correspondence[1]
RD	Registers of deaths
R Deeds	Registers of deeds

  [1] The registers and indexes of correspondence are produced by their Index Room references (see p.109, n.2).

EMBASSY AND CONSULAR ARCHIVES (continued)

RL   Registers of titles to land
RM   Registers of marriages
RP   Registers, etc., of passports
Shipping   Records relating to shipping

For more detailed information on the contents of each class see the *Guide to the Contents of the Public Record Office*, Vol. II, pp.130–151, Vol. III, pp.52–67.

For archives of British legations and embassies, 1568–1789, and of the Levant Company and its consulates, 1606–1866, see *State Papers Foreign*, *Archives of British Legations* (S.P.105) and *Supplementary* (S.P.110).

See also PRIVATE COLLECTIONS (pp.149–150) and Appendix III.

ABYSSINIA (ETHIOPIA): *Addis Ababa* (F.O.915): 1912–1939: Court.
   Various[1] (F.O.742): 1899–1934: C, RC.
AFGHANISTAN (India Office Records, Class R/12) (see p.31, n.4).
ALGIERS (F.O.111–113): 1800–1897; 1939–1942: C, M.
AMERICA, UNITED STATES OF (F.O.115–117, 333): 1791–1942: C, LB, RC, M.
   Baltimore (F.O.703): 1821–1835; 1867–1938: LB, RC.
   Boston (F.O.620, 621, 706): 1871–1940: C, RC, RB, RD.
   Chicago (F.O.862): 1936–1937: C.
   Cincinatti: 1852–1856: C. See F.O.97/34–35.
   Galveston (F.O.701): 1900–1934: C, LB, RC [see also GENERAL CORRE-SPONDENCE BEFORE 1906: *Texas* (F.O.75/18–23) (p.123)].
   Honolulu (F.O.331): 1824–1944: C, RBS, RB.
   Houston (F.O.702): 1909–1932: RC.
   Los Angeles (F.O.740): 1927–1935: C.
   Manila (F.O.275): 1898: Docs. relating to cessation of Spanish rule.
   New Orleans (F.O.581): 1850–1938: RC.
   New York (F.O.281–285): 1816–1911: C, LB, RC, Shipping, M.
   Pensacola (F.O.885): 1880–1905: RB, RD.
   Philadelphia (F.O.879): 1936–1941: C.
   Portland (Oregon) (F.O.707): 1880–1929: RB, RD.
   St. Louis (F.O.739): 1908–1937: RC.
   San Francisco (F.O.600): 1906–1941: RC.
   Savannah (F.O.550): 1880–1937: RC.
   Washington (F.O.598, 599): 1921–1929: C, RC.
   Various (F.O.700): 1880–1936: RC, RB, RD, RBS.
ANGLO-EGYPTIAN SUDAN (F.O.867): 1910–1954: Minutes of proceedings of the Governor-General's Council and boundary papers.
ARGENTINE REPUBLIC (F.O.118, 119, 347): 1820–1941: C, LB, RC.
   Buenos Aires (F.O.446, 807): 1826–1900; 1937–1941: C, RC.
AUSTRIA (F.O.120–122, 657): 1793–1937: C, LB, RC, M.
   Budapest (F.O.114): 1872–1899: RM, M.
   Ragusa (F.O.219): 1862–1885: C, LB, RC.
   Trieste (F.O.590–592): 1775–1915; 1922–1926: LB, RC, Shipping, M [see also *ITALY: Trieste* (p.140)].
   Vienna (F.O.741): 1934–1939: C.
BAHRAIN[2] (F.O.903, 906): 1948–1952: Court.

[1] Formerly *Harar*.
[2] See also India Office Records class R/16 (see p.31, n.4).

EMBASSY AND CONSULAR ARCHIVES (continued)

BELGIUM (F.O.123–125, 300, 603): 1831–1914; 1926–1942: C, LB, RC, IC, M.

  Antwerp (F.O.606, 607): 1815–1941: C, LB, RC.

  Brussels (F.O.744): 1927–1935: C, RC (relating to births, marriages and deaths).

  Congo (F.O.629): 1889–1906; 1926; 1938–1942: C.

BOLIVIA (F.O.126, 127, 745, 758): 1837–1851; 1903–1942: C, RC, IC, M.

BRAZIL (F.O.128–131): 1808–1913; 1932–1942: C, LB, RC, M.

  Bahia (F.O.268–272): 1812–1915: C, LB, RC, Shipping, M.

  Pernambuco (F.O.843): 1823; 1864–1912: C.

  Porto Alegre (F.O.587–589): 1868–1935: LB, RC, M.

  Recife (F.O.865): 1927; 1931: M.

  Rio de Janeiro (F.O.743): 1815–1938; 1942: C, RC, RB.

  Sao Paulo Consular District (F.O.863): 1919; 1932–1936; 1943: C, RB, RM.

BULGARIA (F.O.388–390): 1848–1948: C, RC, M.

  Philippopolis (F.O.868): 1880–1922: RB, RD [see also *TURKEY: Burgas and Philippopolis* (p.144)].

  Sofia (F.O.864): 1934–1940: RB.

  Varna (F.O.884): 1851–1939: RB, RD [until 1908 *TURKEY*].

BURMA[1] (F.O.643): 1942–1947: C of the Burma Secretariat.

CHILE (F.O.132–134): 1829–1847; 1876–1878; 1885–1943: C, LB, RC.

  Coquimbo (F.O.594): 1888–1916: C.

  Punta Arenas (F.O.162, 805): 1891–1939: RC, M.

  Traiguen (F.O.595): 1896–1903: C.

  Valparaiso (F.O.596, 597, 814): 1871–1943: C, RC, Naval Courts.

CHINA[2] (F.O.228–233, 676, 677, 682, 917): 1759–1951: C, LB, RC, IC, M, Superintendent of Trade's records, papers in Chinese language, probate.

  Amoy (F.O.663): 1834–1951: C, RC, RB, RD, RM.

  Canton (F.O.694): 1844–1851: RBS, M.

  Chefoo (F.O.735): 1860–1941: M, copies of C relating to Chinese Maritime Customs Service.

  Chengtu (F.O.664): 1902–1945: RB, RD, RM, M.

  Chinanfu (Tsinan) (F.O.693): 1907–1937: Court.

  Chinkiang (F.O.385–387): 1871–1927: C, RC, RBS, Shipping, RM, M.

  Foochow (F.O.665): 1846–1946: C, RB, RD, RM, RBS.

  Hankow (F.O.666): 1863–1951: C, RB, RD, RM.

  Ichang (F.O.667): 1879–1941: C, RB, RD, RM.

  Kunming (F.O.668): 1945–1951: RB, RD, RM, M.

  Newchwang (F.O.669): 1865–1868: C.

  Ningpo (F.O.670): 1843–1933: C, RB, RD, RM, RBS.

  Peking (F.O.562–564, 692): 1874–1947: C, RC, RM, RBS, RP, M.

  Shanghai (F.O.656, 671, 672, 914): 1845–1949: C, RBS, RB, RD, RM, Court, Registrar of Companies.[3]

  Taku (F.O.673): 1862–1876: C, RB, RD, Court.

  Tientsin (F.O.674): 1860–1952: C, RB, RD, RM, Court.

  Tsingtao (F.O.675): 1911–1951: C, RC, RB, RD, RM, M.

  Wenchow (F.O.851): 1878–1906: C.

  Various (F.O.678–681): 1837–1959: Deeds, R Deeds, RL, RB, RD, RM.

---

[1] See also India Office Records.

[2] For similar material, 1623–1833, see India Office Records class R/10 (see p.31, n.4).

[3] See Keeton, *Development of Extraterritoriality in China*, II, pp.123–126, on the registration of British-owned companies in China.

K

EMBASSY AND CONSULAR ARCHIVES (continued)
COLOMBIA (F.O.135–138): 1823–1943: C, LB, RC, M.
 Bogota (F.O.854): 1823–1940: C.
 Various[1] (F.O.736): 1853–1927; 1945: RBS, RB, RD.
COSTA RICA: San José (F.O.654): 1922–1924: C.
CUBA (F.O.277–280): 1842–1937: C, LB, RC, Shipping, M.
 Antilla (F.O.457): 1925–1932: RC.
 Camguay (F.O.456): 1925–1929: RC.
 Havana (F.O.747): 1931–1936: RC.
 Nuevitas (F.O.455): 1926–1931: RC.
 Santiago (F.O.453, 454): 1832–1876; 1896–1905; 1913–1935: LB, RC.
CZECHOSLOVAKIA (F.O.746, 817): 1934–1951: C, IC.
 Prague (F.O.808): 1920–1939: RC.
DANZIG FREE PORT (F.O.883): 1924–1939: C [see also *GERMANY: Danzig* (p.139)].
DENMARK (F.O.211–213): 1780–1946: C, LB, RC.
 Copenhagen (F.O.749): 1915–1934: C.
 Reykjavik (F.O.321): 1916–1919; 1940; 1943: C.
 Thorshavn (F.O.649, 650): 1917–1950: C, RC.
DOMINICAN REPUBLIC (F.O.140): 1848–1904; 1925–1937: C.
 Ciudad Trujillo (Santo Domingo) (F.O.683): 1811; 1849–1932: RBS, RB, RD, RM, M.
ECUADOR (F.O.144, 145): 1825–1897; 1911–1922: C, RC.
 Guayaquil (F.O.521, 522, 815): 1850–1899; 1905–1939; 1942–1943: C, RC, R Deeds, RBS, RP.
EGYPT (F.O.141–143, 848): 1805–1937; 1942–1952: C, LB, RC, Milner Mission.
 Alexandria (F.O.847, 891): 1855–1952: C, Court.
 Cairo (F.O.841): 1830–1949: Court.
 Port Said (F.O.846): 1858–1859; 1873–1949: Court.
ESTONIA: Tallinn (Reval) (F.O.514): 1866–1940: RM, RBS, M.
ETHIOPIA. See *ABYSSINIA (ETHIOPIA)* (p.136).
FINLAND (F.O.511–513): 1919–1948: C, RC, M.
 Brahestad (F.O.755): 1930: RD.
 Helsinki (Helsingfors) (F.O.753): 1919–1941: RC, RD, M [see also *RUSSIA: Helsingfors* (p.142)].
 Kristinestad (F.O.756): 1928: RD.
 Tampere. See *RUSSIA: Tammerfors (Tampere)* (p.142).
 Turku (Abo) (F.O.754): 1928–1929: RB, RD.
 Viborg (Viipuri) (F.O.757): 1924–1937: RB, RD.
FRANCE (F.O.146–148): 1782–1915; 1924–1925: C, RC, M.
 Bordeaux (F.O.691): 1931–1947: RC.
 Brazzaville (F.O.859): 1940; 1942: C.
 Brest (F.O.293): 1866–1900: C, RC.
 Calais (F.O.452): 1822–1831: LB.
 Damascus (F.O.684): 1922–1944: C, RB, RM [see also *TURKEY: Damascus* (p.144)].
 Diego Suarez (F.O.711): 1907–1921: RB.
 Dieppe (F.O.712): 1871–1894: RB, RD.
 Douala (F.O.912): 1940–1942: C.

[1] Formerly *Santa Marta.*

EMBASSY AND CONSULAR ARCHIVES (continued)

FRANCE (continued)

La Rochelle (F.O.623): 1817–1877: C.

Le Treport (F.O.713): 1899–1929: RB, RD.

Lyons (F.O.751, 752): 1899–1936; 1942: C, RC.

Marseilles (F.O.698): 1815–1934: C, LB, RC.

Nantes (F.O.384, 622): 1825–1895; 1907–1921: C, RC, RM.

Papeete (F.O.687): 1818–1948: C, RC, RB, RD, RM, Shipping, RBS (see also p.95 above).

Paris (F.O.561, 565, 630): 1814–1940: C, LB, RC, RM.

Pondicherry (F.O.708): 1938–1955: C.

Réunion (F.O.322): 1864–1921: RM.

St. Pierre and Miquelon (F.O.349): 1905–1923: RC, RBS.

Strasbourg (F.O.750): 1928–1932: RC.

Tamatave (F.O.714): 1935–1940: RD.

Tananarive (Antananarivo) (F.O.710): 1862–1920: C, LB, RB.

Toulon (F.O.699): 1928–1939: RC.

GERMANY: BAVARIA (F.O.149–151): 1776–1914: C, LB, RC, RP.

    GERMANIC CONFEDERATION (F.O.208–210): 1810–1866: C, LB, RC.

    HAMBURG (F.O.158): 1791–1801: LB.

    HANOVER (F.O.159): 1820–1881: C, RP, M.

    HESSE-DARMSTADT AND BADEN (F.O.234, 255, 356): 1842–1913: C, LB, RC.

    PRUSSIA AND GERMANY (F.O.244–247, 340, 341): 1784–1913; 1925–1939: C, LB, RC, IC, M.[1]

    SAXONY AND SAXON DUCHIES (F.O.215–218): 1816–1914: C, LB, RC, RM, RD, RP, M.

    WÜRTTEMBERG[2] (F.O.163, 164): 1814–1893: C, RC.

Berlin (F.O.601): 1939; 1944–1954: RC, RB, RD.

Bremen (F.O.567–569, 585): 1872–1939: C, RC, RB, RM, RBS.

Bremerhaven (F.O.570, 586): 1897–1924: RC, RM, Shipping.

Breslau (F.O.715): 1929–1938: RB, RD.

Cologne (F.O.153–156): 1796–1806; 1850–1881; 1939: C, LB, RB, RM, RD, RP, Accounts.

Danzig (F.O.634): 1835–1914: C, RB, RD [see also *DANZIG* (p.138)].

Dar-Es-Salaam (F.O.704): 1899–1914: C.

Darmstadt (F.O.716): 1869–1905: RB, RD.

Dresden (F.O.292): 1899–1914: RB, RM, RBS.

Düsseldorf (F.O.298, 604): 1872–1934: C, RB, RM, RD.

Emden (F.O.571): 1910–1914: RC.

Hanover (F.O.717): 1861–1866: RB.

Karlsruhe (F.O.718): 1859–1864: RB, RD.

Königsberg (F.O.509): 1857–1933: RM.

Leipzig (F.O.299): 1836–1872: C.

Stettin (F.O.719): 1857–1939: RB, RD.

GREECE (F.O.286, 287, 381): 1813–1937; 1942–1946: C, RC, M.

Piraeus and Athens (F.O.582): 1841–1879: LB.

---

[1] For archives 1772–1806 in the *Jackson Papers* (F.O.383) see p.167 below; for correspondence 1788–1790 see also S.P.106/67.

[2] Formerly *Stuttgart*.

EMBASSY AND CONSULAR ARCHIVES (continued)

GUATEMALA (F.O.235, 252–254): 1803–1948: C, LB, RC, IC, M.
   Quezaltenango (F.O.659): 1891–1948: C.
HAYTI (F.O.866): 1833–1898; 1906–1914; 1922–1943: C, RB, RM, RD, Claims;
   for C 1826–1827 see F.O.97/245.
   Aux Cayes (F.O.376): 1870–1907: RB, RD.
HOLLAND AND NETHERLANDS (F.O.238–241): 1811–1908; 1940–1946:
   C, LB, RC, RP, Accounts, M.
   Amsterdam (F.O.242, 243, 760): 1816–1870; 1880–1940: C, LB, RC.
   Balik Papan (F.O.221): 1897–1909: C, LB.
   Curaçao Consular District (F.O.907): 1889–1966: RB, RD.
   Djakarta (Batavia) (F.O.810): 1946–1948: C.
   Groningen (F.O.761): 1919–1921: RC.
   Oleh-Leh (F.O.220): 1882–1885: C, LB, RC, RB, RD, RBS, Shipping, M.
   Rotterdam (F.O.759): 1915–1918: RC.
   Samerang (F.O.803): 1869–1941: RB, RD, R Baptisms.
HONDURAS (F.O.632): 1861; 1891–1912; 1936–1937: C, RC.
HUNGARY. See *AUSTRIA: Budapest* (p.136).
ICELAND. See *DENMARK: Reykjavik* (p.138).
IONIAN ISLANDS (F.O.348): 1793–1813: LB.
IRAN (PERSIA) (F.O.248–251): 1807–1954: C, LB, RC, Accounts, M.
   Bushire[1] (F.O.560): 1849–1895: RB, R Baptisms, RM, RD.
   Isfahan (F.O.799): 1941–1946: C.
   Mohammerah (Khorramshahr) (F.O.460): 1880–1929: C.
   Shiraz (F.O.880): 1891–1893: C.
   Tabriz (F.O.449–451): 1837–1923: C, LB, M.
IRAQ (F.O.624): 1921–1952: C.
   Amara (F.O.838): 1941–1951: C.
ITALY: [before 1860 *TUSCANY AND ROME*] (F.O.170–172, 695): 1814–
   1919; 1928–1940: C, LB, RC, IC.
   SARDINIA (F.O.167–169): 1813–1863: C, LB, RC.
   SICILY AND NAPLES (F.O.165, 166): 1764–1801; 1808–1860: C, RC,
   RP.
   Catania (F.O.823): 1930–1940: RC.
   Florence (F.O.904): 1936–1940: C.
   Genoa (F.O.762): 1815–1875; 1939–1940: C, LB, RC.
   Licata (F.O.720): 1871–1900: RB, RD.
   Marsala (F.O.824): 1909–1928: RC.
   Messina (F.O.825): 1925–1939: RC.
   Milan (F.O.795): 1907–1915: LB.
   Palermo (F.O.651–653, 822): 1810–1940: C, LB, RC, M.
   Trapani (F.O.826): 1890–1931: RC.
   Trieste (F.O.593, 842): 1919–1940; 1949–1954: RC, C of Brit. Polit. Adviser to
   Commander of Brit./U.S. Zone [see also *AUSTRIA: Trieste* (p.136)].
JAPAN (F.O.262, 263, 276, 344, 345): 1855–1941: C, LB, RC, Accounts, RM, M.
   Nagasaki (F.O.796): 1859–1937: C, RC, RBS, Court.
   Shimonoseki (F.O.797): 1901–1922: C, IC, RBS.
   Taiwan (Formosa) (F.O.721): 1873–1901: RD.

---

[1] For consular, etc., records from Bushire and other Persian Gulf sheikhdoms see also India Office Records classes R/15 and R/16 (see p.31, n.4).

EMBASSY AND CONSULAR ARCHIVES (continued)
JAPAN (continued)
   Tamsui (F.O.763): 1897–1939: C, RC.
   Tokyo (F.O.798): 1859–1928: C, RC, IC, Court.
   Yokohama (F.O.908): 1924–1927: C.
JORDAN (F.O.816): 1929–1948: C.
KOREA: Seoul (F.O.523): 1891–1902; 1909: C.
LATVIA: Libau (F.O.661): 1883–1939: C, RC [see also *RUSSIA: Libau* (p.142)].
   Riga (F.O.516): 1920–1940: RM, RBS [see also *RUSSIA: Riga* (p.142)].
LIBERIA (F.O.458, 459, 820): 1854–1939: C, LB, RC.
LIBYA (F.O.583): 1950–1951: M [see also *TRIPOLI* (p.143)].
LITHUANIA: Kovno and Memel (F.O.722): 1922–1940: RB, RD.
MEXICO (F.O.203–207, 696): 1822–1934; 1942–1943: C, LB, RC, IC, Accounts,
      Shipping, RP, M.
   Mexico City (F.O.723): 1815–1945: C, RB, RD. [see also F.O.203].
   San Luis Potosi (F.O.877): 1855–1904: C.
MOROCCO (F.O.174, 791, 853, 909): 1785–1891; 1900–1943: C, RC, IC, M. Court.
   Casablanca (F.O.827, 835): 1886–1940: C, RC.
   Marrakesh (F.O.828, 836): 1906–1940: C, RC.
   Mazagan (F.O.829): 1890–1946: RC.
   Mogador (F.O.631, 635, 830): 1813–1816; 1830–1933: C, LB, RC, M.
   Rabat (F.O.442, 443): 1843–1938; 1943: C, LB, RC, IC, RBS.
   Saffi (F.O.831, 832): 1865–1940: C, LB, RC.
   Tetuan (F.O.636): 1830–1843; 1857–1896; 1924–1935: C, LB, M.
NEPAL[1] (F.O.766): 1880–1943: C.
NICARAGUA (F.O.809): 1931–1935: C.
NORWAY (F.O.337, 338): 1905–1945: C, RC.
   Bodo (F.O.724): 1888–1895: RB, RD.
   Drammen (F.O.532): 1896–1906; 1918–1919: RC.
   Flekkefjord (F.O.530): 1881–1921: RC.
   Kragero (F.O.725): 1895: RD.
   Lofoten Islands (F.O.726): 1883–1891: RD.
   Oslo (Christiania) (F.O.236, 237, 330, 529): 1815–1937: C, LB, RC, RM, RBS.
   Porsgrund (F.O.531): 1885–1927: RC.
   Sarpsborg (F.O.764): 1916–1933: RC.
   Trondheim (F.O.765): 1920–1951: RC.
PACIFIC ISLANDS. See *AMERICA, UNITED STATES OF: Honolulu*
      (p.136); *FRANCE: Papeete* (p.139).
PANAMA (F.O.288–290): 1827–1943: C, LB, RC.
   Colon (F.O.806): 1890–1936; 1940: C, RC.
PARAGUAY: Ascuncion (F.O.527): 1855–1860; 1920–1951: C, M.
PERSIA. See *IRAN (PERSIA)* (p.140).
PERU (F.O.177, 178): 1836–1943: C, RC.
   Callao (F.O.855): 1867–1879: LB, Naval Courts.
   Lambayeque (San Jose Lambayeque) (F.O.857): 1868–1897: LB.
   Lima (F.O.856): 1929–1940: C.
POLAND (F.O.688): 1919–1930; 1940–1955: C [before 1919 see *RUSSIA: Warsaw* (p.142)].
   Lodz (F.O.869): 1925–1939: RB.

[1] For Nepal residency records, 1792–1872, see India Office Records, class R/5 (see p.31, n.4).

EMBASSY AND CONSULAR ARCHIVES (continued)

PORTUGAL (F.O.179, 180, 273, 274): 1800–1912: C, LB, RC, M.

  Funchal (F.O.811, 812): 1719–1721; 1750; 1801–1931: C, RC.

  Graciosa (F.O.555): 1863–1903: LB.

  Lisbon (F.O.173): 1809–1876; 1939: LB, RM, M.

  Loanda (F.O.375): 1859–1928: RC, RB, RM, RD.

  Macao (F.O.697): 1835–1866: C.

  Oporto (F.O.641, 642): 1812–1848; 1908–1935: C, LB, M.

  Ponta Delgada (F.O.556–559): 1804–1899; 1907–1929; 1946: C, LB, RC, RB, RM, RD, M.

  St. Vincent (Cape Verde) (F.O.767): 1881–1935: RC, RM.

ROUMANIA (F.O.770, 771): 1879–1915: C, RC.

  Braila (F.O.727): 1921–1930: RB, RD.

  Bucharest (F.O.625): 1851–1948: C, RB, R Baptisms, RD [see also *TURKEY: Bucharest* (p.144)].

  Galatz (F.O.517): 1879–1940: RM [see also *TURKEY: Galatz* (p.144)].

  Jassy (F.O.790): 1921–1923: RC [see also *TURKEY: Jassy* (p.144)].

  Sulina (F.O.728): 1860–1932: RB, RD [see also *TURKEY: Sulina* (p.144)].

RUSSIA AND U.S.S.R. (F.O.181–184): 1801–1920; 1938–1949: C, LB, RC, Shipping, M.

  Archangel (F.O.264–267): 1820–1919: C, LB, RC, Accounts, Shipping, M [see also ARCHIVES OF COMMISSIONS: *Archangel* (p.145)].

  Batum (F.O.397): 1884–1921: RM [see also *TURKEY: Batum* (p.144)].

  Helsingfors (Helsinki) (F.O.768): 1866–1924: RC, LB, RB [see also *FINLAND: Helsinki* (p.138)].

  Leningrad (St. Petersburg) (F.O.378, 379): [1856]–1938: RC, RB, RD,[1] RM, RBS, M.

  Libau (F.O.396, 400, 439, 440): 1813–1940: C, LB, RC, M [see also *LATVIA: Libau* (p.141)].

  Moscow (F.O.447, 448, 518): 1857–1941: C, LB, RC, RM.

  Odessa (F.O.257, 258, 359): 1807–1919: C, LB, RM, M.

  Riga (F.O.377): 1850–1918: RC, RB, RD [see also *LATVIA: Riga* (p.141)].

  Rostov-on-Don (F.O.398): 1891–1918: RM, R Deeds, M.

  Tammerfors (Tampere) (F.O.769): 1906–1934: RB, RD.

  Vladivostok (F.O.510, 537): 1907–1927: RC, RB, RD, RM, RBS [see also ARCHIVES OF COMMISSIONS: *Vladivostok* (p.148)].

  Warsaw (F.O.392–394, 640): 1830–1922: C, LB, RC, IC, RP, M [see also *POLAND* (p.141)].

  Miscellaneous (F.O.399): 1871–1933: RC, RB, Fees.

SALVADOR (F.O.813): 1922–1932; 1940: C.

SAUDI ARABIA (F.O.905): 1934–1941: C [see also *TURKEY: Jedda* (p.144) and WAR OF 1914 TO 1918: *Jedda Agency Papers* (p.126)].

SERBIA (F.O.260): 1869–1899: C [see also *YUGOSLAVIA* and *TURKEY: Serbia* (p.144)].

SIAM. See *THAILAND (SIAM)* (p.143).

SOMALILAND: Hargeisa Protectorate (F.O.844): 1827; 1884–1886; 1891–1899; 1943: C.

[1] For a Register of Births and Baptisms, 1818–1840, and Burials, 1821–1840, of the Independent Church at St. Petersburg, see R.G.4/4605.

EMBASSY AND CONSULAR ARCHIVES (continued)

SPAIN (F.O.185–187, 227): 1704–1939: C, LB, RC, M.

  Balearic Isles (F.O.214): 1773; 1802–1894; 1925–1952: C, LB, RC, M, Deeds.

  Barcelona (F.O.637–639): 1775–1922; 1940: C, LB, Shipping, RP, M.

  Bilbao (F.O.729): 1855–1870: RD.

  Canary Islands (F.O.772): 1764–1770; 1832–1931: LB, RC, IC.

  Madrid (F.O.444, 445): 1835–1931: C, RC, RBS.

  Seville (F.O.332): 1749–1825: M.

  Valencia (F.O.889): 1936–1944: C.

  Vigo (F.O.773): 1916–1940: C.

SUDAN. See *ANGLO-EGYPTIAN SUDAN* (p.136).

SWEDEN (F.O.188–191): 1802–1947: C, LB, RC, Accounts, M.[1]

  Gothenburg (F.O.818, 819): 1819–1936: C, LB, RC.

  Hudiksvall (F.O.730): 1884: RD.

  Oskarshamn (F.O.731): 1887: RD.

  Stockholm (F.O.748): 1812–1900; 1918–1945: C, LB, RC, RB, RM, RD.

SWITZERLAND (F.O.192–194): 1814–1913: C, LB, RC, RM.

  Berne (F.O.644): 1933–1946: RC.

  Davos (F.O.775): 1929–1939: RC.

  Geneva (F.O.778): 1850–1942: C, RC, RB, RD, RM.

  Lausanne (F.O.910): 1886–1948: RB, RD.

  Lucerne (F.O.774): 1899–1923: RC.

  Lugano (F.O.776): 1920–1946: RC.

  Montreux (F.O.911): 1902–1941: RB, RD, RM.

  Neuchatel (F.O.779): 1906–1937: RC.

  Zurich (F.O.777): 1915–1935: RC.

TEXAS: 1842–1845. See GENERAL CORRESPONDENCE BEFORE 1906: *Texas* (F.O.75/18–23) (p.123).

THAILAND (SIAM) (F.O.628, 689, 690): 1856–1937: C, LB, RC.

  Nakawn Lampang (F.O.821): 1896–1939: C, Court.

TRIPOLI (F.O.160, 161): 1742–1940: C, RM, RBS, RD, Wills, M [see also *LIBYA* (p.141)].

TUNISIA (TUNIS) (F.O.335, 339): 1669–1936: C, RC, LB, M.

  Bizerta (F.O.870): 1898–1931: RD.

  Djerba (F.O.871): 1925: RD.

  Gabes (F.O.872): 1925: RD.

  Goletta (F.O.878): 1885–1888: RB.

  Monastir (F.O.873): 1905–1908: RD.

  Sfax (F.O.874): 1896–1931: RD.

  Susa (F.O.875): 1894–1931: RD.

TURKEY (F.O.195–198, 261, 784): 1776–1943: C, LB, RC, IC, M.

  Adana (F.O.609): 1913–1946: RM.

  Aleppo (F.O.861): 1839–1900: C [see also *State Papers Foreign, Supplementary* (S.P.110)].

  Alexandretta (F.O.876): 1835–1857: C.

  Anatolia (F.O.222): 1879–1882: C, LB, IC.

  Angora and Konieh (F.O.732): 1895–1909: RB.

  Basra (F.O.602): 1761–1914: C.

  Batum (F.O.223): 1840–1852: C, LB, RC [see also *RUSSIA: Batum* (p.142)].

---

[1] For RP1806–1810 see F.O.95/454.

EMBASSY AND CONSULAR ARCHIVES (continued)
TURKEY (continued)

Beirut (F.O.226, 615, 616): 1810–1945: C, LB, RC, Shipping, M.

Bucharest (F.O.786): 1826–1884: C, RC, RBS, R Burials, R Actes, Court [see also *ROUMANIA: Bucharest* (p.142)].

Burgas and Philippopolis (F.O.860): 1876–1889; 1906: C [see also *BULGARIA: Philippopolis* (p.137) and ARCHIVES OF COMMISSIONS: *Eastern Roumelia* (p.146)].

Bursa (Brussa) (F.O.785): 1838–1853; 1880–1912: C, RC.

Cyprus (F.O.329): 1784–1878: C, RC, RP, R Deeds.

Damascus (F.O.618): 1837–1844; 1901–1921: C, LB [see also *FRANCE: Damascus* (p.138)].

Dardanelles (F.O.733): 1900–1914: RB.

Edirne (Adrianople) (F.O.783): 1886–1914: RB, RM, RBS.

Galatz (F.O.788): 1852–1873: C, Shipping, M [see also *ROUMANIA: Galatz* (p.142)].

Istanbul (Constantinople) (F.O.441, 780–782): 1784–1943: C, RC, RM, RD, Court, M.

Jaffa (F.O.734): 1900–1914: RB.

Jassy (F.O.789): 1836–1841; 1855–1859: C [see also *ROUMANIA: Jassy* (p.142)].

Jedda (F.O.685): 1859–1914: C, LB, RC [see also WAR OF 1914 TO 1918: *Jedda Agency Papers* (p.126) and *SAUDI ARABIA* (p.142)].

Jerusalem (F.O.617): 1844–1914; 1920–1921: LB.

Kustendje (F.O.887): 1862–1873: RB, RD.

Rustchuk (F.O.888): 1867–1908: RB, RD.

Salonika (F.O.294–297): 1852–1915: C, LB, RC, M.

Samsun (F.O.336): 1837–1863: LB, RC.

Serbia (F.O.224): 1837–1839: LB [see also *SERBIA* (p.142) and *YUGOSLAVIA* (below)].

Smyrna (Izmir) (F.O.626, 858): 1820–1954: C, Court.

Sulina (F.O.886): 1866–1877: RB, RD [see also *ROUMANIA: Sulina* (p.142)].

Tiflis (F.O.225): 1876–1878: LB.

Trebizond (Trabzon) (F.O.524–526): 1830–1913: LB, RC, RBS, Shipping, M.

Tripoli (Syria) (F.O.619): 1899–1900: C.

Varna. See *BULGARIA: Varna* (p.137).

URUGUAY (F.O.505–508): 1823–1924; 1935–1943: C, LB, RC, Naval Courts, M.

U.S.A. See *AMERICA, UNITED STATES OF.*

U.S.S.R. See *RUSSIA AND U.S.S.R.*

VATICAN (F.O.380): 1915–1921; 1937–1943: C.

VENEZUELA (F.O.199–202): 1823–1934; 1951–1952: C, LB, RC, Accounts, M.

YUGOSLAVIA (F.O.536): 1919; 1941–1951: C [see also *SERBIA* (p.142) and *TURKEY: Serbia* (above)].

ARCHIVES OF COMMISSIONS, ETC.
See pp.84–85.

Albania: International Commission of Control (British Delegation) (F.O.320) 1913–1914

America: Fisheries (F.O.301) 1873–1888
Commissions at Halifax (1873–1876) and Washington (1887–1888).

America: North-West Boundary (F.O.302) 1872–1876

ARCHIVES OF COMMISSIONS (continued)

America: Treaty of Ghent (F.O.303)   1796–1829
   Commissions under Articles 4 and 5 of the Treaty.

American Claims, 1794 (F.O.304)   1796–1806
   Commissions under Articles 5 and 7 of Treaty of Amity, Commerce and Naviga-
tion, 1794, and under Stat. 43 Geo. III c.39. For archives of the Commission under
Article 6 of the Treaty see F.O.95/513–514.

America, see also *British and American Claims, 1877* (F.O.305), *Mixed Arbitral Tribunals: Anglo-American Pecuniary Claims* (F.O.897), *Slave Trade: Sierra Leone* (F.O.
   315) and *Miscellaneous* (F.O.317).

Archangel: Allied High Commission: Correspondence (F.O.175)   1918–1919
Archangel: Allied High Commission: Registers of Correspondence, etc. (F.O.176)   1918–
   1919
   Established to render military assistance to the anti-Bolshevik forces in North
Russia.
   Formerly EMBASSY AND CONSULAR ARCHIVES: *RUSSIA, Archangel*
(*British Expedition*).
   See also *Vladivostok: Allied High Commission* (F.O.538).

Argentine Republic, see *British and Buenos Airean Claims* (F.O.307).

Austria: Inter-Allied Commission of Control (F.O.896)   1926–1928
   Established in 1921 to administer industrial disarmament of Austria prescribed
by Treaty of St. Germain.

Austria: Klagenfurt Plebiscite Commission (*British Section*) (F.O.895)   1920
   Established under Treaty of St. Germain.

Austria, see also *Mixed Arbitral Tribunals: Anglo-Austrian* (F.O.324).

Brazil, see *British and Brazilian Claims, 1858* (F.O.306) and *Slave Trade: Sierra Leone*
   (F.O.315).

British and American Claims, 1871 (F.O.305)   1871–1875
   Claims under Article 12 of the Treaty of Washington, 1871. For a register of
correspondence with the Foreign Office, 1871, see *Miscellaneous* (F.O.317/2).

British and Brazilian Claims, 1858 (F.O.306)   1858–1877
   Commission under the convention of 1858 for settling claims between subjects of
both powers.
   For a register of correspondence, 1858–1861, see EMBASSY AND CONSU-
LAR ARCHIVES: *BRAZIL: Registers of Correspondence* (F.O.130/9) (p.137).

British and Buenos Airean Claims (F.O.307)   1831–1834
   Commission under the convention of 1830 for settling British claims for acts of
violence committed by Argentine privateers during the war with Brazil.
   See p.94.

British and Mexican Mixed Commission, 1866 (F.O.318)   1835–1867
   Commission under the convention of 1866 for the settlement of outstanding
claims by British Subjects.

ARCHIVES OF COMMISSIONS (continued)

British and Mexican Commission, 1884 (F.O.319)   1885–1889

Commission under the Parliamentary Agreement of 1884 for the settlement of claims by British subjects on the Mexican government.

British and Portuguese Mixed Commission, 1817, see *Slave Trade: London* (F.O.308).

British and Portuguese Claims, 1840 (F.O.309)   1840–1849

Commission to examine claims of British subjects who served in the Portuguese Army and Navy during the war of liberation in Portugal.

For papers and documents referred to in the minutes see GENERAL CORRESPONDENCE BEFORE 1906: *Supplement to General Correspondence* (F.O.97/307) (p.124).

See p.94.

British and Venezuelan Claims, 1903 (F.O.310)   1903

Commission under the protocol of 1903 to satisfy claims by British subjects against the Venezuelan government.

Buenos Ayres, see *British and Buenos Airean Claims* (F.O.307).

Bulgaria, see *Eastern Roumelia, 1878–1879* (F.O.901) and *Mixed Arbitral Tribunals: Anglo-Bulgarian* (F.O.325).

Denmark, see *French, Danish and Spanish Claims Commission* (T.78) and *Schleswig: International Plebiscite Commission* (F.O.852).

Eastern Roumelia, 1878–1879 (F.O.901)   1878–1879

European Commission under Article 18 of Treaty of Berlin, 1878, to organize the autonomous state of Eastern Roumelia.

Received from a private source.

For 1880 see GENERAL CORRESPONDENCE BEFORE 1906: *Supplement to General Correspondence* (F.O.97/527–530) (p.124).

French, Danish and Spanish Claims (TREASURY) (T.78)   1787–1855

Various French Claims Commissions, 1815–1833, dealt with claims by British subjects under Article 2 of the Treaty of Commerce of 1786. The same Commissioners were instructed in 1834 to investigate claims on Denmark by British subjects arising from the confiscation of property in 1807 in retaliation for seizing the Danish fleet. They were further instructed in 1838 to deal with claims on Spain by British subjects whose property was confiscated on the declaration of war in 1804.

Germany: Inter-Allied Rhineland High Commission (F.O.894)   1920–1930

Supreme Allied administrative authority in the Rhineland under the Treaty of Versailles, 1920.

Germany, see also *Inter-Allied Armistice Commission* (W.O.144), *Mixed Arbitral Tribunals: Anglo-German* (F.O.326), *Schleswig: International Plebiscite Commission* (F.O.852) and *Upper Silesia (British Section): Inter-Allied Administrative and Plebiscite Commission* (F.O.890).

Hungary, see *Mixed Arbitral Tribunals: Anglo-Hungarian* (F.O.327).

Inter-Allied Armistice Commission (WAR OFFICE) (W.O.144)   1918–1920

Formed on 12 November 1918 to deal with prisoners of war and the handing

ARCHIVES OF COMMISSIONS (continued)

Inter-Allied Armistice Commission (continued)

over of materials, transport and stores under the terms of the Armistice. It later assumed administrative functions and became the channel of communication with German representatives until the ratification of the Peace Treaty.

Mexico, see *British and Mexican Mixed Commission, 1866* (F.O.318) and *British and Mexican Mixed Commission, 1884* (F.O.319).

Mixed Arbitral Tribunals
    Anglo-American Pecuniary Claims (F.O.897)   1923
      Claims to the Permanent Court of Arbitration at the Hague under the Arbitral Convention of 1908.
    Anglo-Austrian (F.O.324)   1921–1930
      Tribunal under Article 258 of Treaty of St. Germain, 1919.
    Anglo-Bulgarian (F.O.325)   1921–1927
      Tribunal under Article 188 of Treaty of Neuilly-sur-Seine, 1919.
    Anglo-German (F.O.326)   1921–1931
      Tribunal under Article 304 of Treaty of Versailles, 1919.
    Anglo-Hungarian (F.O.327)   1921–1931
      Tribunal under Article 239 of Treaty of Trianon, 1920.
    Clause 4 Arbitrations (F.O.328)   1922–1930
      Arbitral procedure under clause 4 of annex to Articles 249 and 250 of Treaty of St. Germain, Articles 297 and 298 of Treaty of Versailles and Articles 232 and 233 of Treaty of Trianon.

Netherlands, see *Slave Trade: Havana* (F.O.313), *Sierra Leone* (F.O.315), and *Surinam Absentees Sequestered Property Commission* (T.75).

Paris Exhibition, 1900 (F.O.311)   1897–1901
See p. 94.

Poland, see *Upper Silesia (British Section): Inter-Allied Administrative and Plebiscite Commission* (F.O.890).

Portugal, see *British and Portuguese Claims, 1840* (F.O.309) and *Slave Trade* (F.O. 308; F.O.312–315).

Reparation Commission 1919 (F.O.801)   1919–1931
    Set up by Treaty of Versailles, 1919, to assess damage done to Allied countries in war-time.

Rhineland, see *Germany: Inter-Allied Rhineland High Commission* (F.O.894).

Roumelia, Eastern, see *Eastern Roumelia, 1878–1879* (F.O.901).

Russia, see *Archangel: Allied High Commission* (F.O.175–176) and *Vladivostok: Allied High Commission* (F.O.538).[1]

Schleswig: International Plebiscite Commission (F.O.852)   1919–1921
    International Commission under Article 109 of Treaty of Versailles.

Silesia, see *Upper Silesia (British Section): Inter-Allied Administrative and Plebiscite Commission* (F.O.890).

---

[1] For correspondence of H.J.Mackinder, British High Commissioner for South Russia, 1919–1920, see p.168.

ARCHIVES OF COMMISSIONS (continued)

Slave Trade

Cape Town (F.O.312)   1843–1870
Mixed British and Portuguese Commission under Treaty of 1842.

Havana (F.O.313)   1819–1869
Commissions under treaties with Spain, Portugal and the Netherlands of 1817 and 1818 and subsequent years.

Jamaica (F.O.314)   1843–1851
Mixed British and Portuguese Commission under Treaty of 1842.

London (F.O.308)   1819–1824
Mixed British and Portuguese Commission under the convention of 1817.
Formerly known as *British and Portuguese Mixed Commission, 1817.*

Sierra Leone (F.O.315)   1819–1868
Commissions under various treaties with Spain, Portugal, the Netherlands, U.S.A., Brazil, etc.
See also *Miscellaneous* (F.O.317).

Spain: International Committee for the Application of the Agreement regarding Non-Intervention (F.O.849)   1936–1939
Spain: International Committee for the Application of the Agreement regarding Non-Intervention (CABINET OFFICE) (Cab.62)   1936–1945
This Committee was established in London and held meetings from September 1936 to April 1939. Related material will be found in the Hemming Papers at Corpus Christi College, Oxford.

Spanish Claims, 1823 and 1828 (F.O.316)   1790–1833
Commission under conventions of 1823 and 1828.

Spain, see also *French, Danish and Spanish Claims* (T.78) and *Slave Trade: Havana* (F.O.313) and *Sierra Leone* (F.O.315)

Surinam Absentees Sequestered Property Commission (TREASURY) (T.75)   1813–1822
Commission appointed by Treasury minute of 9 March 1813 to manage the estates in Surinam which belonged to persons residing in the French dominions.

Upper Silesia (British Section): Inter-Allied Administration and Plebiscite Commission (F.O.890)   1920–1922
Set up under Treaty of Versailles to administer Upper Silesia until a plebiscite could decide whether the population wished to be part of Germany or Poland.

Vladivostok: Allied High Commission (F.O.538)   1918–1921
Allied High Commission set up in 1918 to give military assistance to anti-Bolshevik forces in Siberia.
See also *Archangel: Allied High Commission* (F.O.175–176).

Miscellaneous (F.O.317)   1868–1892
Comprises: Royal Commission for inquiring into the Laws of Naturalization and Allegiance, 1868–1869; register of correspondence with the Foreign Office of Commission of Washington, 1871; Commission to revise Instructions to British Naval Officers engaged in Suppression of the Slave Trade, 1881–1882; Behring Sea Commission, 1891–1892.

ARCHIVES OF CONFERENCES
See pp.85–86.

Allied (War) Conferences (CABINET OFFICE) (Cab.25)   1915–1919[1]

Continent (F.O.139)   1813–1822
Conferences of Paris, 1814 and 1815; Congress of Vienna, 1814–1815; Conferences of Aix-la-Chapelle, 1818, and Vienna, 1822.

Formerly classified as EMBASSY AND CONSULAR ARCHIVES: *CONTINENT: Correspondence.*

Eastern Conference, Lausanne, 1922 to 1923 (F.O.839)   1922–1923
Conference of the Allied Powers with Turkish and Greek representatives to discuss the revision of Treaty of Sèvres and general question of peace in Near East.

Genoa (International Economic) Conference (CABINET OFFICE) (Cab.31)   1922

International Conferences (CABINET OFFICE) (Cab.29)   1916–1939
Papers of various international conferences and less formal meetings with representatives of foreign governments, including the Peace Conference, 1919–1920, the London Reparations Conference, 1924, the Hague Conference, 1929–1930, and the Lausanne Conference, 1932.

Locarno Conference, 1925 (F.O.840)   1925
Conference between representatives of Belgium, France, Germany, Great Britain and Italy leading to Treaty of Mutual Guarantee.

PEACE CONFERENCE OF 1919 to 1920 [see also *International Conferences*]
    Acts of the Conference (F.O.374)   1919; 1922–1935
    Conference of Ambassadors, Paris (F.O.893)   1920–1930
    Correspondence (F.O.608)   1919–1920
    Handbooks (F.O.373)   1918–1919

Washington (Disarmament) Conference (CABINET OFFICE) (Cab.30)   1921–1922

VARIOUS
Seals and Ink Stamps (F.O.365)
Matrices of seals of Secretaries of State, of the Chief Clerk of the Foreign Office, and of various missions, consulates and commissions; and franking stamps of missions and consulates.

Originally two classes: *Seals* (F.O.365) and *Ink Stamps* (F.O.346). In 1953 the latter class was abolished, its contents being destroyed with the exception of ten specimens which were added to F.O.365, the title being changed to that above.

For impressions of consular ink stamps see *Public Record Office: Various: Impressions of Ink and Rubber Stamps* (P.R.O.29/1).

Specimens of Classes of Documents Destroyed (F.O.900)   1824–1862; 1927–1951
Specimens of documents relating to Foreign Service Messengers destroyed under the *Second Foreign Office Schedule* of 1923 and of consular archives destroyed under the *Foreign Office (Consular Archives) Schedules* of 1920 and 1953 (see p.95).

PRIVATE COLLECTIONS
See Appendix III and pp.86–88.
Ampthill Papers (F.O.918) c. 1852–1884.
Aston Papers (F.O.355)   1827–1843

[1] For this and other Cabinet Office *Conference* classes see *Records of the Cabinet Office to 1922* (P.R.O. Handbook No. 11), pp.34–35.

PRIVATE COLLECTIONS (continued)

Bloomfield Papers (F.O.356)   1823–1871
Clarendon Papers (F.O.361)   1867–1870
Cowley Papers (F.O.519)   1774; 1802–*c*.1935
Cromer Papers (F.O.633)   1872–1929
English Church at the Hague (F.O.259)   1658–1822
Granville Papers (F.O.362)   1870–1874
Hammond Papers (F.O.391)   1831–1834; 1854–1885
Henderson Papers (F.O.357)   1818–1831
Hertslet Papers (F.O.351)   1730–1854
Hervey Papers (F.O.528)   1778–1794; 1830–1840
Howard de Walden Papers (F.O.360)   1817–1834
Jackson Papers (F.O.353)   1763–1856
Jordan Papers (F.O.350)   1901–1919
Malet Papers (F.O.343)   1884–1895
Ministers and Officials: Various (F.O.800)   1824–1949
Miscellaneous (F.O.323)   1636–1887
Pierrepont Papers (F.O.334)   1791–1807
Pottinger Papers (F.O.705)   1797–1798; 1809–1860; 1879
Simmons Papers (F.O.358)   1857–1896
Stratford Canning Papers (F.O.352)   1778–1863
Stuart de Rothesay Papers (F.O.342)   1801–1814
Tenterden Papers (F.O.363)   1873–1882
White Papers (F.O.364)   1857–1891
Woodbine Parish Papers (F.O.354)   1813–1855

Appendix I: Foreign Office Clerks 1782–1851

From 1852 lists of Clerks serving in the Foreign Office have been published in the annual *Foreign Office Lists*. These *Lists* also include brief official biographies, although it is only since 1854 that biographies have been included for retired as well as serving Clerks. Before 1852 there is no single source for information on the careers of the Clerks and the following list is intended to remedy to some extent this lack.

It includes Clerks, Private Secretaries and Précis Writers who retired before 1852 and died before 1854 or who otherwise do not appear in the *Foreign Office Lists*. Only those Under Secretaries who had previously served in the Foreign Office in one of the above capacities are included.

The list has been compiled from the following printed and manuscript sources: *The Royal Kalendars 1783–1795; App. to 1st Rpt. of Commrs. on Fees* (1785), pp.27–32; *H.C. Sessional Papers* 1833 (267) XXIII, pp.367–375; *Dictionary of National Biography;* Hertslet, *Recollections; Brit. Diplomatic Representatives 1789–1852;* F.O.83/10; F.O.95/591; F.O. 366/280, 369, 380–383, 386, 392, 542, 553, 669–674, 685.

ANCELL, *Richard*
Clerk in State Paper Office from Nov. 1776; Librarian 1801–1810

ANCRAM, *John William Robert Kerr, Earl of (later 7th Marquis of Lothian)*
Private Secretary 1819–1820

ARBUTHNOT, *Charles*
Précis Writer 1793;
Subsequently entered Parliament, became Under Secretary of State, 1803–1804, and later served in Diplomatic Service;
Died 1850

ASHBURNHAM, *Hon. Charles*
Précis Writer 1828–1829;
Previously and subsequently served in Diplomatic Service

AUST, *George*
Second Senior Clerk in 1782 with about 20 years' service;
Under Secretary of State 20 Feb. 1790–5 Jan. 1796

BANDINEL, *James*
Appointed Clerk April 1799;
Superintendent of Slave Trade Department from about 1819;
4th Senior Clerk 1822; 2nd Senior Clerk 1824;
Retired 12 Dec. 1845; Died 29 July 1849

BARTLETT, *Richard*
Appointed Extra Clerk 4 June 1806;
Permanently attached as Supernumerary Clerk 5 Jan. 1819;
Appointed Consul at Corunna 14 Jan. 1822;
Consul at Teneriffe 19 June 1830

BENTINCK, *Lord William George Frederick Cavendish*
Private Secretary 1822–1824;
Subsequently entered Parliament;
Died 1848

BIDWELL, *Thomas, Senior*
A Clerk in 1782 with about 15 years' service;
2nd Senior Clerk 1787;
Chief Clerk 18 April 1792;
Died 28 Sept. 1817

BIDWELL, *Thomas, Junior*
Appointed Clerk 20 Oct. 1790;
Senior Clerk 1806;
Chief Clerk 2 Feb. 1824;
Retired 5 April 1841; Died 1 May 1852

BODE[1]
An Assistant Clerk in the Treaty Department in 1846

BOUVERIE, *Hon. Edward Pleydell*
Précis Writer 1840;
Subsequently entered Parliament;
Died 1889

---

[1] Probably William Bode the last head of the Secretary of State's Secret Office in the Post Office, abolished in 1844. See Ellis, *Post Office*, pp.138, 141.

BROUGHTON, *Bryan*
1st Senior Clerk in 1782 with over 20 years'
service; also Clerk in Treasury;
Retired 1787

BROUGHTON, *Charles Rivington*
Appointed Clerk 22 April 1788;
2nd Senior Clerk 1803;
Retired 4 Feb. 1824; Died 14 Nov. 1832

BROWN, *John Henry Torrens Temple*
Appointed Extra Copying Clerk 13 Dec.
1837;
Transferred to Slave Trade Department
14 March 1838;
Resigned between 1839 and 1841

BRUCE, *Hon. James*
Précis Writer 1797–1798

BRUCE, *Stuart Crawford*
Served in Foreign Office 1826–1827;
Subsequently served in Diplomatic Service

CARTER, *Richard*
Clerk in 1782; had resigned by 1784

CARTWRIGHT, *Thomas (later Sir Thomas)*
Précis Writer 1817–1821;
Previously and subsequently served in
Diplomatic Service;
Died 1850

CASAMAJOR, *Justinian*
Appointed Clerk 18 Aug. 1797;
Resigned 1799;
Subsequently served in Diplomatic Service

COCKBURN, *Alexander*
Clerk 1795–1799;
Subsequently served in Diplomatic Service

DOWLING, *Daniel Morton*
Clerk in Slave Trade Department 21 Aug.
1841–20 Oct.1845

FLINT, *Charles William*
Appointed Clerk 1795;
Salary became dormant 2 July 1798 on
appointment as Superintendent of Aliens

FORBES, *John*
Private Secretary 1810–1812

FRANCKLIN, *George Fairfax*
Attaché (unpaid) in Chief Clerk's Dept. from
6 Jan. 1827;
Transferred to Consular Dept. April 1835;
Resigned 19 July 1837

FRASER, *John Henry David*
Served in Foreign Office 1826;
Subsequently served in Diplomatic Service

FRASER, *William*
Under Secretary 1782–1789 (formerly Under
Secretary in the Northern Department);
Translator of the German Language, 21 June
1797–11 Dec. 1802[1]

GODDARD, *Charles*
Private Secretary 1795–1796;
Subsequently Transmitter of State Papers

GRAHAM, *David*
Appointed Clerk 18 Oct. 1805;
Retired 21 July 1817; Died 11 Sept. 1824

GREVILLE, *Algernon Frederick*
Private Secretary, 1834–1835 (Private
Secretary to Duke of Wellington, 1827–1842);
Died 1864

GREY, *W. Henry, Junior*
Copying Clerk in Consular Department
1842–1846

HAMILTON, *William Richard*
Private Secretary 1804;
Précis Writer 1804–1806;
Under Secretary of State 1809–1822;
Minister to Sicily 1822–1825;
Died 1859

HAY, *James William*
Appointed Clerk 17 Oct. 1788;
Retired 5 July 1805; Died 18 Jan. 1806

HERVEY, *Lord William*
Appointed Clerk 21 Jan. 1825;
Appointed Paid Attaché at Vienna 5 Jan. 1828
and subsequently served in the Diplomatic
Service (see p.166 below)

---

[1] He earlier held this sinecure conjointly with his Under Secretaryship. See Ellis, *Post Office*,
p.133.

HINCHLIFFE, *John*
Appointed Clerk 16 July 1782;
1st Senior Clerk 1794;
Retired 1 April 1799 and died shortly
afterwards

HUSKISSON, *William Milbanke*
Appointed Clerk 17 Nov. 1834;
Died 13 January 1849

HUTTNER, *John Christian*
Translator of the Spanish, Portuguese, Italian
and Danish Languages from about 1808 (see
p.11);
Died May 1847

JACKSON, *Francis James*
Appointed Clerk 12 Jan. 1781;
Appointed Secretary of Legation at Berlin
1789 and had a subsequent career in the
Diplomatic Service (see p.167);
Died 5 Aug. 1814

JACKSON, *John*
Appointed Clerk 27 Jan. 1806, having been
previously employed for 7 years as an Extra
Clerk;
Retired 5 July 1830

JENKINS, *John W.*
A Clerk in 1782 (appointed Nov. 1760);
2nd Senior Clerk 1790;
Retired 1794

JENKINSON, *Hon. Charles Cecil Cope (later
3rd Earl of Liverpool)*
Précis Writer 1803–1804;
Subsequently entered Parliament and was
Under Secretary at Home Office, 1807–1809,
and War Office, 1809;
Died 1851

JOHNSON
Served in Slave Trade Department for a
period before 14 March 1838

LAMBE, *Thomas Davis*
Private Secretary 1801–1802

LIDDELL, *Hon. Thomas*
Clerk 1824–1826

MANBY, *James*
A Clerk in 1782 (appointed 15 Aug. 1780);
Died before 12 Jan. 1787

L

MARSHALL, *Samuel Gregory*
Supernumerary Clerk for a period from
5 July 1812

MASTERTON, *Charles*
Assistant Translator Oct. 1823–5 April 1831;
Consul at Cochabamba (Bolivia) March 1838

MILDMAY, *Hugo Cornwall St. John*
Clerk 1824–1844

MONEY, *William*
A Clerk in 1782 (appointed 15 Aug. 1780;
formerly served in Diplomatic Service);
2nd Senior Clerk 1792;
Retired 1794

MOORE, *Francis*
Appointed Clerk 5 July 1784;
2nd Senior Clerk 1 April 1799;
Retired January 1803; Died 21 Aug. 1803

NOEL, *Charles Noel*
Clerk 1798–1799

PETTINGAL, *Charles*
Clerk attached to Slave Trade Department
before 1839;
Appointed Arbitrator (Slave Trade) at Cape
Verde Islands 30 Aug. 1843

PIERREPONT, *Hon. Henry Manvers*
Private Secretary 1802–1804;
Subsequently served in Diplomatic Service
(see p.168 below)

PLANTA, *Joseph, Junior*
Appointed Clerk 27 Sept. 1802;
Précis Writer 1809–1817; Private Secretary
1814–1817;
Appointed Under Secretary 25 July 1817;
Retired 19 April 1827;
Subsequently entered Parliament and was
Joint Secretary of the Treasury 1827–1830;
Died 5 April 1847

QUICK, *William Fortescue*
Appointed Clerk in Librarian's Department
24 Aug. 1841;
Died 19 Aug. 1844

RICH, *Henry O.L.*
Appointed Temporary Clerk in Librarian's
Department 24 Aug. 1841;
Dismissed 15 April 1845

ROBINSON, *Henry Stirling*
Appointed Clerk 20 Sept. 1826;
Resigned 27 Aug. 1829

ROLLESTON, *Stephen*
Appointed Clerk 31 July 1783;
2nd Senior Clerk 1795; 1st Senior Clerk
1 April 1799;
2nd Chief Clerk 10 Aug. 1804;
sole Chief Clerk from 28 Sept. 1817;
Retired 5 Jan. 1824; Died 19 Nov. 1828

ROSS, *James Tyrrell*
Private Secretary 1807–1809

RUPERTI, *Christian*
Employed as Clerk and Translator (not on the
establishment) since before 1791;
Joint Translator of the German Language
1806–1809

RYDER, *Hon. Frederick Dudley*
Appointed Clerk 1827;
Dismissed 29 Oct. 1834
[There is an incorrect entry for him in the
early *Foreign Office Lists*]

SCHEENER, *Edward*
Appointed Supernumerary Clerk 5 Aug. 1809;
Put on establishment 1814;
Ordered to absent himself permanently from
the Foreign Office 12 Sept. 1826;
Retired 5 July 1830
[Many papers relating to his case are in F.O.
95/591]

SCOTT, *Charles*
Appointed Clerk 11 Jan. 1828;
Died in Persia 28 Oct. 1841

SEALE, *Robert B.*
Appointed Clerk in Librarian's Department
24 Aug. 1841;
Dismissed 23 Oct. 1844

SMITH, *Lt.-Col.*
Private Secretary 1805–1806

SNEYD, *Jeremy*
Chief Clerk in 1782 with about 35 years'
service, about 13 of them as Chief Clerk;
Retired 18 April 1792

STAPLETON, *Augustus Granville*
Appointed Clerk 12 Nov. 1823;
Private Secretary 1824–1827;
Retired 31 Aug. 1828 on appointment as
Commissioner for Customs;
Died 26 Feb. 1880

TALBOT, *Robert*
Private Secretary 1806–1807

TAUNTON, *Walter G.*
Extra Clerk in Librarian's Department
28 Nov. 1844 to 23 June 1845

TAYLOR, *Brook (later Sir Brook)*
Appointed Clerk 1795;
Resigned on becoming Private Secretary to
Secretary of State 1796 (to 1801); also Précis
Writer 1798–1801;
Subsequently served in Diplomatic Service;
Died 1846

TAYLOR, *Herbert (later Lt.-Gen. Sir Herbert)*
Appointed Clerk 2 Aug. 1792;
Resigned on receiving Army Commission
25 May 1794;
Died 20 March 1839

TAYLOR, *William Watkinson*
Clerk 1795–1797

TROTTER, *John Bernard*
Private Secretary 1806;
Précis Writer 1806–1807;
Died 1818

TURNER, *Adolphus*
Appointed Clerk 1824;
Appointed Consul-General at Monte Video
11 April 1843

VAUGHAN, *Charles Richard (later Sir Charles)*
Private Secretary 1809–1810;
Subsequently served in Diplomatic Service;
Died 1849

WARD, *Edward Michael*
Private Secretary 1812–1814;
Subsequently served in Diplomatic Service

WARREN, *Charles*
Appointed Clerk 20 Oct. 1790;
3rd Senior Clerk 1806;
Retired 16 June 1818

WESLEY (*later Wellesley*), *Hon. Henry (later
1st Baron Cowley*)
Précis Writer 1795–1797;
Subsequently served in Diplomatic Service
(see p.165);
Died 1847

WILSON, *Robert*
Assistant in Librarian's Department 1826;
Died 1839

WOODCOCK, *Charles*
PrivateSecretary 1804–1805;
Extra Clerk 1805

WRANGHAM, *Digby Cayley*
Clerk and Private Secretary 1827–25 April
1831

WYNN, *Thomas Edward*
Appointed Clerk 21 April 1796;
Resigned 17 Feb. 1802

L*

Appendix II: Signs and Codes used in Registers and Indexes

(a) Signs in Use in Departments in 1890[1]

	Eastern	Western	American	Commercial	Consular and African	Treaty
Confidential	Cf.	C	Conf.		Conf$^{l.}$	Conf$^{l.}$
Consuls	[Separate]	Underlined in black	[Separate]			
Cross-references: in	Black	Black	Black	Black $\sim$	Black $\sim$	Black
out	Red	Red	Red	23	23	23
Immediate	Imm. or Imm$^{te.}$	Imm$^{t.}$	Immte.		Imm$\underline{^{te.}}$	Imm$\underline{^{te.}}$
No draft; or printed letter	B (in red)	X	PL	PL	PL	PL
Paper returned without covering letter				27		
Printed	P (in black)					
Telegram	[Separate]	Red	Red	Tel.	Tel.	Tel.
Telegram paraphrased	P (in red)	P (in black)	P (in red)			
Transmitting	Tr.	Trs.	Trans.	Transmits	In orig$^{l.}$ or copy	Trs.

The abbreviations used for Public Offices varied somewhat from department to department but are always obvious.

(b) Standard Signs introduced in 1891[2]

Conf.	Confidential.
Dom.	Domestic.
Imm.	Immediate.
Mess.	Sent by Messenger.
O.	No draft kept of letter sent; or printed letter used.
P (next to register number)	Despatch printed.[3]
P (in red)	Telegram paraphrased.
Post.	Sent by post.
Sends (256)	Paper returned without covering letter.
Tr. $\overline{\quad\quad}$	Transmitting.

Cross references are in black for incoming correspondence and in red for drafts.
Public Offices are referred to by their initials.

(c) Country Code Letters 1891–1905 (see p.43)

In 1891 each department assigned code letters to the countries with which it dealt and these were used to index the departmental registers. Because of the breakdown and subsequent revision of the

---

[1] From a list in F.O.97/565.
[2] From F.O.366/724, p.475. A list of permitted abbreviations is in F.O.881/6017, p.2.
[3] In 1898 the sign for a despatch which had been printed was changed to X. See F.O.881/7034*, p.15.

indexing system these code letters now have a practical application only in the indexes of the Consular, Commercial and Treaty Departments.[1] The code letters usually appear on the spines of the registers for this period in F.O.566.

	POLITICAL DEPARTMENTS			NON-POLITICAL DEPARTMENTS		
	Western	*Eastern*	*American and Asiatic*[2]	*Consular*[3]	*Commercial*[4]	*Treaty*[5]
A	France	Turkey	U.S.A.	Russia	France	Austria–Hungary
Af.				African Protectorates; Liberia (1900)		
AF.X						Africa (*from* 1897)
B	Italy	Russia	China; *and* Korea (*from* 1900)	Sweden; Norway	Belgium	Belgium
BS.B						Balkan States
C	Switzerland	Central Asia	Japan	Denmark	Netherlands	Coronation and Illness of King Edward VII
C.A.						Central America* (*to* 1895)
Ch. *or* China				China		
C.J.S.						China; Japan; Siam (to 1897)[6]
D	Spain	Egypt	Siam	Netherlands	Austria–Hungary	Denmark
D.Q.						Death of Queen Victoria
E	Portugal	Persia	Brazil	Belgium; *and* Congo (*from* 1901)	Germany	Egypt
F	Tunis	Greece	River Plate Countries	Germany	Switzerland	France
F.E.						Free Entries
F.S.						Foreign Ships
G	Morocco	Roumania	Mexico	Austria–Hungary	Sweden; Norway	Germany
Gr.G.						Greece
H		Serbia	Central America	France	Denmark	

[1] The Commercial Department index uses country code letters only to 1899; the Treaty Department index for the period 1891–1899 is wanting. The African Departments did not use country code letters.

[2] Two separate departments from 1899.

[3] See the lists at tne front of F.O.804/51.

[4] See the lists at the front of F.O.804/57.

[5] See the lists at the front of F.O.804/56.

[6] From 1898 see under W: Asia.

	POLITICAL DEPARTMENTS			NON-POLITICAL DEPARTMENTS		
	Western	*Eastern*	*American and Asiatic*	*Consular*	*Commercial*	*Treaty*
H.D.						Hayti; S. Domingo* (*to* 1895)
I	Pacific Islands		Peru; Bolivia	Switzerland	Russia	Italy
J			Chile	Italy		
Jap. *or* Japan				Japan		
K		Bulgaria	Colombia	Greece	Italy	
L	Austria	Montenegro	Venezuela	Turkey; *including* Bulgaria; Monte-negro; Muscat (*from* 1901); Crete (*from* 1904)		
L.O.						Law Officers
M	Hungary		Ecuador	Roumania; Serbia	Portugal	
Me						Mexico* (*to* 1895)
Misc.				Miscel-laneous; *including* Pacific Islands (*from* 1901)		
Mo						Morocco (*to* 1897)
N	Germany		Hayti; S. Domingo	Egypt; *including* Abyssinia (*from* 1901)	Turkey	Netherlands
O	Bavaria			Morocco	Balkan States	
O/C						Orders in Council (*to* 1897)
P	Coburg			Persia	Persia	
Pa						Persia (*to* 1897)
Pl						Portugal
Q	Darmstadt			Borneo		
R				Spain	Greece	Russia
S	Württemberg			Portugal	Egypt	
S.A.						South America* (*to* 1895)
Siam				Siam		
S.N.						Sweden; Norway
Sp.						Spain

| | POLITICAL DEPARTMENTS | | | NON-POLITICAL DEPARTMENTS | | |
	Western	*Eastern*	*American and Asiatic*	*Consular*	*Commercial*	*Treaty*
Sw.						Switzerland
T	Denmark			U.S.A.; *and* Cuba (*from* 1903)	Morocco	Turkey
T.S.						Treaty Series
U	Sweden			Central America; Colombia; Mexico		
U.S.						U.S.A.
V	Norway			Brazil	U.S.A.	Mexico; Central and South America[1] (*from* 1896)
W	Netherlands			Peru; Chile	Central America; Mexico	Asia (*from* 1898)
X	Belgium			River Plate Countries	South America	Miscellaneous (*to* 1897)
Y	Borneo			Hayti; S. Domingo	Miscellaneous	
Y.A.						Russo–Japanese War: Miscellaneous
Y.B.						Russo–Japanese War: coaling general
Y.C.						Russo–Japanese War: Foreign Enlistment Act.
Y.D.						Russo–Japanese War: Japanese seizures
Y.E.						Russo–Japanese War: Russian seizures
Y.F.						Russo–Japanese War: Telegraphs, Mails, etc.

[1] V is the symbol used in F.O.804/56; the registers are labelled H.D., V., S.A., C.A., M. (see the entries marked* above). Until 1895 there are separate registers for Central America, South America (sub-divided by countries), Hayti and S. Domingo, and Mexico.

POLITICAL DEPARTMENTS			NON-POLITICAL DEPARTMENTS		
Western	*Eastern*	*American and Asiatic*	*Consular*	*Commercial*	*Treaty*
Z			Pacific Islands (*to* 1900); African Protectorates; Liberia (1901–1904); Zanzibar; Liberia (1905)	Circulars	Zanzibar (*to* 1897); Miscellaneous (*from* 1898)

(*d*) *Index Numbers 1906–1939* (see pp.63, 65, 68)

1 Abyssinia (*known as* Ethiopia *from* 1936); *also* Africa (1914–19) [*see also* 60]
2 Argentina
3 Austria (Austria–Hungary *to* 1919)
4 Belgium; *and* Congo (*to* 1928); *and* Luxembourg (*from* 1929)
5 Borneo (*to* 1907); Bolivia (*from* 1911) [*see also* 35]
6 Brazil
7 Bulgaria
8 Central America (Guatemala, Honduras, Nicaragua, El Salvador)
9 Chile
10 China
11 Colombia
12 Corea (*to* 1910); Czechoslovakia (*from* 1920)
13 Crete (*to* 1913); Communications and Transit (*from* 1931)
14 Cuba
15 Denmark
16 Egypt; *and* Sudan (*from* 1925)
17 France
18 Germany
19 Greece; *also* Balkans (1914–19)
20 Hayti and San Domingo
21 Hungary (*from* 1920)
22 Italy
23 Japan
24 Liberia
25 Maskat (*to* 1926); Hejaz and Nejd (1931–33); Saudi Arabia (*from* 1934)
26 Mexico
27 Montenegro (*to* 1919); Commercial Aviation (*from* 1936)
28 Morocco
29 Netherlands
30 Norway; *also* Scandinavia (1914–19)
31 Pacific Islands (*to* 1913); Palestine and Transjordan (*from* 1931) [*see also* 88]
32 Panama and Costa Rica
33 Paraguay
34 Persia
35 Peru; *including* Bolivia (*to* 1910) *and* Ecuador (*to* 1913)
36 Portugal
37 Roumania
38 Russia (*known as* Soviet Union *from* 1927)
39 Serbia (*to* 1919); *also* War (1914–19)
40 Siam
41 Spain
42 Sweden
43 Switzerland
44 Turkey
45 United States
46 Uruguay
47 Venezuela
48 Zanzibar (*to* 1913)
49 Western: Co-ordination (1939)
50 General *or* Miscellaneous (*to* 1919); Western: General (*from* 1920)
51 America: General (*from* 1912)
52 Contract Labour (*from* 1914; *known as* Slavery and Native Labour *from* 1930)
53 Albania (1914–16) [*see also* 90]; Western: Economic (1939)
54 Ecuador (*from* 1914) [*see also* 35]
55 Poland (*from* 1918)
56 Finland (*from* 1918)
57 Siberia (1918–24)
58 Caucasus (1918–24)
59 Baltic States (*from* 1919)
60 Africa: General (*from* 1920) [*see also* 1]
61 Far Eastern: General (*from* 1920)
62 Central: General (*from* 1920)
63 Northern: General (*from* 1920)

65   Eastern: General (*from* 1920)
66   Egyptian: General (*from* 1925; *known as*
      Egyptian and Ethiopian: General,
      1936–38)
67   Southern: General (*from* 1934)
68   Dominions: Intelligence (1939) [*see also*
      Supplementary Numbers 384 *and* 750]
85   Russian Conference (1924)
87   Opium (*from* 1923)
88   Palestine (1920–25) [*see also* 31]
89   Syria (*from* 1920)
90   Albania (*from* 1920) [*see also* 53]
91   Arabia (*from* 1920)

92   Jugo-Slavia (from 1920; *known as*
      Serb-Croat-Slovene Kingdom, 1925–29,
      and as Jugoslavia *from* 1930)
93   Mesopotamia (1920–24); Irak (1925);
      Iraq (*from* 1929)
94   Health (1920–37) [*see also Supplementary*
      Number 494]
95   Arms Traffic (*from* 1920)
96   International Rivers and Transport (*from*
      1920)
97   Central Asia (*from* 1920)
98   League of Nations (*from* 1920)
99   Repayments (1920–23) [*see also*
      Supplementary Number 299]

The above index numbers when appearing on their own refer to the main series of political correspondence. When reference is to other series, the following numerical or alphabetical prefixes are used.

1   Commercial (*to* 1920);[1]
      News (1920–25) [*from* 1926 *see*
      Supplementary Numbers)
2   Consular [*from* 1924 *see also Supplementary*
      Numbers]
3   Treaty (to 1923)[2] [*from* 1924 *see*
      Supplementary Numbers]

4   Africa (*to* 1913)
11   Contraband (1915–20) [*see below for*
      Supplementary Numbers]
12   Prisoners of War and Aliens
      (1915–19)
21   Contraband: Coal and Tonnage
      (1917–20)

N[3]   News (1916–20)
P *or* Prize   Treaty: Prize Court (1914–19)
                [followed not by a country num-
                ber but by an abbreviated form of
                the country name]
PF   News (*from* 1938)

P.I.D.   Political Intelligence Department
                (1918–19) [not followed by a
                country number]
W   War (1914–20) [a sub-division of
                the political correspondence].

The following *Supplementary Numbers* were used instead of country index numbers in those non-political departments whose correspondence was arranged by subjects and also to supplement the normal country index numbers in the Consular and Contraband Departments.

                NEWS (*from* 1926)
150   General

                CONSULAR
285   Ships' Agreements (*from* 1928)
286   Life Certificates (*from* 1924)
299   Repayments (*from* 1924) [*see also* 99]

                TREATY (*from* 1924 *unless otherwise stated*)
370   Cargoes and Prize Court
371   Civil Procedure
372   Decorations and Awards
373   Diplomatic and Consular (*to* 1932);
      Privilege (*from* 1933)

374   Extradition
375   Lunatics
376   Marriages
377   Miscellaneous
378   Nationality
379   Royal Matters
380   Territorial Waters
381   Treaty Formalities
382   Postal Agreements (*from* 1925)
383   Arbitration Agreements (1926–30);
      Appointments: Diplomatic (*from* 1932)
384   Empire Foreign Policy (1927–28);
      Dominions Intelligence (1934–38) [*see*
      also 68 *and* 750]

[1] In 1914 Contraband correspondence is in the Commercial series with the suffix X, but the registers are now bound up with later Contraband Department ones.
[2] From 1919 to 1923 Decorations were indicated by the suffix D after the normal 300 series index numbers.
[3] Also used as a suffix for the War Miscellaneous General (News) correspondence (W50N), 1914–1916, now in F.O.371.

TREATY (*continued*)

385   Appointments: Consular (*from* 1932)
388   Nationality: Immigration Laws in
      U.S.A. (1930–32);
      Deportation (*from* 1933)

LIBRARY (*from* 1920 *unless otherwise
stated*)

401   Presents (*to* 1921)
402   State Papers
403   Printed Books (*to* 1921);
      Conferences (*from* 1938)
404   Maps (*to* 1921);
      Examinations (*from* 1938)
405   Miscellaneous
406   Facilities and Information
407   Publications (*from* 1938)
408   Parliamentary Domestic (*to* 1921)
409   Legalization of Documents
412   Newspapers (*to* 1921)
413   Assistance to Authors (1921)
414   Registrar (*to* 1921)
494   Health (*from* 1938) [*see also* 94]

CHIEF CLERK (*from* 1920; *does not appear
in printed indexes until* 1931; *after* 1933
ESTABLISHMENT AND FINANCE*)

501   Claims (*from* 1930)
502   Communications (1924–26)
503   Diplomatic
504   Domestic
505   General

COMMUNICATIONS (*from* 1927; *for* 1924–
26 *see* CHIEF CLERK)

650   General

DOMINIONS INFORMATION (1929–33)

750   General [*see also* 68 *and* 384]

CONTRABAND

1122A   Italy (Exports to) (1915)
1129A   Netherlands (Exports to) (1915)
1129S   Netherlands (Ships) (1916–19)
1130A   Denmark (Exports to) (1915–19)
1130B   Norway (Exports to) (1915–19)
1130C   Sweden (Exports to) (1915–19)
1130D   Denmark (Ships) (1916–19)
1130DN Denmark (Navicerts) (1917)
1130F   Scandinavia (Fish and Oil) (1916–18)
1130N   Norway (Ships) (1916–18)
1130NN Norway (Navicerts) (1917)
1130S   Scandinavia and Sweden (Ships)
        (1915–20)
1130SN Scandinavia (Navicerts) (1917)
1130W   Europe (North and West) (1917–18)
1150M   Mails (1917–18); Censorship (1919)
1150R   Relief (1916–20)
1150T   Tonnage (1917)
1151A   America (Jute) (1916–17)
        See also p.161 n.1.

(e) Departmental Designations 1920–1939 (see p.68)

A   American and African
C   Central
E   Eastern
F   Far Eastern
J   Egyptian (*from* 1925; *known* as Egyptian
    and Ethiopian *from* 1936)
K   Consular
L   Library
N   Northern
P   News

R   Southern (*from* 1934)
T   Treaty
V   Dominions Information (1929–33)
W   Western (*known as* League of Nations and
    Western *from* 1930)
X   Chief Clerk (*does not appear in printed
    indexes until* 1931; *known as* Establishment
    and Finance *from* 1933); *also*
    Communications (*to* 1926)
Y   Communications (*from* 1927)

Appendix III: Analysis of Private Collections in the Public Record Office relating to Foreign Affairs

In addition to the *Foreign Office Private Collections* listed on pp.149–150 there are several other Private Collections in the Public Record Office which include material on foreign affairs, chiefly in classes of *Public Record Office, Documents Acquired by Gift, Deposit or Purchase* (P.R.O.30). These include collections of papers of Secretaries of State for Foreign Affairs, of diplomats and of prominent politicians who, while not directly responsible for the conduct of foreign affairs, were yet involved, in Cabinet and in other ways, in the formulation of foreign policy.

All these are included in the analysis which follows. This is in three sections: (i) a short list of General and Miscellaneous Collections; (ii) a list of persons concerned with foreign affairs for whom Private Collections are preserved in the Public Record Office or who are represented in the General and Miscellaneous Collections; and (iii) a Country Index to (ii).

(i) *General and Miscellaneous Collections*

Ministers and Officials: Various (F.O.800) 1824–1949

This class includes the Private Office papers of Secretaries of State, 1900–1935 and 1937–1940, and of many Under Secretaries of State, 1886–1948, and private papers of many senior diplomats and other officials and individuals connected with foreign affairs.

Miscellaneous (Foreign Office) (F.O.323) 1636–1881

Miscellaneous (Public Record Office) (P.R.O.30/26)

(ii) *List of Persons concerned with Foreign Affairs represented in Private Collections in the Public Record Office*

Entries marked † relate to material in the General and Miscellaneous Collections in (i) above.

Entries marked * relate to persons not directly responsible for the conduct of foreign affairs yet involved in the formulation of foreign policy.

The appointments held by each person during the period for which his papers exist are given and it is to these appointments that the Index of Countries, etc., in (iii) below relates. It will not always follow that each appointment will be represented by correspondence or papers.

Abbott, see *Tenterden Papers* (F.O.363)

Adams, see *Dacres Adams Papers* (P.R.O. 30/58)

†*Ainslie* (P.R.O.30/26/72) 1776–1793
Entry book of correspondence with the Levant Company of Sir Robert Ainslie, Ambassador to Turkey, 1776–1794.

†*Alston* (F.O.800/244–248) 1908–1915
Correspondence of [Sir] Beilby Francis Alston, Senior Clerk in Far Eastern Department, 1907–1911, 1912–1913, special mission in Siam, 1911, acting Counsellor in China, 1912 and 1913–1918.

Ampthill Papers (F.O.918) *c.* 1852–1884
Correspondence of Lord Odo Russell, first Lord Ampthill, employed in Foreign Office, 1850–1852 Attaché in Austria, 1849–1850, 1852–1853, in France, 1853–1854, in Turkey, 1854–1857, in U.S.A., 1857–1858, Secretary of Legation in Italy, residing at Rome, 1858–1870, Assistant Under Secretary of State, 1870–1871, Ambassador to Germany, 1871–1884.

Aston Papers (F.O.355) 1827–1843
Correspondence of [Sir] Arthur Aston, Secretary of Legation in Brazil, 1826–1833, Secretary of Embassy in France, 1835–1839, and Minister to Spain, 1840–1843.[1]

†*Backhouse* (F.O.323/6) 1834
Correspondence and papers of John Backhouse, Under Secretary of State, on a Special Mission to Don Carlos of Spain at Portsmouth.

[1] For the acquisition of these papers by the Foreign Office see F.O.83/909.

Baker, see *Noel Baker*

*Balfour Papers (P.R.O.30/60) [1880]–1907
Papers of A.J.Balfour as Chief Secretary of Ireland, 1887–1891 (see also next entry); and of his brother, Gerald William Balfour, later second Earl of Balfour, Chief Secretary of Ireland, 1895–1900, President of the Board of Trade, 1900–1905, and President of the Local Government Board, 1905. The papers of G.W.Balfour include many Cabinet Papers and Foreign Office Confidential Prints and Print Sections.

†*Balfour* (F.O.800/199–217) 1916–1922
Correspondence of Arthur James Balfour, later first Earl of Balfour, Secretary of State, 1916–1919, Lord President of the Council, 1919–1922.[1]

Baring, see *Cromer Papers* (F.O.633)

†*Bertie* (F.O.800/159–191) 1896–1918
Correspondence of Sir Francis Bertie, later first Lord Bertie of Thame, Assistant Under Secretary of State, 1894–1903, Ambassador to Italy, 1903–1905, and to France, 1905–1918.

Bloomfield Papers (F.O.356) 1823–1871
Entry books of correspondence of Sir Benjamin Bloomfield, later first Baron Bloomfield, Minister to Sweden, 1823–1833; and correspondence, entry books and a register of correspondence of his son, John Arthur Douglas Bloomfield, later second Baron Bloomfield, Secretary of Legation in Sweden, 1826–1839, Secretary of Embassy, 1839–1844, and Minister to Russia, 1844–1851, Minister to Prussia, 1851–1860, and to Austria, 1860–1871.

Brodrick, see *Midleton Papers* (P.R.O.30/67)

†*Bryce* (F.O.800/331–335) 1904–1921
Correspondence of James Bryce, later Viscount Bryce of Dechmount, Ambassador to the U.S.A., 1907–1913.

†*Bulwer* (F.O.800/232) 1848–1851
Papers of Sir Henry Bulwer, Minister to the U.S.A., 1849–1851, mainly relating to the Clayton-Bulwer Treaty.

†*Cadogan* (F.O.800/293–294) 1934–1939
Correspondence of Sir Alexander Cadogan, Minister, 1933–1935, and Ambassador to China, 1935–1936, Deputy Under Secretary of State, 1936–1937, Permanent Under Secretary of State, 1938–1946.

*Cairns Papers (P.R.O.30/51) 1856–1885
Papers of Hugh McCalmont Cairns, first Earl Cairns, Solicitor-General, 1858–1859, Attorney-General, 1866, Lord Chancellor, 1868 and 1874–1880.

†*Canning* (F.O.800/229–231) 1824–1827
Papers relating to Spain, 1824–1825, and Greece, 1824–1827, of George Canning, Secretary of State, 1822–1827.[2]

Canning, see also *Stratford Canning Papers* (F.O.352)

†*Caradoc* (F.O.323/3) 1834–1835
Papers of Lt.-Col. Hon. J.H.Caradoc, later Lord Howden, Military Commissioner with the Spanish army operating in the Basque provinces.

*Carnarvon Papers (P.R.O.30/6) 1833–1898
Papers, including Foreign Office Confidential Prints relating to Turkey, Russia and Egypt, of Henry Howard Molyneux Herbert, fourth Earl of Carnarvon, Under Secretary of State for the Colonies, 1858–1859, Secretary of State for the Colonies, 1866–1867 and 1874–1878, Lord-Lieutenant of Ireland, 1885–1886.

Carnock, see *Nicolson*

Casement Diaries (Home Office: H.O.161) 1901–1911
Diaries kept by Sir Roger Casement, chiefly relating to his missions to the Congo, 1903, and Putumayo (Peru), 1910–1911.
Closed to public inspection for 100 years.

Cave Papers (P.R.O.30/7) 1811–1822
Correspondence of Andrew Snape Douglas, Secretary of Legation in Sicily and Naples, 1809–1811 and 1813–1824.

†*Cecil* (F.O.800/195–198) 1915–1919
Correspondence of Lord Robert Cecil, later first Viscount Cecil of Chelwood, Parliamentary Under Secretary of State, 1915–1918, Minister of Blockade, 1916–1918, Assistant Secretary of State, 1918. Includes correspondence of Baron Hardinge (q.v.), Permanent Under Secretary, Sir Eric Drummond (q.v.), Private Secretary to the Secretary of State, and [Sir] Cecil Francis Dormer, Assistant Private Secretary to the Secretary of State, 1915–1919.

Cecil, see also *Cranborne*

†*Chamberlain* (F.O.800/256–263) 1924–1929
Correspondence of Sir Austen Chamberlain, Secretary of State, 1924–1929.[3]

---

[1] See also Appendix IV.
[2] See also Appendix IV and p.58.
[3] See also Appendix IV.

Chartwell Trust Papers: Microfilm (Public
    Record Office Transcripts: P.R.O.31/19)
    *c.*1882–1945
    Microfilm of the correspondence and
papers of Sir Winston Churchill.

Chatham Papers (P.R.O.30/8)
    Correspondence of William Pitt, first
Earl of Chatham; and of his son, William
Pitt the younger, Chancellor of the Exchequer, 1782–1783, Prime Minister, 1783–
1801 and 1804–1806.

Churchill, see *Chartwell Trust Papers*
    (P.R.O.31/19)

Clarendon Papers (F.O.361) 1867–1870
    A single volume of correspondence of
George William Frederick Villiers, fourth
Earl of Clarendon, Secretary of State, 1853–
1858, 1865–1866 and 1868–1870.[1]

Clark-Kerr, see *Inverchapel*

†*Corbett* (P.R.O.30/26/124) 1892–1893
    A letter book of [Sir] Vincent Edwin
Henry Corbett, when Second Secretary in
Turkey.

Cornwallis Papers (P.R.O.30/11) 1614–1854
    Include the papers of Charles Corn-
wallis, second Earl and first Marquis Cornwallis, mainly relating to the American War,
1780–1782, and to India, 1786–1797, but
also to his mission as Plenipotentiary at the
Congress of Amiens, 1801–1802.

Cowley Papers (F.O.519) 1774; 1802–*c.*1935
    Correspondence and papers of Henry
Wellesley, first Baron Cowley, Minister,
1810–1811, and Ambassador to Spain, 1811–
1821, Ambassador to Austria, 1823–1831,
and to France, 1835 and 1841–1846; of his
son, Henry Richard Charles Wellesley,
second Baron and first Earl Cowley, Secretary of Legation in Württemberg, 1832–
1843, Secretary of Embassy in Turkey, 1843–
1848, Special Mission, 1848–1851, and
Minister to Germanic Confederation, 1851–
1852, Ambassador to France, 1852–1867;
and of Colonel Hon. Frederick Wellesley,
Military Attaché in Russia, 1871–1878, and
First Secretary in Austria, 1878–1879.

†*Cranborne* (F.O.800/296) 1935–1938
    Correspondence of Robert Arthur James
Gascoyne-Cecil, Viscount Cranborne, later
fifth Marquess of Salisbury, Parliamentary
Under Secretary of State, 1935–1938.

†*Crewe* (F.O.800/330) 1926
    Reports to Robert Offley Ashburton

Crewe (continued)
Crewe-Milnes, first Marquess of Crewe,
Ambassador to France, 1922–1928, from Sir
Charles Mendl, Press Attaché in France,
1926–1940.

Cromer Papers (F.O.633) 1872–1929
    Correspondence and papers of Evelyn
Baring, first Earl of Cromer, Commissioner
of the Egyptian Public Debt, 1877–1879,
Controller General in Egypt, 1879–1880,
Agent and Consul General in Egypt, 1883–
1907.

†*Crowe* (F.O.800/243) 1907–1925
    Correspondence of Sir Eyre Crowe,
Senior Clerk in the Western Department,
1906–1912, Assistant Under Secretary of
State, 1912–1920, Permanent Under Secretary of State, 1920–1925.

†*Currie* (F.O.800/114) 1893–1896
    Papers of Sir Philip Currie, later first
Baron Currie, Permanent Under Secretary of
State, 1889–1893, Ambassador to Turkey,
1894–1898, and later to Italy.

†*Curzon* (F.O.800/28; 147–158) 1895–1898;
    1919–1924
    Correspondence of George Nathaniel
Curzon, first Marquess Curzon of Kedleston,
Parliamentary Under Secretary of State,
1895–1898, Secretary of State, 1919–1924.[1]

†*Cushendun* (F.O.800/227–228) 1922–1923;
    1927–1929
    Correspondence of Ronald McNeill,
later first Baron Cushendun, Parliamentary
Under Secretary of State, 1922–1924 and
1924–1925, Chancellor of the Duchy of
Lancaster, 1927–1929, acting Secretary of
State, 1928.

Dacres Adams Papers (P.R.O.30/58) 1676;
    1783–1856
    Papers of William Dacres Adams, Pri-
vate Secretary to William Pitt the Younger,
1804–1806, and the Duke of Portland, 1807–
1809.

Dormer, see *Cecil*

Douglas, see *Cave Papers* (P.R.O.30/7)

†*Drummond* (F.O.800/329, 383–385) 1915–
    1918
    Correspondence of Sir Eric Drummond,
Private Secretary to the Secretary of State,
1915–1918, Senior Clerk and member of
British Delegation to Peace Conference,
1918–1919, Secretary-General of League of
Nations, 1919–1933. See also *Cecil.*

[1] See also Appendix IV.

M

†*Elliot* (F.O.800/255) 1924–1925
Correspondence of Sir Charles Elliot, Ambassador to Japan, 1920–1926.

English Church at the Hague (F.O.259) 1658–1822
Legal papers, inventories, receipts, accounts, etc.

†*Errington* (F.O.800/235–239) 1881–1885
Correspondence of George Errington, M.P., on a special mission to the Vatican, 1881–1885.

†*Fergusson* (F.O.800/25–28) 1886–1891
Correspondence of Sir James Fergusson, Parliamentary Under Secretary of State, 1886–1891.

Granville Papers (P.R.O.30/29) 1604–1909
Granville Papers (F.O.362) 1870–1874
P.R.O.30/29 includes correspondence of Granville Leveson-Gower, first Earl Granville, Ambassador to Russia, 1804–1806 and 1807, to the Netherlands, 1824, and to France, 1824–1828, 1831–1835 and 1835–1841; and of Granville George Leveson-Gower, second Earl Granville, Under Secretary of State, 1840–1841, Secretary of State, 1851–1852, 1870–1874 and 1880–1885.
F.O.362 is correspondence of the second Earl Granville relating to America, Austria and France.
A volume of the second Earl's Foreign Miscellaneous correspondence, 1880–1885, relating to Siam, Persia, China, Japan, Morocco, Mexico and Madagascar is in GENERAL CORRESPONDENCE BEFORE 1906: *Supplement to General Correspondence* (F.O.97/621).

†*Grey* (F.O.800/35–113) 1892–1895; 1905–1916
Correspondence of Sir Edward Grey, later first Viscount Grey of Fallodon, Parliamentary Under Secretary of State, 1892–1895, Secretary of State, 1905–1916.

Hague, see *English Church at the Hague* (F.O.259)

†*Halifax* (F.O.800/309–328) 1937–1940
Correspondence of Edward Frederick Lindley Wood, third Viscount (later first Earl) of Halifax, Secretary of State, 1938–1940.[1]

Hammond Papers (F.O.391) 1831–1834; 1854–1885
Correspondence of Edmund Hammond, later first Baron Hammond, Clerk in the Foreign Office, 1824–1854, accompanied Stratford Canning (q.v.) on Special Mission, 1831–1932, Permanent Under Secretary of State, 1854–1873.

†*Hardinge* (F.O.800/192) 1906–1911
Correspondence of Sir Charles Hardinge, first Baron Hardinge of Penshurst, Permanent Under Secretary of State, 1906–1910 and 1916–1920, Viceroy of India, 1910–1916, Ambassador to France, 1920–1922. See also *Cecil* and *Villiers*.

†*Harmsworth* (F.O.800/250) 1919
Correspondence of Cecil Bisshopp Harmsworth, Parliamentary Under Secretary of State, 1919–1922.

Harmsworth, see also *Northcliffe*

†*Harvey* (F.O.800/194) 1913
Correspondence of Sir Henry Paul Harvey, British Delegate on the International Commission at Paris for the Settlement of Financial Questions arising out of the Balkan War, 1913–1914.

Henderson Papers (F.O.357) 1818–1831
Correspondence of James Henderson, Consul-General in Colombia, 1823–1830.

†*Henderson* (F.O.800/280–284) 1929–1931
Correspondence of Arthur Henderson, Secretary of State, 1929–1931.

†*Henderson* (F.O.800/264–271) 1924–1941
Correspondence of Sir Nevile Henderson, Minister to Egypt, 1924–1928, Counsellor-Minister in France, 1928–1929, Minister to Yugoslavia, 1929–1935, to Argentina, 1935–1937, Ambassador to Germany, 1937–1939.

Hertslet Papers (F.O.351) 1730–1854
Papers of Lewis Hertslet, Librarian, 1810–1857, and Superintendent of Queen's Messengers, 1824–1854, in his capacity as Private Agent to the Foreign Service Messengers before 1824, with some earlier and later papers relating to Messengers. See p.75

Hervey Papers (F.O.528) 1778–1794; 1830–1840
Papers of John Augustus Hervey, Lord Hervey, Minister to Tuscany, 1787–1794; and of Lord William Hervey, Secretary of Legation in Spain, 1830–1839.

[1] See also Appendix IV.

†*Hoare* (F.O.800/295) 1935

Correspondence of Sir Samuel Hoare, later first Viscount Templewood, Secretary of State, 1935[1]

Howard de Walden Papers (F.O.360) 1817–1834

Correspondence of Charles Augustus Ellis, sixth Baron Howard de Walden, Précis Writer to the Secretary of State, 1822–1824, Under Secretary of State, 1824–1828, Minister to Sweden, 1833, to Portugal, 1834–1846, and later to Belgium. See p.47.

Howden, see *Caradoc*

†*Inverchapel* (F.O.800/298–303) 1935–1949

Correspondence of Sir Archibald Clark-Kerr, first Baron Inverchapel, Ambassador to Iraq, 1935–1938, to China, 1938–1942, to the U.S.S.R., 1942–1946, to the U.S.A., 1946–1948.

Isaacs, see *Reading*

Jackson Papers (F.O.353) 1763–1856

Papers of Francis James Jackson, Clerk in Foreign Office, 1781–1789 (see p.153), Secretary of Legation in Prussia, 1789–1791, Secretary of Embassy in Spain, 1791–1795, Special Mission to Austria, 1795, Minister *ad interim* to France, 1801–1802, Minister to Prussia, 1802–1806, Minister *ad interim* to Denmark, 1807, Minister to the U.S.A., 1809–1810; and of his brother, Sir George Jackson, Secretary of Legation in Prussia, 1806–1807 and 1813–1815, Secretary of Embassy in Russia, 1816, Special Mission to Spain, 1822, Commissioner at Washington, 1822–1827, Slave Trade Commissioner at Rio de Janeiro, 1832–1841, at Surinam, 1841–1845, at London, 1845–1859. The collection includes official archives of the Berlin mission, 1772–1806.[2]

†*Johnson* (P.R.O.30/26/70) 1809–1814

Entry books of correspondence, with a few papers, of John Mordaunt Johnson, Chargé d'Affaires in Brussels, 1814.

Jordan Papers (F.O.350) 1901–1919

Correspondence of Sir John Newell Jordan, Minister Resident in Korea, 1901–1906, Minister to China, 1906–1920.

†*Keith* (P.R.O.30/26/93) 1791

Note by Lt.-Gen. Sir Robert Murray Keith, Minister to the Holy Roman Empire, to Congress of Sistoria announcing British guarantee of Austro-Prussian agreement of 1790.

†*Kennedy* (F.O.800/4–5) 1873–1893

Correspondence of Sir Charles Malcolm Kennedy, Senior Clerk in the Commercial Department, 1872–1894, including correspondence as Commissioner at Paris, 1874–1875.

Kerr, see *Inverchapel*

Kitchener Papers (P.R.O.30/57) 1877–1959

Papers of Field Marshal Horatio Herbert Kitchener, first Earl Kitchener of Khartoum, relating among others to his service on the Palestine Survey, 1874–1878, the Cyprus Survey, 1878–1879, 1880–1882, as Vice-Consul at Kastamuni, 1879–1880, Commissioner for the Zanzibar Boundary, 1885, Governor-General of the Eastern Sudan, 1886–1888, Sirdar of the Egyptian Army, 1892–1899, Agent and Consul General in Egypt, 1911–1914, Secretary of State for War, 1914–1916.

†*Knatchbull-Hugessen* (F.O.800/297) 1936–1938

Correspondence of Sir Hughe Knatchbull-Hugessen, Ambassador to China, 1936–1938.

†*Langley* (F.O.800/29–31) 1886–1919

Correspondence of Sir Walter Langley, Clerk in the Foreign Office from 1878, Private Secretary to Parliamentary Under Secretaries of State, 1887–1898, Senior Clerk in Far Eastern Department, 1902–1907, Assistant Under Secretary of State, 1907–1919.

†*Lansdowne* (F.O.800/115–146) 1898–1913; 1920–1924

Correspondence of Henry Charles Keith Petty Fitzmaurice, fifth Marquess of Lansdowne, Secretary of State, 1900–1905.[3] Includes also correspondence of T. H. Sanderson (q.v.).

†*Lascelles* (F.O.800/6–20) 1874–1908

Correspondence of Sir Frank Lascelles, Second Secretary in Italy, 1873–1876, in the U.S.A., 1876–1878, in Greece, 1878–1879, Agent and Consul-General to Bulgaria, 1879–1887, Minister to Roumania, 1887–1891, to Persia, 1891–1894, Ambassador to Russia, 1894–1895, to Germany, 1895–1908.

League of Nations Assembly and Council Documents (P.R.O.30/52) 1920–1946

Records of the London Office of the League of Nations and *Journals* of the League; presented by U.N.O.

---

[1] See also Appendix IV.
[2] For the recovery of these papers from Lady Jackson see F.O.83/460.
[3] See also Appendix IV.

Leveson-Gower, see *Granville Papers* (P.R.O. 30/29 and F.O.362)

†*Locker-Lampson* (F.O.800/227) 1925–1929

Correspondence of Godfrey Locker-Lampson, Parliamentary Under Secretary of State, 1925–1929.

†*Lowther* (F.O.800/193) 1908–1913

Correspondence of Sir Gerald Lowther, Ambassador to Turkey, 1908–1913.

†*Lowther* (F.O.800/28; 34) 1891–1894

Correspondence of James William Lowther, later first Viscount Ullswater, Parliamentary Under Secretary of State, 1891–1892.

†*MacDonald* (F.O.800/218–219) 1923–1924

Correspondence of James Ramsay MacDonald, Prime Minister and Secretary of State, 1924. Other papers are under arrangement in the Public Record Office.[1]

†*Mackinder* (F.O.800/251) 1919–1920

Correspondence of [Sir] Halford John Mackinder, British High Commissioner for South Russia, 1919–1920.

†*MacLeod* (P.R.O.30/26/85) 1895–1929; 1937

Correspondence with Sir Ernest Satow (q.v.) of Sir James MacIver MacLeod, Vice-Consul at Fez, 1892–1894, 1896–1907, accompanied Satow on mission to Morocco, 1894–1895, Consul at Fez, 1907–1917, employed in Foreign Office, 1917–1919, Consul-General in Chile, 1919–1923, at Tunis, 1923–1930; also notes of persons and subjects connected with Morocco, 1937.

McNeill, see *Cushendun*

Malet Papers (F.O.343) 1884–1895

Correspondence of Sir Edward Baldwin Malet, Ambassador to Germany, 1884–1895.

Mance Papers (P.R.O.30/66) 1899–1924

Papers of Brig. Gen. Sir H. Osborne Mance, communications expert on British Delegation to Paris Peace Conference, 1919–1920, served on Committees, etc., of League of Nations dealing with transport, 1920–1924.

Manchester Papers (P.R.O.30/15)

Includes correspondence of George Montagu, fourth Duke of Manchester, Ambassador to France, 1783–1784.

Mendl, see *Crewe* and *Tyrrell*

Middleton Papers (P.R.O.30/67) 1885–1941

Correspondence of William St. John Fremantle Brodrick, later first Earl of Midleton, Financial Secretary to War Office, 1886–

Midleton Papers (continued)

1892, Under Secretary of State for War, 1895–1898, for Foreign Affairs, 1898–1900, Secretary of State for War, 1900–1903, for India, 1903–1905.

Milner Papers (P.R.O.30/30) 1915–1920

Correspondence and papers of Alfred, Viscount Milner, a member of the War Cabinet, 1916–1918, Secretary of State for War, 1918, and for the Colonies, 1918–1921. For papers relating to his mission to Egypt, 1919–1920, see EMBASSY AND CONSULAR ARCHIVES: *EGYPT: Milner Mission* (F.O.848) (p.138).

Nicholl Papers (P.R.O.30/42) 1787–1832

Includes draft reports and opinions of Sir John Nicholl, King's Advocate General, 1798–1809, for the Secretary of State for Foreign Affairs.

†*Nicolson* (F.O.800/336–381) 1889–1916

Correspondence of Arthur Nicolson, later first Lord Carnock, Consul-General in Budapest, 1888–1893, Secretary of Embassy in Turkey, 1893–1894, Agent and Consul-General to Bulgaria, 1894–1895, Minister and Consul-General to Morocco, 1895–1904, Ambassador to Spain, 1905–1906, to Russia, 1906–1910, Permanent Under Secretary of State, 1910–1916. See also *Villiers*.

†*Noel Baker* (F.O.800/249) 1918–1919

Correspondence of Philip Noel Baker, member of League of Nations Section of British Delegation to Peace Conference, 1919, and of League of Nations Secretariat, 1919–1922.

†*Oliphant* (F.O.800/252–254) 1921–1928

Correspondence of Sir Lancelot Oliphant, Acting Counsellor, 1920–1923, and Counsellor in Eastern Department, 1923–1928, Assistant Under Secretary of State, 1928–1936, later Deputy Under Secretary of State and Ambassador to Belgium.

Parish, see *Woodbine Parish Papers* (F.O.354)

†*Pelly* (F.O.800/233–234) 1859–1863

Correspondence of [Sir] Lewis Pelly, acting Secretary of Legation in Persia, 1859–1860, acting Agent and Consul at Zanzibar, 1861–1862, Political Resident on Persian Gulf, 1862–1871.

Pierrepont Papers (F.O.334) 1791–1807

Correspondence of Henry Manvers Pierrepont, Minister to Sweden, 1804–1807, and again on a Special Mission in the latter year. Includes an entry book of correspon-

---

[1] See also Appendix IV.

Pierrepont Papers (continued)
dence of Alexander Stratton, Minister to Sweden in the intervening months. See also p.153.

†*Piggott* (F.O.323/7) 1884–1887
Papers of [Sir] Francis Taylor Piggott, Barrister, employed by the Foreign Office on a special mission to Italy to discuss a proposed convention for the mutual execution of legal judgements, 1887.

Pitt, see *Chatham Papers* (P.R.O.30/8) and *Dacres Adams Papers* (P.R.O.30/58)

†*Ponsonby* (F.O.800/3) 1870–1894
Correspondence with the Foreign Office and British diplomatic representatives of Major General Sir Henry Frederick Ponsonby, Private Secretary to Queen Victoria, 1870–1895.

†*Ponsonby* (F.O.800/227) 1924
Correspondence of William Ponsonby, later first Baron Ponsonby, Parliamentary Under Secretary of State, 1924.

Portland, see *Dacres Adams Papers* (P.R.O.30/58)

Pottinger Papers (F.O.705) 1797–1798; 1809–1860; 1879
Papers of Sir Henry Pottinger, relating to India and also to his period as Chief Superintendent of Trade and Plenipotentiary on a Special Mission to China, 1841–1844.

†*Private Office* (F.O.800/329,383–399) 1915–1924; 1931–1941
Mainly correspondence of Private Secretaries to the Secretary of State. See also *Drummond.*

†*Reading* (F.O.800/222–226) 1918–1919; 1931
Correspondence of Rufus Daniel Isaacs, first Marquess of Reading, Ambassador to the U.S.A., 1918–1919, Secretary of State, 1931.[1]

†*Runciman* (F.O.800/304–308) 1938
Correspondence of Walter Runciman, first Viscount Runciman, relating to his Special Mission to Czechoslovakia, 1938.

Russell Papers (P.R.O.30/22) 1804–1913
Correspondence of Lord John Russell, first Earl Russell, Prime Minister, 1846–1852, Secretary of State, 1852–1853 and 1859–1865, Prime Minister, 1865–1866.

Russell, see also *Ampthill Papers.*

†*Ryan* (F.O.800/240) 1881–1929
Papers relating to Turkey of Sir Andrew

Ryan (continued)
Ryan, who occupied various diplomatic and consular posts in Turkey, 1897–1914 and 1918–1924, served in Foreign Office, 1914–1918, Consul-General in Rabat, 1924–1930.

Salisbury, see *Cranborne*

†*Sanderson* (F.O.800/21) 1876–1908
Correspondence of Sir Percy Sanderson, Consul and later Consul-General in Roumania, 1876–1894, Consul-General in New York, 1894–1907.

†*Sanderson* (F.O.800/1–2) 1860–1922
Correspondence of Thomas Henry Sanderson, first Baron Sanderson, Foreign Office Clerk from 1859, Senior Clerk in Eastern Department, 1885–1889, Assistant Under Secretary of State, 1889–1894, Permanent Under Secretary of State, 1894–1906. See also *Lansdowne.*

†*Sargent* (F.O.800/272–279) 1926–1948
Correspondence of Sir Orme Sargent, Counsellor in Central Department, 1926–1933, Assistant Under Secretary of State, 1933–1939, Deputy Under Secretary of State, 1939–1946, Permanent Under Secretary of State, 1946–1949.

Satow Papers (P.R.O.30/33) *c.*1856–1927
Correspondence and diary of Sir Ernest Mason Satow, Student Interpreter, 1861–1865, Interpreter, 1865–1868, Japanese Secretary, 1868–1876, and Second Secretary in Japan, 1876–1884, Agent, later Minister, and Consul-General to Siam, 1884–1888, Minister to Uruguay, 1888–1893, to Morocco, 1893–1895, to Japan, 1895–1900, to China, 1900–1906, British Member of Permanent Court of Arbitration at the Hague, 1906–1912, British Plenipotentiary at Second Hague Peace Conference, 1907. See also *MacLeod.*

Simmons Papers (F.O.358) 1857–1896
Papers of General (later Field Marshal) Sir John Lintorn Arabin Simmons, mainly arising from his appointment as British Military Delegate at the Congress of Berlin, 1878.

†*Simon* (F.O.800/285–291) 1931–1935
Correspondence of Sir John Simon, later first Viscount Simon, Secretary of State, 1931–1935.[2]

†*Spring-Rice* (F.O.800/241–242) 1903–1918
Correspondence of Sir Cecil Arthur Spring-Rice, Clerk in Foreign Office, 1882–

[1] See also Appendix IV.
[2] See also Appendix IV.

Spring-Rice (continued)

1889, Assistant Private Secretary to Secretary of State, 1884–1885, Précis Writer, 1886, acting Third Secretary in U.S.A., 1886–1888, acting Second Secretary in U.S.A., 1889–1891, Second Secretary in Belgium, 1891, Japan 1891 and 1893, U.S.A., 1891–1892, 1893–1895, Germany, 1895–1898, Turkey, 1898, Secretary of Legation in Persia, 1898–1901, Commissioner for Egyptian Debt, 1901–1903, Secretary of Embassy in Russia, 1903–1906, Minister to Persia, 1906–1908, to Sweden, 1908–1913, Ambassador to the U.S.A., 1913–1918. See also *Villiers*.

Stratford Canning Papers (F.O.352) 1778–1863

Correspondence of Stratford Canning, first Viscount Stratford de Redcliffe, Précis Writer, 1807–1809, Secretary of Embassy in Turkey, 1809–1812, Minister to Switzerland, 1814–1819, to the U.S.A., 1820–1823, Special Mission to Russia, 1825, Ambassador to Turkey, 1826–1827, Plenipotentiary to Greece, 1828, Ambassador to Turkey, 1832, Special Mission to Spain, 1833, Ambassador to Turkey, 1842–1858, Special Mission to Switzerland, 1847–1848, to Austria, Belgium, Greece and German States, 1848.

Stratton, see *Pierrepont Papers* (F.O.334).

Stuart Papers (P.R.O.30/36) 1858–1888

Correspondence of Sir William Stuart, Secretary of Legation in Brazil, 1858–1859, Sicily, 1859–1861, Greece, 1861, the U.S.A., 1861–1864, Secretary of Embassy in Turkey, 1864–1866, in Russia, 1866–1868, Minister to Argentine Republic, 1868–1871, to Greece, 1872–1877, to the Netherlands, 1877–1888.

Stuart de Rothesay Papers (F.O.342) 1801–1814

Correspondence of Sir Charles Stuart, later first Baron Stuart de Rothesay, Secretary of Legation in Austria, 1801–1806, Secretary of Embassy in Russia, 1806–1808, Special Mission to Spain, 1808–1809, to Austria, 1809, Minister to Portugal, 1810–1814, Minister *ad interim* to France, 1814, later Ambassador to Netherlands, France, Russia.

†*Sykes* (F.O.800/221) 1918

Correspondence of Sir Mark Sykes, Adviser on Arab Affairs, 1916–1919.

Templewood, see *Hoare*

Tenterden Papers (F.O.363) 1873–1882

Correspondence of Charles Stuart Aubrey Abbot, third Baron Tenterden, Permanent Under Secretary of State, 1873–1882.

†*Tyrrell* (F.O.800/220) 1924

Correspondence of Sir William Tyrrell, later first Baron Tyrrell, Assistant Under Secretary of State, 1918–1925, later Permanent Under Secretary of State and Ambassador to France, with Sir Charles Mendl, News Department Representative in France, 1920–1926, later Press Attaché in France.

†*Vambéry* (F.O.800/32–33) 1889–1911

Correspondence of Professor A. Vambéry of the University of Budapest, a notable Turkish scholar with the ear of the Sultan, who reported secretly on Turkish affairs to successive Permanent Under Secretaries of State.

†*Various Sources* (F.O.800/382) 1831–1874

Minutes and correspondence of various Secretaries of State and Foreign Office officials, mainly relating to handwriting, etc., and to arrangements in the Librarian's Department.

†*Villiers* (F.O.800/22–24) 1883–1923

Correspondence of Sir Francis Hyde Villiers, Private Secretary to successive Permanent Under Secretaries of State, 1882–1892, and to the Secretary of State, 1892–1894, Assistant Clerk, 1894–1896, Senior Clerk, 1896, Assistant Under Secretary of State, 1896–1906, Minister to Portugal, 1906–1911, to Belgium, 1911–1920. The correspondence is chiefly with Sir Charles Hardinge (q.v.), 1907–1908; Sir Arthur Nicolson (q.v.), 1893–1908; and Sir Cecil Spring-Rice (q.v.), 1883–1905.

†*Watson* (P.R.O.30/26/83) 1818; 1821

Copies of correspondence of Edward Watson relating to his dismissal as British Vice-Consul at Leghorn (Tuscany).

Wellesley, see *Cowley Papers* (F.O.519)

White Papers (F.O.364) 1857–1891

Papers of Sir William Arthur White, clerk, later Vice-Consul and often acting Consul-General at Warsaw, 1857–1864, Consul at Danzig, 1864–1875, Agent and Consul-General to Serbia, 1875–1878, to Roumania, 1878–1879, Minister to Roumania, 1879–1885, Minister *ad interim* to Turkey, 1885, Ambassador to Turkey, 1886–1891.

†*Whitworth* (F.O.323/4) 1802–1803

Correspondence of Charles Whitworth

Whitworth (continued)
first Baron (later first Earl) Whitworth, Ambassador to France, 1802–1803.

†*Wigram* (F.O.800/292) 1932–1936
Lectures on British Foreign Policy by Ralph Follett Wigram, First Secretary in France, 1924–1933, Acting Counsellor in Foreign Office, 1933–1934, Counsellor, 1934–1936.

Woodbine Parish Papers (F.O.354) 1813–1855
Correspondence and papers of Sir Woodbine Parish, accompanied Castlereagh to Paris, 1815, employed on Commission in Greece, 1816–1817, Clerk in Foreign Office, 1817–1823, Consul-General in Argentine Republic, 1823–1832, also Plenipotentiary, 1824–1825, Chargé d'Affaires, 1825–1826, 1828–1831, Commissioner in France, 1833, Commissioner in Sicily, 1840–1841, Plenipotentiary to Sicily, 1842–1845.

(iii) *Index of Countries, etc.*
[N.B. This relates to the appointments held by the persons listed in (ii) above. It will not always follow that each appointment will be represented by correspondence or papers.]

CABINET MINISTERS, ETC. (EXCLUDING SECRETARIES OF STATE FOR FOREIGN AFFAIRS)
[marked * in list]

1782–1806	*Chatham Papers*
1804–1809	*Dacres Adams Papers*
1846–1852;	*Russell Papers*
1865–1866	
1858–1880	*Cairns Papers*
1858–1886	*Carnarvon Papers*
1886–1898;	*Midleton Papers*
1900–1905	
1895–1905	*Balfour Papers*
1914–1916	*Kitchener Papers*
1916–1921	*Milner Papers*
c.1882–	*Chartwell Trust Papers: Micro-*
1945	*film*

FOREIGN OFFICE (INCLUDING VARIOUS GENERAL APPOINTMENTS)

1798–1809	*Nicholl Papers*
1807–1809	*Stratford Canning Papers*
1817–1823	*Woodbine Parish Papers*
1822–1828	*Howard de Walden Papers*
1831–1834	*Hammond Papers*
1840–1841;	*Granville Papers*
1851–1852	
1852–1853	*Russell Papers*
1730–1854	*Hertslet Papers*

FOREIGN OFFICE, ETC. (continued)

1859–1865	*Russell Papers*
1867–1870	*Clarendon Papers*
1870–1871	*Ampthill Papers*
1854–1873	*Hammond Papers*
1831–1874	*Various Sources*
1870–1874	*Granville Papers*
1873–1882	*Tenterden Papers*
1880–1885	*Granville Papers*
1886–1891	*Fergusson*
1891–1892	*Lowther (J.W)*
1873–1893	*Kennedy*
1893	*Currie*
1870–1894	*Ponsonby (H.F)*
1892–1895	*Grey*
1895–1898	*Curzon*
1898–1900	*Midleton Papers*
1896–1903	*Bertie*
1900–1905	*Lansdowne*
1860–1906	*Sanderson (T.H)*
1883–1906	*Villiers*
1906–1910	*Hardinge*
1906–1912	*Satow*
1908–1913	*Alston*
1905–1916	*Grey*
1910–1916	*Nicolson*
1918	*Sykes*
1886–1919	*Langley*
1915–1919	*Cecil*
1915–1919	*Drummond*
1917–1919	*MacLeod*
1919	*Harmsworth*
1919–1920	*Mance Papers*
1916–1922	*Balfour*
1922–1923	*Cushendun*
1915–1924	*Private Office*
1919–1924	*Curzon*
1924	*MacDonald*
1924	*Ponsonby (W)*
1924	*Tyrrell*
1907–1925	*Crowe*
1921–1928	*Oliphant*
1924–1929	*Chamberlain*
1925–1929	*Locker-Lampson*
1927–1929	*Cushendun*
1929–1931	*Henderson (A)*
1931	*Reading*
1931–1935	*Simon*
1935	*Hoare*
1932–1936	*Wigram*
1935–1938	*Cranborne*
1937–1940	*Halifax*
1931–1941	*Private Office*
1936–1946	*Cadogan*
1926–1948	*Sargent*

ARGENTINE REPUBLIC
1823–1832   *Woodbine Parish Papers*
1868–1871   *Stuart Papers*
1935–1937   *Henderson (N)*

AUSTRIA
1791   *Keith*
1795   *Jackson Papers*
1801–1806;   *Stuart de Rothesay Papers*
1809
1823–1831   *Cowley Papers*
1848   *Stratford Canning Papers*
1849–1850;   *Ampthill Papers*
1852–1853
1860–1871   *Bloomfield Papers*
1878–1879   *Cowley Papers*
1888–1893   *Nicolson [Budapest]*

BALKANS
1913   *Harvey*

BELGIUM (and SOUTHERN NETHERLANDS)
1814   *Johnson*
1848   *Stratford Canning Papers*
1911–1920   *Villiers*

BRAZIL
1827–1833   *Aston Papers*
1858–1859   *Stuart Papers*

BULGARIA
1879–1887   *Lascelles*
1894–1895   *Nicolson*

CHILE
1919–1923   *MacLeod*

CHINA
1841–1844   *Pottinger Papers*
1900–1906   *Satow Papers*
1912–1915   *Alston*
1906–1920   *Jordan Papers*
1933–1936   *Cadogan*
1936–1938   *Knatchbull-Hugesson*
1938–1942   *Inverchapel*

COLOMBIA
1818–1831   *Henderson Papers*

CONGO
1903   *Casement Diaries*

CYPRUS
1881–1882   *Kitchener Papers*

CZECHOSLOVAKIA
1938   *Runciman*

DENMARK
1807   *Jackson Papers*

EGYPT AND SUDAN
1877–1880   *Cromer Papers*
1886–1888;   *Kitchener Papers*
1892–1899
1883–1907   *Cromer Papers*
1911–1914   *Kitchener Papers*
1924–1928   *Henderson (N)*

FRANCE
1783–1784   *Manchester Papers*
1801–1802   *Cornwallis Papers*
1801–1802   *Jackson Papers*
1802–1803   *Whitworth*
1814   *Stuart de Rothesay Papers*
1815   *Woodbine Parish Papers*
1824–1828   *Granville Papers*
1833   *Woodbine Parish Papers*
1831–1835   *Granville Papers*
1835   *Cowley Papers*
1833–1839   *Aston Papers*
1835–1841   *Granville Papers*
1841–1846   *Cowley Papers*
1853–1854   *Ampthill Papers*
1852–1867   *Cowley Papers*
1905–1918   *Bertie*
1926   *Crewe*
1928–1929   *Henderson (N)*

GERMAN STATES (see also PRUSSIA, WÜRTTEM-
    BERG)
1848   *Stratford Canning Papers*

GERMANIC CONFEDERATION
1848–1852   *Cowley Papers*

GERMANY
1871–1884   *Ampthill Papers*
1884–1895   *Malet Papers*
1895–1908   *Lascelles*
1937–1939   *Henderson (N)*

GREECE
1816–1817   *Woodbine Parish Papers*
1824–1827   *Canning*
1828;   *Stratford Canning Papers*
1848
1861;   *Stuart Papers*
1872–1877
1878–1879   *Lascelles*

APPENDIX III

IRAQ
1935–1938   Inverchapel

ITALY (see also SICILY AND NAPLES, TUSCANY,
    VATICAN)
1874–1876   Lascelles
1884–1887   Piggott
1903–1905   Bertie

JAPAN
1861–1884;   Satow Papers
1895–1900
1924–1925   Elliott

KOREA
1901–1906   Jordan Papers

LEAGUE OF NATIONS
1918–1919   Noel-Baker
1919–1921   Drummond
1920–1924   Mance Papers
1920–1946   League of Nations Assembly and
             Council Documents

MOROCCO
1893–1895   Satow Papers
1895–1904   Nicolson
1892–1917;   MacLeod
1937

NETHERLANDS
1658–1822   English Church at the Hague
1824   Granville Papers
1877–1888   Stuart Papers

PALESTINE
1877–1878   Kitchener Papers

PERSIA AND PERSIAN GULF
1859–1860;   Pelly
1862–1863
1891–1894   Lascelles
1906–1908   Spring-Rice

PERU
1910–1911   Casement Diaries

PORTUGAL
1810–1814   Stuart de Rothesay Papers
1834   Howard de Walden Papers
1906–1911   Villiers

PRUSSIA
1772–1807;   Jackson Papers
1813–1815
1851–1860   Bloomfield Papers
1864–1875   White Papers [Danzig]

ROUMANIA
1878–1885   White Papers
1887–1891   Lascelles
1876–1894   Sanderson (P)

RUSSIA AND U.S.S.R.
1804–1807   Granville Papers
1806–1808   Stuart de Rothesay Papers
1816   Jackson Papers
1825   Stratford Canning Papers
1839–1851   Bloomfield Papers
1857–1864   White Papers [Warsaw]
1866–1868   Stuart Papers
1871–1878   Cowley Papers
1894–1895   Lascelles
1903–1906   Spring-Rice
1906–1908   Nicolson
1919–1920   Mackinder
1942–1946   Inverchapel

SERBIA
1875–1878   White Papers

SIAM
1884–1888   Satow Papers
1911   Alston

SICILY AND NAPLES
1811–1822   Cave Papers
1840–1845   Woodbine Parish Papers
1859–1861   Stuart Papers

SLAVE TRADE
1832–1856   Jackson Papers

SPAIN
1791–1795   Jackson Papers
1808–1809   Stuart de Rothesay Papers
1810–1821   Cowley Papers
1822   Jackson Papers
1824–1825   Canning
1833   Stratford Canning Papers
1834   Backhouse
1834–1835   Caradoc
1830–1839   Hervey Papers
1840–1843   Aston Papers
1905–1906   Nicolson

SWEDEN
1804–1807   Pierrepont Papers
1833   Howard de Walden Papers
1823–1839   Bloomfield Papers
1908–1913   Spring-Rice

SWITZERLAND
1814–1819;   *Stratford Canning Papers*
1847–1848

TUNIS
1923–1929   *MacLeod*

TURKEY
1776–1793   *Ainslie*
1809–1812;   *Stratford Canning Papers*
1826–1827;
1832
1843–1848   *Cowley Papers*
1854–1857   *Ampthill Papers*
1842–1858   *Stratford Canning Papers*
1864–1866   *Stuart Papers*
1878   *Simmons Papers*
1879–1880   *Kitchener Papers*
1885–1891   *White Papers*
1892–1893   *Corbett*
1893–1894   *Nicolson*
1894–1896   *Currie*
1889–1911   *Vambéry*
1908–1913   *Lowther* (*G*)
1881–1929   *Ryan*

TUSCANY
1787–1794   *Hervey Papers*
1818;   *Watson*
1821

UNITED STATES OF AMERICA
1809–1810   *Jackson Papers*
1820–1823   *Stratford Canning Papers*
1822–1827   *Jackson Papers*
1848–1857   *Bulwer*
1857–1858   *Ampthill Papers*
1861–1864   *Stuart Papers*
1876–1878   *Lascelles*
1894–1907   *Sanderson* (*P*)
1907–1913   *Bryce*
1913–1918   *Spring-Rice*
1918–1919   *Reading*
1946–1948   *Inverchapel*

URUGUAY
1888–1893   *Satow Papers*

VATICAN
1858–1870   *Ampthill Papers*
1881–1885   *Errington*

WÜRTTEMBERG
1832–1843   *Cowley Papers*

YUGOSLAVIA
1929–1935   *Henderson* (*N*)

ZANZIBAR
1861–1862   *Pelly*
1885   *Kitchener Papers*

Appendix IV: Private Collections of Papers of Secretaries of State for Foreign Affairs

Date of Appointment	Secretary of State	Location
27 March 1782	Charles James Fox	British Museum, Add. MSS. 47559–47601
17 July 1782	Thomas Robinson, 2nd Lord Grantham	Lady Lucas Coll., Bedford County R.O.
2 April 1783	Charles James Fox	(See under 1782)
19 December 1783	George Nugent-Temple-Grenville, 3rd Earl Temple (1st Marquess of Buckingham 1784)	Stowe MSS., Henry E. Huntingdon Library, San Marino, California, U.S.A.
23 December 1783	Francis Godolphin Osborne, Marquess of Carmarthen, 5th Duke of Leeds 23 March 1789	British Museum, Add. MSS. 28060–28067*
8 June 1791	William Wyndham Grenville, 1st Lord Grenville	Mrs. G.G.Fortescue, Boconnoc, Cornwall†
20 February 1801	Robert Banks Jenkinson, Lord Hawkesbury (2nd Earl of Liverpool 1808)	British Museum, Add. MSS. 38190–38489, 38564–38581*
14 May 1804	Dudley Ryder, 2nd Lord Harrowby (1st Earl of Harrowby 1809)	The Earl of Harrowby, Sandon Hall, Stafford*
11 January 1805	Henry Phipps, 2nd Lord Mulgrave (1st Earl of Mulgrave 1812)	Not known*
7 February 1806	Charles James Fox	(See under 1782)*
24 September 1806	Charles Grey, Viscount Howick (2nd Earl Grey 1807)	The Prior's Kitchen, The College, Durham*
25 March 1807	George Canning	Archives Department, Leeds City Library; also F.O.800/229–231‡
11 October 1809	Henry Bathurst, 3rd Earl Bathurst	Earl Bathurst§
6 December 1809	Richard Wellesley, 1st Lord Wellesley [G.B.], 1st Marquess Wellesley [Irish]	British Museum, Add. MSS. 12564–13915, 37274–37318, 37414–37416*

* For Précis and Entry Books in F.O.95 see pp.57–59 above.
† *Manuscripts of J.B.Fortescue, Esq., at Dropmore*, H.M.C., 10 vols. (1892–1927); for Précis and Entry Books (F.O.95/99–101, 271–278) see p.57 above.
‡ See Appendix III; for Précis and Entry Books (F.O.95/253–258 and 474) see p.58 above.
§ *Report on the Manuscripts of Earl Bathurst*, H.M.C. (1923); for Précis and Entry Books (F.O. 95/470–471) see p.58 above.

Date of Appointment	Secretary of State	Location
4 March 1812	Robert Stewart, Viscount Castlereagh, 2nd Marquess of Londonderry [Irish] 6 April 1821	Mount Stewart, Newtownards, Co. Down*
16 September 1822	George Canning	(See under 1807)
30 April 1827	John William Ward, 4th Viscount Dudley and Ward, 1st Earl of Dudley 5 October 1827	Not known
2 June 1828	George Hamilton-Gordon, 4th Earl of Aberdeen [Scot.], 1st Viscount Gordon [U.K.]	British Museum, Add. MSS. 43049–43358
22 November 1830	Henry John Temple, 3rd Viscount Palmerston [Irish]	Trustees of Broadlands Archives Trust, on temporary deposit with Historical Manuscripts Commission
15 November 1834	Arthur Wellesley, 1st Duke of Wellington	The Duke of Wellington, on temporary deposit with Historical Manuscripts Commission
18 April 1835	Viscount Palmerston	(See under 1830)
2 September 1841	Earl of Aberdeen	(See under 1828)
6 July 1846	Viscount Palmerston	(See under 1830)
26 December 1851	Granville George Leveson-Gower, 2nd Earl Granville	P.R.O.30/29; F.O.362†
27 February 1852	James Howard Harris, 3rd Earl of Malmesbury	The Earl of Malmesbury
28 December 1852	Lord John Russell (1st Earl Russell 1861)	P.R.O.30/22.†
21 February 1853	George William Frederick Villiers, 4th Earl of Clarendon	Bodleian Library; also F.O.361†
26 February 1858	Earl of Malmesbury	(See under 1852)
18 June 1859	Lord John Russell	(See under 1852)
3 November 1865	Earl of Clarendon	(See under 1853)
6 July 1866	Edward Henry Stanley, Lord Stanley (15th Earl of Derby 1869)	The Earl of Derby
9 December 1868	Earl of Clarendon	(See under 1853)
6 July 1870	Earl Granville	(See under 1851)

* For Précis and Entry Books see pp.58–59 above.
† See Appendix III.

Date of Appointment	*Secretary of State*	*Location*
21 February 1874	Earl of Derby	(See under 1866)
2 April 1878	Robert Arthur Talbot Gascoyne-Cecil, 3rd Marquess of Salisbury	The Marquess of Salisbury, on temporary deposit at Christ Church, Oxford
28 April 1880	Earl Granville	(See under 1851)
24 June 1885	Marquess of Salisbury	(See under 1878)
6 February 1886	Archibald Philip Primrose, 5th Earl of Rosebery [Scot.], 2nd Lord Rosebery [U.K.] (1st Earl of Midlothian [U.K.] 1911)	The National Library of Scotland
3 August 1886	Stafford Henry Northcote, 1st Earl of Iddesleigh	British Museum, Add. MSS. 50013–50064, 50209–50210
14 January 1887	Marquess of Salisbury	(See under 1878)
18 August 1892	Earl of Rosebery	(See under 1886)
11 March 1894	John Wodehouse, 1st Earl of Kimberley	The Earl of Kimberley
29 June 1895	Marquess of Salisbury	(See under 1878)
12 November 1900	Henry Charles Keith Petty-Fitzmaurice, 5th Marquess of Lansdowne	The Marquess of Lansdowne; *also* F.O.800/115–146*
11 December 1905	Sir Edward Grey, 1st Viscount Grey of Fallodon 27 July 1916	F.O.800/40–113*
11 December 1916	Arthur James Balfour (1st Earl Balfour 1922)	British Museum, Add. MSS. 49683–49962; *also* F.O.800/199–217*
24 October 1919	George Nathaniel Curzon, 1st Earl Curzon, 1st Marquess Curzon 28 June 1921	India Office Library, MSS. Eur. F.112; *also* F.O.800/149–158*
23 January 1924	James Ramsay MacDonald	F.O.800/218–219;* other papers under arrangement in the P.R.O.
7 November 1924	Sir Joseph Austen Chamberlain	University of Birmingham Library; *also* F.O.800/256–263*
8 June 1929	Arthur Henderson	F.O.800/280–284*
26 August 1931	Rufus Isaacs, 1st Marquess of Reading	The Marquess of Reading; *also* F.O.800/226*

* See Appendix III.

Date of Appointment	Secretary of State	Location
9 November 1931	Sir John Allsebrook Simon (1st Viscount Simon 1940)	Viscount Simon; *also* F.O.800/285–291*
7 June 1935	Sir Samuel John Gurney Hoare, bt. (1st Viscount Templewood 1944)	Cambridge University Library; *also* F.O.800/295*
22 December 1935	Robert Anthony Eden (K.G.1954; 1st Earl of Avon 1961)	The Earl of Avon
1 March 1938	Edward Frederick Lindley Wood, 3rd Viscount Halifax (1st Earl of Halifax 1944)	The Earl of Halifax; *also* F.O.800/309–328*

* See Appendix III.

SELECT INDEX

Printed in England for Her Majesty's Stationery Office
by The Campfield Press, St. Albans

(22434) Dd. 143793. K.16 7/69.